Dreaming of Justice, Waking to Wisdom

Dreaming of Justice, Waking to Wisdom

ROUSSEAU'S PHILOSOPHIC LIFE

Laurence D. Cooper

The University of Chicago Press CHICAGO AND LONDON

The University of Chicago Press, Chicago 60637
The University of Chicago Press, Ltd., London
© 2023 by The University of Chicago
All rights reserved. No part of this book may be used or
reproduced in any manner whatsoever without written
permission, except in the case of brief quotations in critical articles
and reviews. For more information, contact the University of
Chicago Press, 1427 E. 60th St., Chicago, IL 60637.
Published 2023
Printed in the United States of America

32 31 30 29 28 27 26 25 24 23   1 2 3 4 5

ISBN-13: 978-0-226-82499-4 (cloth)
ISBN-13: 978-0-226-82501-4 (paper)
ISBN-13: 978-0-226-82500-7 (e-book)
DOI: https://doi.org/10.7208/chicago/9780226825007.001.0001

Library of Congress Cataloging-in-Publication Data

Names: Cooper, Laurence D., 1962– author.
Title: Dreaming of justice, waking to wisdom : Rousseau's philo-
sophic life / Laurence D. Cooper.
Other titles: Rousseau's philosophic life
Description: Chicago : The University of Chicago Press, 2023. |
Includes bibliographical references and index.
Identifiers: LCCN 2022036159 | ISBN 9780226824994 (cloth) |
ISBN 9780226825014 (paperback) | ISBN 9780226825007 (ebook)
Subjects: LCSH: Rousseau, Jean-Jacques, 1712–1778. Rêveries du
promeneur solitaire. | Philosophy. | Philosophy in literature.
Classification: LCC PQ2040.R53 C66 2023 | DDC 194—dc23/
eng/20220926
LC record available at https://lccn.loc.gov/2022036159

♾ This paper meets the requirements of ANSI/NISO Z39.48-1992
(Permanence of Paper).

For Jessica

Contents

Citations and Abbreviations

References to *The Reveries of the Solitary Walker* are first to the "Walk" (i.e., the chapter) being cited and then to the paragraph(s). Walks are signified by a roman numeral, paragraphs by arabic numbers.

References to Rousseau's other writings are first to the pages in the *Œuvres complètes* (hereafter *OC*) and then, after a semicolon, to the pages of the *Collected Writings of Rousseau* (hereafter *CW*). Volume numbers are as follows:

Confessions: *OC*, volume 1; *CW*, volume 5.

Discourse on the Origin and Foundations of Inequality, or *Second Discourse* (hereafter *SD*): *OC*, volume 3; *CW*, volume 3.

Discourse on the Sciences and the Arts, or *First Discourse* (hereafter, *FD*): *OC*, volume 3; *CW*, volume 2.

Discourse on the Virtue Most Necessary for a Hero: *OC*, volume 2; *CW*, volume 4.

Emile, or On Education: *OC*, volume 4; *CW*, volume 13.

Final Reply of J.-J. Rousseau of Geneva: *OC*, volume 3; *CW*, volume 2.

Government of Poland: *OC*, volume 3; *CW*, volume 11.

Letter to d'Alembert: *OC*, volume 5; *CW*, volume 10.

Letter to Beaumont: *OC*, volume 4; *CW*, volume 8.

Letters to Malesherbes: *OC*, volume 1; *CW*, volume 5.

Observations by Jean-Jacques Rousseau of Geneva: *OC*, volume 3; *CW*, volume 2.

Preface to Narcissus: *OC*, volume 2; *CW*, volume 2.

Rousseau, Judge of Jean-Jacques: Dialogues (hereafter *Dialogues*): *OC*, volume 1; *CW*, volume 1.

Social Contract (hereafter *SC*): *OC*, volume 3; *CW*, volume 4.

Translations into English follow those in the *Collected Writings* though with occasional revisions of my own.

Preface

Is it good to pursue something that you can never have? Sometimes, surely. Can it be good to devote your whole life to such a pursuit? That would seem more doubtful. Yet that is precisely the claim made by and on behalf of the life of philosophy. Philosophers, by which I mean lovers of wisdom who orient their whole lives to its passionate pursuit,[1] have by and large conceded that wisdom in the strict sense is beyond human reach. Indeed, many philosophers, including some who seem to say otherwise, give us cause to doubt whether human beings can lay claim to any knowledge at all. For to truly know a thing would require knowing how it relates to other things, or how it is situated in the Whole of which it is a part. To know anything would seem to require that we know everything. Yet the same philosophers who give the lie to the pretensions of human intellect also celebrate the life dedicated to the pursuit of wisdom as the most rational life, the life of greatest clarity and insight, the most virtuous life—indeed, the only life in which true virtue is realized at all—and for these reasons also the freest life, arguably the most natural life, and altogether the best and happiest of lives for a human being. They even claim that their quixotic pursuit can benefit the larger world—this despite acknowledging that most human beings find meaning and well-being in beliefs that philosophy by its nature calls into question and inevitably finds wanting. What can they be thinking? What should *we* think? One thing we should not

---

1. *Lovers of wisdom who orient their whole lives to its passionate pursuit.* This is not the whole of my conception of what it means to be a philosopher, but it is the essential first element. In this I follow the lead of classical philosophy. When Socrates undertakes to explain what distinguishes the philosopher from other human beings in Plato's *Republic*, he begins by describing the philosopher as a passionate, indeed erotic, lover and desirer of wisdom (475b). Alternative conceptions of philosophy and the philosopher abound. But whatever their merits, those that do not begin with this monomania are not part of my subject.

think is that we may dismiss philosophers' praise of the philosophic life for being self-serving. For as Plato and others have shown, the philosophic life—the philosophic life *properly understood*—requires of its practitioners such an impressive array of natural gifts that those who live it will surely have chosen it over more envied ways of life (*Republic*, 485a–486e). Or might it be that the philosophic life is so compelling to those of a certain nature that they never really had a choice at all? But that would only make it harder to dismiss the case for the philosophic life as the best and freest of human lives.[2]

One who did *not* declare the philosophic life good in itself was Jean-Jacques Rousseau. When Rousseau spoke explicitly of "philosophy" and "philosophers," it was almost always to disparage them for working against the good of society and even the pursuit of truth, if not intentionally then heedlessly. Most whom he referred to as philosophers he deemed creatures of vanity, more interested in their own renown than in truth or wisdom for its own sake. Even the honest pursuit of truth was seen by Rousseau as problematic, at least where the truth being sought concerns the greatest and most needful matters, for there is no getting at these matters except by rigorously inquiring into the presuppositions underlying our beliefs about them. Human beings in Rousseau's view are first and (almost always) last creatures of belief and opinion: there are none among us who have not begun life subjected to authoritative opinion and few who will ever come to see how deep that subjection goes, let alone free themselves from it. To inquire into our foundational beliefs—to question not only justice, good and evil, and God, but also the *goodness* of justice, the *source* of good and evil, and the *being* of God—is to render them questionable. For some people this may prove the gateway to freedom of mind. Such people may come to see that they have been living like prisoners in a cave, mistaking mere shadows for the truth about what *is*, and that now, having achieved this awareness, they have begun an ascent to the sunlit world above (*Republic*, 514a–517c). For many more people, however, the result of such radical questioning is apt to be one or another kind of demoralization: either the de-moralizing "liberation" from salutary restraint (to say nothing of noble aspiration) or else a pervasive disorientation and disquiet—either anarchy or enervation—or perhaps both. On this Rousseau is at one with the classical philosophers: philosophy relentlessly employs reason and eschews all authorities in its effort to replace opinion with truth, yet society rests on and is held together by authoritative opinion. Most will resist challenges to

2. On experiencing compulsion as freedom, see Nietzsche, *Beyond Good and Evil*, section 213.

authoritative opinion as best they can. (An exception that proves the rule is "the Frenchman" in Rousseau's *Dialogues*, who accepts the truth about Jean-Jacques only after experiencing great anxiety, self-doubt, and perhaps even terror.)[3] Even at its best philosophy inevitably threatens popular faith and civic health. And of course philosophy (or pseudophilosophy) is far more often *not* at its best, especially when, as in Rousseau's time, there is growing faith in the possibility of popular enlightenment.

Rousseau did express enormous admiration for a small number of philosophers—namely, those whose great theoretical gifts were animated by ardent intellectual eros and governed in their public discourse by the prudence and beneficence needed to shield society from philosophy and even to improve society by tempering popular passions. But in his writings Rousseau rarely referred to these philosophers, whom he perhaps regarded as the only *true* philosophers, *as* philosophers. Socrates he praised for being wise [*sage*] and virtuous [*vertueux*], and Plato he called a "noble genius" [*beau genie*].[4] More generally, he referred to thinkers whom he admired as "celestial intelligences" or "sublime geniuses" or "preceptors of the human race."[5] But the language with which he praised these rare few hardly obviates his critique of the vast majority of those the world has called philosophers—quite the contrary. Nor did he claim that the efforts of such lofty souls could redound to much good for the world. Philosophy as Rousseau presented it certainly has its uses and may even be necessary to happiness and good governance, but its value lies almost exclusively in finding palliatives for ills that it fomented in the first place. Rousseau even questioned whether philosophy is good for the philosopher. In his own case, as he tells it, philosophizing incited enmity while yielding little pleasure in return. He avows that while he sometimes thought deeply, "thinking was always a painful and charmless occupation" for him (VII, 5; also see *SD*, 138; 23).

In denying that he found thinking intrinsically pleasurable, Rousseau seemed to put himself in maximal contradiction with the classical philosophers and the long line of medieval and modern philosophers who followed them in this regard, albeit often under cover of one kind of piety or another.

---

3. See Pagani, *Man or Citizen*, 30.

4. See *FD*, paragraphs 26–30; *Final Reply of J.-J. Rousseau of Geneva*, paragraph 5; and *Emile*, 700; 537. A rare instance in which Socrates and Plato are referred to as philosophers appears in *Final Reply*, paragraph 38, where they are less praised than *excused* for being philosophers—and excused only because the cause of virtue had already suffered defeat.

5. See, for example, *Preface to Narcissus*, 970–71; 94–195; *Final Reply of J.-J. Rousseau of Geneva*, 72–73; 111–12; and *FD*, 29–30; 22.

This appearance, however, belies reality. Rousseau was not at odds with his predecessors regarding the goodness and choiceworthiness of the philosophic life *properly understood*. The sweep of his critique was not so complete as to obscure from careful readers his deep kinship with the spirit of the classical philosophers concerning the philosophic life. Rousseau was a philosopher; he knew himself to be a philosopher; and he found in the life of philosophy the same things that the overt celebrants of the philosophic life had found—namely, a life of naturalness, freedom, and happiness for the one who lives it, and a potential source of benefaction for others and even for society at large. That he understood himself to be a philosopher is indicated by any number of passages stretching across the whole of his mature output, from the *First Discourse* and the *Second Discourse* in which, respectively, he likened himself to Prometheus and he invoked Plato and Xenocrates as his only worthy judges, to *The Reveries of the Solitary Walker*, his final work, in which he lambasted contemporary "philosophers" while expressing the confidence that he belonged to the ranks of the "celestial intelligences."[6] But the chief indication that Rousseau was a philosopher and must surely have regarded himself as one is that his writings are works of political philosophy of the first order that contend, philosophically, with and against other philosophers of the highest rank.

That Rousseau embraced the philosophic life for its intrinsic freedom and happiness will become clear over the course of the investigation to come. The focus of the investigation will be *The Reveries of the Solitary Walker*, the only one of his works specifically devoted to the philosophic life. For now I can offer only two pieces of suggestive evidence: first, the observation that in the *Reveries* Rousseau exults in various kinds of contemplative activity—not only self-described reveries but also profound, rational inquiry into the greatest matters; and, second, the "argument" from performance—that is, from the fact that he chose to live a life of deep and persistent philosophic inquiry.

Many readers will surely greet my reading of the *Reveries* with deep skepticism. To be sure, Rousseau *had* lived the life of a productive philosopher. But isn't the retired life that he depicts in the *Reveries* at most a *post*philosophic life? Is it not simply the life of, well, *reverie*? And where the life depicted in the *Reveries* includes episodes of philosophizing proper, which it does, is it really a happy life?

To these challenges I offer the following provisional reply as a preview

---

6. *First Discourse*: see frontispiece; starting at paragraph 36n. *Second Discourse*: see exordium and paragraph 7.

of the argument to be unfolded over the course of this book. Even an ada-
mant skeptic must concede that there is far more serious thought in the
Reveries than the title or the opening pages would have one believe. That
Rousseau regarded the philosophic life as intrinsically choiceworthy—as
the life of maximum freedom and happiness—is communicated with similar obliqueness. This obliqueness veils but ultimately enhances the depth,
texture, and artistry that make the *Reveries* not only a major philosophic
accomplishment but also a literary work of the first order. As we'll see,
even Rousseau's claim that thinking has always been for him a "painful and
charmless occupation" proves upon careful reading to apply to only *one*
kind of thinking—namely, the thinking about oneself that is necessitated
by something outside oneself. And some of his seemingly unphilosophic
reveries—some, not all—enhance sight of what *is* and thus belong to the
philosophic life.[7]

Rousseau's reflections on philosophy and the philosophic life are not
confined to the *Reveries*. Almost all his books reveal something about
philosophy. As indeed they must: like his Socratic forebears, Rousseau
understood that one cannot adequately probe such fundamental matters
as human nature (*Discourse on Inequality*), political right (*On the Social
Contract*), or the education of the soul (*Emile*) without reflecting on the
nature of philosophic inquiry or taking account of what the philosophic
life reveals about these matters. But it is only in the *Reveries* that he thema-
tized the philosophic life, and even there he took great care not to adver-
tise philosophy in such a way as to burnish its appeal to those unsuited to it
or not apt to practice it prudently. As in his prior works, so in the *Reveries*
he mentions philosophy and philosophers almost only to criticize them. It
is precisely this rhetorical shield that seems to place him at such a distance
from those who overtly declared the philosophic life the best of lives. In
fact, however, this rhetorical shield indicates Rousseau's *kinship* with his
predecessors. He, like they, sought to protect philosophy. His seeming
disdain for philosophy was necessary for philosophy's protection. In prior
eras, whether in classical antiquity or under the watchful eye of Christian,
Jewish, or Islamic authorities, philosophy needed protection against suspicion and persecution: it needed to be seen as consistent with authoritative
beliefs. In his own era, Rousseau seems to have determined, philosophy
needed protection against popularization. Rousseau's end was the same

---

7. *Sight of what is.* Is this any less naive an aspiration for philosophy than knowledge
of the Whole? In fact it is. Sight is a more modest attainment than knowledge, and "what
is" refers not to "the true world" but to the world as it presents itself to us, as mediated
by human consciousness.

as Plato's—the same end for the same reasons. What had changed was the terrain to be navigated.

But if one purpose of this book is to show that Rousseau is in accord with a prior tradition of thought in important respects, my greater purpose is to uncover elements of Rousseau's teaching on the philosophic life that are not evident in the works of his predecessors—nor in the works of his successors, for that matter. Here I must make two clarifying points. First, by "Rousseau's *teaching* on the philosophic life" I mean both the substance of what he communicates and his way of communicating it—both the what and the how. Second, in saying that I mean to uncover elements of his teaching that are *not evident* in other philosophers' treatments I mean only that. What is not evident in philosophers' writings may or may not have been known to them. It is beyond the compass of this study to determine the full extent to which what is new in Rousseau's teaching about the philosophic life was known to his predecessors. But I shall try to show that the most distinctive elements of his teaching, even as they go beyond the teachings propounded by his Socratic predecessors, especially Plato, do not contradict them.

Rousseau stood to the Socratic tradition as heir and would-be restorer. But he was also positioned by history to modify and deepen that tradition precisely so that it might live on. He could *modify* the Socratic tradition because he wrote for a world shaped by Christian and post-Christian universalism. He could *deepen* it because he had confronted the challenge posed to philosophy by biblical religion. Philosophy emerged from the confrontation with biblical religion in some ways chastened—at least it did so in the eyes of the most clear-seeing and honest thinkers. Such thinkers had received from biblical religion a more refined education regarding the ways in which pride can insinuate itself into and thus compromise one's philosophizing.[8] But such chastening of philosophy, reflecting as it does a deepened honesty and self-awareness, makes philosophy *more* philosophic, not less. And so we are led back to my chief reason for examining the *Reveries* and my overarching hope in writing this book, which is not to assess Rousseau's relation to other thinkers but to shed light on the philosophic life itself. Irrespective of his relation to other thinkers, Rousseau, in my view, offers much to *us*, who live within a horizon that has

---

8. The seriousness and longevity of Rousseau's engagement with the Bible is indicated most succinctly at *Confessions*, 580; 485. Regarding his view that even the purest of philosophers (namely, Socrates) is subject to inherently unphilosophic pride, see his "Fiction or Allegorical Piece on Revelation" as well as Christopher Kelly's interpretation thereof in *Rousseau's Exemplary Life*, 58–60 and 71–73.

much in common with the one within which he wrote and which, where it differs from his, does so in considerable part *because of* what he wrote.[9]

But should we accept Rousseau's offer? Doesn't he mean to warn most of us *away* from philosophy? Indeed he does, but timing is all. Those who have picked up this book will likely already have been ensnared by the idea of achieving freedom and well-being through philosophy. For them—for us—a philosopher's warnings about philosophy's dangers are at least as apt to intensify philosophy's appeal as to diminish it. But what about agnostic or diffident readers? Shouldn't they put down this book, breathe a sigh of relief, and step outside into the *real* sunshine?

Perhaps they should—but not without considering the possibility that Rousseau's teaching on the philosophic life can be valuable, and was meant to be valuable, even for them. This not because Rousseau believes in the realistic possibility of popular enlightenment—he doesn't—but because his teaching on the philosophic life is in the first instance an advertisement for a rustic life centered on innocent pursuits. With his charming depictions of country life, Rousseau means to cultivate love of goodness and appreciation of virtue. And by lamenting his unjust consignment to solitude, he takes care not to degrade civic life and responsibility—quite the contrary (VI, 7). Even those who deem Rousseau's prior works subversive of moral and political health (subversive either by stimulating revolutionary fanaticism or by promoting self-indulgence) should be able to see in the *Reveries* the promotion of goodness and indeed the way to a deeper *understanding* of goodness. These, in turn, might render readers less susceptible to noxious prejudices and therewith freer of mind, for the primary requirement of freedom of mind is not philosophic eros but rather moral strength, without which there is little hope of resisting the distorting urges of pride and vanity.[10] That Rousseau regards considerable freedom of mind to be possible, at least in principle, for those with ordinary natural gifts is established by *Emile*. Emile, chosen for Rousseau's elaborate thought experiment precisely because he has an ordinary nature, does not become a philosopher; but the view of the world at which he arrives, especially the understanding that the wicked are to be pitied rather than hated, has much in common with the philosopher's view (548, 533–36; 410, 397–400).

In order to make his teaching on the philosophic life beneficial to

---

9. See Orwin and Tarcov, *Legacy of Rousseau*.
10. See *Preface to Narcissus*, 970; 195; and *Observations*, 39; 39–40.

nonphilosophers—to those nonphilosophers for whom it *could* be beneficial—Rousseau needed to employ a pedagogical art that would elicit and educate certain longings and intimations without stoking pride or vanity. He had to appeal to something in these readers akin to the philosophic nature. What might this something be? The answer, I think, is *amour de soi*, the natural, benign, nonrelative form of self-love—more specifically, the *expansiveness* of amour de soi. The challenge is to keep expansive amour de soi from curdling into amour-propre, or relative self-love.[11] Amour-propre will always be present, but it must be kept moderate both in magnitude and in temper. The means to this moderation is for amour-propre to be governed by amour de soi—by amour de soi equipped with prudence. Optimally, and perhaps necessarily, amour-propre would be not only moderated by amour de soi but also enlisted into its service, much as how, in the healthy Platonic soul, reason enlists spiritedness into *its* employ (*Republic*, 441e). If this can be accomplished, the nonphilosopher's study and contemplation—including study and contemplation of the philosophic life—might yield goods that are of the same kind if not the same magnitude as those yielded by the philosophic life proper: enhanced freedom of mind; joy in the exercise of one's highest faculties; appreciation of the wondrousness of nature and of one's place in it; and a more fully felt sentiment of being. These goods are not discrete experiences so much as conditions of soul—conditions that, with habituation, might become characteristics of soul.

Have we not already absorbed what philosophy has to offer us? A great many of us today, particularly among the more educated classes, lay claim to Socrates's "human wisdom" (*Apology*, 20d), or something quite like it. As Socrates professed epistemic humility, so do we. Indeed, the skepticism that Socrates confessed is for many of us a creed. Yet somehow our skepticism doesn't look, or rather feel, altogether like his. It is hard to say about ourselves what we can say about him—namely, that his ignorance and skepticism don't seem to have undermined his happiness and well-being. Has that which permitted or even caused Socrates's happiness been a source of unhappiness for us? If so, we might stand to benefit from Rousseau's account of the philosophic life, which takes account of the very challenges we face.

Why *have* we fallen short of Socrates's happiness and well-being? Is it

---

11. The two kinds of self-love are not as separate or separable as this treatment may make them sound: they are versions of a single thing. Yet the difference between the two versions is vitally important to any understanding of morality, politics, and individual well-being.

that we lack the strength to abide happily amid uncertainty regarding the most important things? Have we gone too far in our skepticism? Or have we perhaps failed to go far *enough*? Neither of these hypotheses can be summarily dismissed. Nor, as it happens, are they mutually exclusive. We may be insufficiently skeptical in some areas and too skeptical in others. But rather than think in terms of magnitude or degree, let's compare the *character* of our skepticism to that of Socrates. For whatever we may think or say, it's far from clear that the two are the same.

Students of political thought know that philosophers have sometimes insincerely professed the popular or official faith of their societies. Less familiar is the reverse, that is, that philosophers may sometimes have overstated their skepticism. Socrates professed what must have sounded like wholesale ignorance before five hundred Athenian jurors. But his profession was qualified more than is normally recognized: he didn't say that he knew nothing at all but that he knew "*practically* nothing," or "nothing *so to speak*" (*hōs epos eipein*). Indeed he proceeded in the very same speech to make several claims to knowledge. He said that he *knew* that it is disgraceful and terrible to quit one's post in war. And in exhorting fellow citizens to virtue, he implied that he *knew* what virtue was (*Apology*, 28d and 29e). Even his unqualified admission that he didn't know "anything noble and good" can be understood to have been an indication of knowledge: he might have lacked knowledge of anything noble and good because he knew that no single thing *could be* both noble and good in the senses we normally attach to those words.[12] In short, "ignorance that knows itself, that judges itself and condemns itself, is not complete ignorance: to be that, it must be ignorant of itself."[13]

And yet these qualifications do not obviate Socrates's skepticism or contradict his confession of ignorance, for it was always the case, and Socrates knew it to be the case, that his "knowledge" rested on or was constructed from elements that he did not know and never *could* know. If he knew that it is bad or ignoble to desert one's post in wartime, he never claimed to know the whole of what badness or baseness is. How could he have? To know the bad would have required that he first know the good, and although he had a highly developed *opinion* of the good (*Republic*, 506e), he never claimed knowledge of it. To know in the strictest sense what is good for this or that being in this or that situation would require

12. The mutual exclusivity of nobility and goodness as these are typically understood is indicated in a number of Platonic dialogues, including the *Apology*. For an unusually frank explication of this matter, see Leibowitz, *Ironic Defense of Socrates*, 96–97 and 178–80.

13. Montaigne, "Apology for Raymond Sebond," in *Complete Essays of Montaigne*, 372.

that one know the nature of that being and that situation, which in turn would require that one know the Whole of which that being is part. Yet somehow, to repeat, Socrates's happiness and well-being do not seem to have been compromised by any of this—to the contrary. Such knowledge as he had, qualified and incomplete though it was, sufficed for a life that cannot but strike one as happy in a remarkably full if peculiar sense. To borrow a useful pair of terms from Descartes, even as Socrates bowed to the impossibility of "metaphysical certitude," he demonstrated the possibility and sufficiency of "moral assurance," if not for everyone at least for himself.[14]

Descartes's distinction pertains to degree. But, again, the case of Socrates suggests that we consider instead the character or nature of skepticism. Socrates was not simply a skeptic. He was a *zetetic* skeptic, one who knew the limits of human understanding yet sought the truth or sight of what *is* with confidence born of experience.

And *our* skepticism?

The initial returns seem encouraging. As Socrates proved to know some things after all, or acted for all practical purposes *as if* he knew some things, so do we. And we too don't seem to be pained by the lack of metaphysical certitude. Indeed, we often forget this lack: consider the certainty with which we routinely judge any number of moral and political phenomena. Not that we all hold the *same* certitudes as one another. But no matter: lack of consensus rarely seems to diminish our conviction. Indeed, conflict often seems to ratify our self-certainty, or so one might guess from the ferocity with which we so often condemn views that oppose our own and the people who hold those views. Skepticism and epistemic humility may be the watchwords of our day, but indignation remains a driving force of moral and political life. It is here, regarding morality, that our skepticism reveals itself to be something very different from Socrates's. If proof is wanted, consider the anger with which we so often argue about morality and politics and then look for anger in Socrates.

We might or might not wish to be like Socrates. But most of us aspire, or say that we aspire, to qualities for which he serves as paradigm: honesty, freedom of mind, and a certain grace or lightness of spirit. How might we progress toward those qualities? Paradigm though he be, Socrates cannot serve as a model for us. He is too idiosyncratic, too distant, too little known. And we have no idea of his ever having traversed anything quite like the confusing terrain in which we late moderns or postmoderns find

14. Descartes, *Discourse on Method*, part 4, paragraph 8.

ourselves. Rousseau, however, has. His exploration of this terrain in the effort to escape it is the very story of *The Reveries of the Solitary Walker*.

There is one more reason to linger "in the shade of the study" (*FD*, 22; 16) reflecting on the philosophic life—the best reason of all. Philosophy plausibly promises a deeper and more sustained engagement with reality. It teaches us how to see—not by opening our eyes but by turning them, by turning *us*, toward what *is* (*Republic*, 518d). To be sure, many books divert us from reality. But some books intensify our engagement with reality. And a few, such as the *Reveries*, by exploring this engagement itself and how it came about, can help us in our own pursuit of the same. Contemplation of the philosophic life can render us more alive to actual sunshine and all that it illuminates.

After the Cave

There is no more powerful representation of the philosophic life and its relation to other ways of life than the celebrated Image of the Cave in the seventh book of Plato's *Republic* (514a–516c). According to that image, the cave is one place, and the land above and beyond it is another. The way out of the cave is steep and arduous, requiring many steps and several stages. But one is either in or out—and once out, completely out. Whereas there are multiple conditions and perspectives within the cave—the puppeteer's experience of life, for example, versus that of the enchained prisoners—there is no indication of a diversity of stations or perspectives outside the cave, nor indeed any mention of forthcoming challenges beyond waiting for one's eyes to adjust to the sunlight.

But nonmention does not imply nonexistence. The Image of the Cave does not preclude the possibility or even the necessity of further travel and ascent for the one who has been liberated. Indeed, it is only above ground that we encounter clouds, bad weather, and a broad and alternating spectrum of light and darkness; and there is considerably more variety above ground than below with respect to climate and topography. Few readers of the *Republic*, I would wager, have given this matter much thought. And why would they? It's not just that the Image of the Cave culminates where it does, that is, in the sunlight, but also that this culmination purports to represent a perfect wisdom. The liberated one, once his eyes have adjusted to the light, sees the things that *are*; and this *seeing*, as the preceding Images of the Sun and the Divided Line will have told the reader, represents *understanding* (*noesis*; 507c–511d). Careful readers will already have a pretty good idea that Socrates's depiction of philosophers in these images and the surrounding text is a deliberate idealization. They will have noted the wide discrepancy between philosophers as Socrates *describes* them and the philosopher that he himself *is*—a discrepancy, with respect to wisdom, not just of degree but of kind. The philosophers that Socrates describes in the *Republic* know things that Socrates himself never claims to know and indeed cannot know. In truth the "philosophers" he describes in the *Republic* are less philosophers than "perfect sophists" (*Symposium*, 208c). They are less *lovers* of wisdom than *possessors* of it, whereas Socrates himself, a mere human being, has and *can* have only "human wisdom." Yet these same careful readers regard the ascent to the philosophic *life* as something comparable to liberation from a cave—if not with respect to wisdom then with respect to clarity and freedom of mind. Socrates does somehow seem to live in a different place from the rest of us. However imperfect his wisdom, there is something about him, something about his life and soul, that strikes one as in some way perfect or fully realized. Little wonder, then, that we don't ask what further journey might be possible, let alone necessary, outside the cave.

And yet we might. For even if Socrates has already achieved some kind of completeness, he continues to devote himself to active inquiry and pedagogy. Is there a self-perfecting direction to this activity? Is Socrates seeking through his mature philosophic activity not only to deepen his understanding of things but to *be* something more? This question that we hardly think to ask also isn't asked by anyone in the *Republic*. Yet the question is perhaps posed and even answered—affirmatively—by the *Republic* as a whole, in which we see Socrates engaging a room full of young interlocutors. Might not his educating others also be an exercise in self-perfection? The Image of the Cave, the paradigmatic representation of what we might call the perfectionist view of philosophy, leaves open the possibility of further challenges and further perfection for the one who has gained liberation. And the conversation in which the Image is introduced suggests that Socrates might be trying to actualize that possibility.

What Plato *allows*, Rousseau *articulates*. In *The Reveries of the Solitary Walker* Rousseau depicts the ongoing development or perfection of the philosophic life by one who is already living it. To show this, if I am successful, may be the chief contribution of my book. For I believe that Rousseau's articulation of the ongoing perfection of the philosophic life and soul—his articulation of the philosophic life and soul in their ongoing becoming—may be *his* chief contribution on the subject of the philosophic life and one that, as far as I can tell, has barely begun to be understood.

Let me be careful not to seem to be saying something I'm not. That Rousseau regards the philosophic life as allowing for and even demanding further development does not keep him from regarding the philosophic life as such—from its outset—as radically distinct from other ways of life, including the life that immediately preceded and gave rise to it. For all that Rousseau contravenes the perfectionist view of philosophy, he nevertheless accepts much of what belongs to it. Like Plato, he treats philosophy as a rare way of life centered on the pursuit of knowledge for its own sake, especially self-knowledge. Like Plato, he embraces philosophy as the freest, most sufficient, and most choiceworthy life for one whose nature and circumstances permit it. Like Plato (*Republic*, 521e), he regards the turn to philosophy as a turning of the soul, a turning so decisive—and permanent—as to make it the decisive step of one's life as a whole, notwithstanding that further steps remain to be taken.

So decisive a transformation is indeed comparable to stepping out of a cave into daylight. But perhaps the better comparison is one provided by Rousseau himself. His sweeping account of humanity's development in the *Second Discourse* designates several epochal moments "revolutions" but only one of them a "*great* revolution" (171; 152; emphasis added). The reference is to the onset of property, inequality, and forced labor in consequence of the invention of metallurgy and agriculture. The *Reveries* too recounts one and only one "great revolution." As Rousseau depicts it, *this* great revolution, precipitated by a profound inquiry, consisted in his settling once and for all his opinions about God and the soul (III, 9). Close reading, however, reveals that his "great review" was the start of a life of unending questioning, and that the only opinion it yielded that he would continue to hold (though not without questioning) was the choiceworthiness or needfulness of the philosophic life. His great review, in short, was the beginning of his philosophic life.[1]

Revolutions are important. A *great* revolution is epochal. It sets the terms on which all subsequent life will take place. What was it that led Rousseau to accord unique importance to the changes brought about by metallurgy and agriculture and not, say, to the onset of sustained cohabitation of men and women, or the founding of the first state, or various other events that are apt to strike us as equally epochal? And what does this suggest about the great revolution recounted in the *Reveries*? The unique importance of metallurgy and agriculture lay in their uniquely important role with respect to personal dependence, which Rousseau regards as the most powerful extrinsic shaper of human life. Metallurgy and agriculture radically extended, intensified, and anchored personal dependence, not only material dependence but also psychic dependence, by making the division of labor outside the home possible and profitable and therefore

---

1. Meier too sees the Third Walk as recounting the beginning of Rousseau's philosophic life. See Meier, *On the Happiness*, 51, 54, and 58.

necessary and permanent.[2] And the philosophic life? Its "great revolution," which transforms a nonphilosopher into a philosopher, is the *reversal* of humanity's great revolution. For to live as a philosopher is to live with enormous *in*dependence.

That personal dependence can be reversed—if not completely, then considerably—is good news. Yet this good news would seem to be cruelly limited in scope. Whereas metallurgy and agriculture transformed the condition of human life as such, the philosophic life transforms only the rare individual who has the capacity for it and is drawn to it without being corrupted along the way. The consequences for the larger world would seem to be negligible, not least because these few are apt to be regarded, when they are regarded at all, as weird if not wicked (*Republic*, 487e–495a). In fact, though, the possibilities are greater than that. As we'll see, Rousseau believes that philosophers can influence the wider world—not by publicly philosophizing but by assuming something very much like the part of the Legislator, the larger-than-life figure who forms peoples (*SC*, 381–82; 155).

The political activity of true philosophers *follows from* their being philosophers; it does not *make* them philosophers. As Socrates's choice of interlocutors suggests, disenchanted political aspirants may be among the likeliest candidates for philosophy. But the turn to philosophy, to *true* philosophy, requires that the disenchantment with politics be complete. Disenchantment with politics belongs to a more comprehensive liberation of *la conscience* (meaning both conscience and consciousness) from political and indeed all external authority. The heart of this liberation, finally—and thus what marks the philosophic life as conceived by Rousseau—is a certain transformation: *The philosopher is one who has overcome what I will call the ordinary moral consciousness in favor of what I will call the cognitivist view of morality.* By the ordinary moral consciousness I mean the presuppositions that underpin moral judgment as we normally understand it, according to which right and wrong actions are done by individuals who know or should have known right and wrong and who may therefore be praised or blamed in accordance with the *free choice* they have made. What I am calling the cognitivist view of morality, by contrast, holds that everyone acts in pursuit of what he or she takes to be good—that one's actions necessarily follow from, indeed are *compelled* by, what one takes to be good—and thus that right and wrong actions arise, respectively, from

2. On the signal importance of personal dependence in Rousseau's thought, particularly as a cause of unhappiness and corruption, see Melzer, *Natural Goodness of Man*, 70–85. Also see Dent, *Rousseau*, 52–67 and 70–85.

right judgment (either knowledge or right opinion) and wrong judgment (error or ignorance). The cognitivist view does not rest on any teleological metaphysics but only on the recognition that action follows from desire and that desire instantiates what seems desirable, or good, to the desirer. Overcoming the ordinary moral consciousness in favor of the cognitivist view of morality is necessary to the philosophic life as understood by Rousseau—and not only by Rousseau.[3] It is necessary in the first instance because it is true: we *are* compelled by the apparent good. It is also necessary because the incoherence of the ordinary moral consciousness inevitably skews our sight of much else. Whether overcoming the ordinary moral consciousness is sufficient for the philosophic life is harder to say. If it *is* sufficient, it is so by virtue of producing or allowing a number of additional qualities.

As transcending the ordinary moral consciousness in favor of the cognitivist view of morality signifies that one has embarked on the philosophic life, more perfectly transcending the ordinary moral consciousness in favor of the cognitivist view signifies that one has further perfected the philosophic life. This further perfection is the main plotline of the *Reveries*. More precisely, the main narrative thrust of the book is Rousseau's movement toward perfecting and securing the transcendence of the ordinary moral perspective in favor of the cognitivist view of morality. Rousseau already knows at the outset of the book that the philosophic life entails overcoming the ordinary moral consciousness in favor of the cognitivist view of morality. He already knows that this wholesale transformation of consciousness is both demanded by reason and required for his happiness. Its necessity for happiness is twofold, both negative and positive. Negative: Overcoming the ordinary moral consciousness would allow him, the victim of a sustained, unjust conspiracy, to regard this injustice with some detachment. He wouldn't need to worry that he deserves the punishment he's receiving or fear that his world (his worldview) has been refuted. Positive: having been relieved of the foregoing anxieties and resentment, he would have easier access to the wonders of being. Yet although he understands these things *in principle* at the start of the book, he continues to labor under a very compromising self-deception. During most of the narrative, he believes or at least tells himself that he has already overcome the

3. The Platonic Socrates argues in several dialogues for the cognitivist view of morality—not straightforwardly, but in the end, I think, emphatically. See Lorraine Pangle's remarkable study *Virtue Is Knowledge*. Whether Socrates considers embrace of the cognitivist view a requirement to be a true philosopher is less certain but is arguably suggested by the action of several dialogues.

ordinary moral consciousness—that he has already attained resignation, acceptance, and calm—when he clearly has not done so. His further perfection as a philosopher, his more complete overcoming of the ordinary moral consciousness, will depend on his seeing through this deception.

If "seeing through" seems to imply a conscious and canny deceiver, that's because it does. Readers of Rousseau's other works won't be surprised to learn that the deceiver is amour-propre. Rousseau's amour-propre, in this instance taking the form of "petty self-pride," has been disguising itself as a noble passion for justice (VIII, 15). Amour-propre's cunning and tenacity indicate that for Rousseau, as for Plato, the self is a kind of polity whose various factions pursue their own agendas unless they are adequately governed.

Rousseau's discovery of his long-standing self-deception is what finally allows him to embrace the cognitivist view of morality more firmly. The discovery is recounted in the Eighth Walk. It is made possible by a more general philosophic breakthrough that occurs in the Seventh Walk, a breakthrough concerning how to look at and see things. Rousseau articulates the breakthrough with reference to botany. Where once he had seen only a mass of foliage, he now can see an intricate, variegated, and hierarchical system of beings (VII, 16). He develops an astounding new conceptual depth perception—and not only with respect to plants. Everything that Rousseau says about his newly deepened and clarified way of botanizing applies to the study of nature as such, very much including human nature and one's own particular nature (*naturel*).

Overcoming the ordinary moral consciousness—not the most reassuring phrase, to be sure. Yet it does not mean overcoming morality as such or moral concern and obligation, though it might seem to from the perspective of the ordinary moral consciousness. These terms are understood differently, however. Just and unjust now refer respectively to what serves and what detracts from *the good* or *the health* of the parties concerned.

What is at issue between the ordinary moral consciousness and the cognitivist view of morality is, at bottom, the question of human freedom. Those governed by the ordinary moral consciousness presume that we have freely chosen to do what we have done and that our choices and deeds are therefore rightly subject to moral praise and blame. They admit, however, that this rule doesn't always hold: sometimes we act unfreely, either because we have been compelled or because we have acted in ignorance, and in those instances we should not be held blameworthy. The critique of the ordinary moral consciousness begins by asking whether what it allows as an exception isn't in fact the rule—not because someone is coercing us or keeping important information from us, but simply because we always do, we are always compelled to do, whatever seems good for us to do. And to be compelled by anything is to be, in some sense, unfree. If we act badly, it is because we are in error regarding what would be good to do. But are we not responsible for that error? In part, yes: we think for ourselves and we habituate ourselves to certain views by acting as we do. But in deeper part, no. Yes, we think for ourselves; but we began to do so only when released from the tutelage of others. Yes, we play a great role in shaping our own judgment and character; but the self that took on this role of character shaping was not self-created. This is by no means to deny human freedom, though, again, it is bound to seem so to the ordinary moral consciousness. Rather, it is to identify the true locus and nature of our freedom. Our freedom is freedom of *mind*. We can reflect on and change what it is that seems good to us. We can make progress toward a truer vision of the good (as, of course, we can devolve toward a more erroneous vision of the good). But this freedom, though natural, must be won; and according to Rousseau, as to the Socratics he follows in this, the winning is a rare and difficult thing.

The Plan of This Book

This book has a dual character. On the one hand, it is a study of the philosophic life as treated by one of its most illuminating expositors. On the other hand, it is a commentary on a particular text by a particular author—an understudied and underappreciated book by a much-studied and much-appreciated author. Fortunately, ambidexterity isn't required—just a modest degree of coordination. For although the two tasks are analytically discrete and to some extent discretely treated (with part 1 roughly dedicated to the first task and part 2 to the second), they are so intertwined as to ensure that neither hand operates independently of the other.

Part 1 is organized thematically. In chapter 1, I present an overview of Rousseau's teaching on the philosophic life as articulated in *The Reveries of the Solitary Walker*. My purpose there is to adumbrate major elements of this teaching and how they relate to one another. In keeping with the *Reveries'* narrative or developmental character, my account will particularly emphasize development and dynamics, that is, the coming-to-be of the philosophic life and its ongoing perfection after it has come to be. So developmentally oriented is Rousseau's teaching, though, that it cannot be adequately uncovered without sustained attention to the shape and character of the book. Literary analysis in such a case is not a diversion from philosophic inquiry but rather a part of it. Such analysis is the task of chapter 2, in which I sketch the arc of the *Reveries'* narrative and introduce other general features of the book.

Rousseau's teaching on the philosophic life is too rich, too subtle, and too developmental both in conception and in depiction to be distilled. The education he offers requires close reading of the *Reveries* in its entirety. In part 2, I present one such reading.

PART I

CHAPTER 1

The Life of Philosophy and the Life of Rousseau

Whatever else it may be, *The Reveries of the Solitary Walker* is a book about Rousseau. Yet given that the book consists in far more than reveries and that Rousseau is never quite as solitary as his title suggests, perhaps we shouldn't be surprised that the advertised particularism belies a more general teaching. Yes, the book tells the story of the philosophic life of Jean-Jacques Rousseau. But it also, necessarily, says much about the philosophic life as such and human life as such.

So Rousseau says. But how much can a single case tell us about the general phenomenon or the species as a whole? *Is* the philosophic life a general phenomenon? Forget about a species—are philosophers even a breed? And how can such a peculiar human type deepen our understanding of humanity in general? Rousseau knows himself to be a most unusual, not to say idiosyncratic, man. Yet precisely *because* of his idiosyncrasy he also regards himself as a kind of paradigm for all human beings. As Michael Davis puts it, "what operates in all men, and may even be their defining feature, is much more powerfully manifest in Rousseau. What is special about Rousseau is what is common to us all."[1] My reading of Rousseau's singularity is not identical with Davis's. What I regard as perhaps most special about Rousseau as he presents himself in the *Reveries* (and other writings) is the degree to which natural goodness has remained alive in him despite a youth marked by harsh and perverse circumstances and an adulthood spent mostly in and around Paris, capital of a corrupt monarchy and an even more corrupt "republic" of letters. And if Rousseau exemplifies the defining feature of men, if indeed there *is* such a thing, the feature

---

1. Davis, *Autobiography of Philosophy*, 169. Rousseau's view of his universal significance, which is implied in the *Reveries,* is stated at the outset of the *Confessions*: "I wish to show my fellows a man in all the truth of nature; and this man will be myself" (5; 5).

I would nominate is the ongoing interplay and negotiation between his natural goodness on the one hand and the unnatural elements of both his own being and the surrounding society, on the other. What it means to be a natural human being is no small question, and it won't do to work out the whole matter here. But the core of the matter, the sine qua non of naturalness in a human being, is the predominance in the soul of amour de soi.[2] To be sure, Rousseau like the rest of us lives a life full of convention and artifice; and he experiences his share of unnatural passions and probably more than his share of peculiar ones, owing to the copresence in his soul of an exquisitely subtle and intelligent sensibility and an exceedingly touchy amour-propre. Yet as we can discern from the *Reveries* (as from the *Confessions*), amour-propre has never completely overtaken him: it has never choked off his natural goodness.[3] It is because he has somehow retained or remained in touch with what, in the rest of us, has been more completely suppressed that he can present himself as the paradigm for us all.

We can go even further than that. Rousseau's resistance to succumbing entirely to amour-propre not only keeps nature meaningfully alive in him; it also allows him to become a "celestial intelligence" (to use his term) or true philosopher (to use mine). For becoming a true philosopher means coming to see the world as much as possible as it *is*, without distortion; and only those who have freed themselves from the tyranny of amour-propre can begin to approach this condition. Now let us consider: If Rousseau is a paradigm for all of us by virtue of his naturalness, he is all the more so for being a philosopher. For philosophers, who resist succumbing to the tyranny of amour-propre even as they develop their reason—who free themselves from amour-propre all the more through the *use* of their reason—are not only natural beings but natural *human* beings. Philosophers are the most natural human beings among us; indeed they may be the only natural human beings the world has ever known. The men and

2. See my study *Rousseau, Nature, and the Problem of the Good Life*.

3. Why Rousseau was never completely overtaken by amour-propre is ultimately unknowable, but the proximate causes seem to include a rare nature, including great strength of soul (however idiosyncratically expressed), and various strokes of good fortune, some of which seemed anything but good fortune at the time. A stroke of good fortune that *did* seem good at the time was his being admitted into the tender care of Madame de Warens at an especially formative time of his life (X). His natural goodness may also have found crucial support from beneficent clergy prior to his sojourn with Madame de Warens. See *Emile*, 559–64; 419–24; and *Confessions*, 119; 100. For more on what the *Confessions* has to say about what sustained Rousseau's natural goodness or his access to it, see my "Nearer My True Self to Thee."

women who inhabited the pure state of nature were undeniably natural, if in fact they ever existed; but it is questionable whether such beings really ought to be considered human.

The Philosophic Life

The details of Rousseau's philosophic life, as of any life, are accidental and idiosyncratic. Yet behind the details—or, perhaps more accurately, within them—are basic elements and themes that belong to the philosophic life as such as conceived by Rousseau. These same elements and themes are adumbrated in the *Republic* and arguably by the Socratic tradition more generally: what the philosophic life *is*, or the activities and pursuits in which it consists; its prerequisites; its goodness for those for whom it *is* good; and the dangers it poses. Most of these matters are best encountered as Rousseau tells them, that is, as we work through the *Reveries* Walk by Walk. But there are a few matters that we'd do well to note now: matters that seem to have proven particularly easy either to miss or to misunderstand.

ACTIVITIES AND PURSUITS

The philosophic life is distinguished both by philosophizing proper and by distinctive ways of conducting oneself in activities other than philosophizing. Philosophizing is the passionate, relentless pursuit of truth regarding the Whole through one's own reason, a pursuit that cannot help but call into question one's original foundational beliefs but which is not made any the less resolute or joyful for that, though, to be sure, the *initial* challenge to one's beliefs is bound to be enormously difficult and even searing. This questioning is bound to leave one with more questions than one had started with and many more questions than answers. But not with *no* answers. One answer that counts for a lot is the goodness and happiness of the philosophic life. This goodness and happiness are knowable only through experience, however, which means that one undertakes the life of philosophy with at best only intimations of or trust in its joys even as one is subjected immediately to its difficulties. As for the ways in which philosophers conduct themselves in activities other than philosophizing proper, much will surely depend on the particular philosopher's unique nature and on the character and condition of the surrounding society. This is especially true concerning activity that bears on politics or religion.

The philosopher as understood by Rousseau—the philosopher *as* philosopher, as seeker of self-knowledge and knowledge of the world—must engage the political. There can be no clear sight of the Whole without considering oneself and one's place in relation to the Whole, that is, without a certain degree of self-consciousness and self-knowledge, and there can be no self-knowledge without reflection on how one has been formed by the regime in which one came to consciousness. In holding this view Rousseau is at one with the classical philosophic tradition, which was born with Socrates's "second sailing" away from the natural philosophy of his predecessors in favor of examining *logoi* (*Phaedo*, 99c–d). Whatever we may be by nature and whatever or whoever we have become, we have been formed in the first place by authoritative opinion. And authoritative opinion—the *most* authoritative opinion, opinion concerning the most authoritative matters, beginning with what should count as the ultimate *source* of authority—will always have been determined by the *politiea*, or regime. Not even the freest minds can avoid having been reared with and thus shaped by a slew of prejudices and presuppositions. Their freedom will have been won precisely by becoming aware of and then critically examining authoritative opinion according to the best lights of their reason. Nor does the necessity of political philosophy to self-knowledge or philosophy as such stop there. Political philosophy is necessary not only to philosophy's *coming-into*-being but also to its *being* itself. If philosophy is to be true to itself as the practice of relentless, rational inquiry, it must confront its most powerful alternatives and critics. This too is a political inquiry, and one that must be sustained continually if philosophy is to remain philosophy. In Greece this meant confronting the city's gods and myths and the poets who propounded them. In Rousseau's time, it meant confronting both revealed religion and the modern rationalism that claimed to have refuted that religion. In our time it would mean confronting revealed religion, modern rationalism, and the postmodern critique of reason.

There is another reason that philosophy needs to be political philosophy: as philosophy requires freedom from authoritative opinion, so too it requires a certain freedom from, meaning no enslavement to, the passions. Now most passions spring from or owe their intensity to amour-propre. Thus the philosopher must break free of amour-propre's grip. This does not mean, nor should we want it to mean, *purging* oneself either of amour-propre or of the passions. What is wanted is that the philosopher *understand* amour-propre, which requires, again, a kind of political inquiry, since it is in politics that amour-propre shows itself most vividly and comprehensively and since amour-propre's primary expression is the passion for (what it sees as) justice. Even the solitary in his solitude must engage the political, though this is easily lost on those not attuned to society's formative influence on the polity that is the soul.[4]

As noted earlier, Rousseau also undertook political *activity*, indeed political activity arguably of the grandest kind. And he seems to have done so for positive and intrinsic reasons rather than defensive and instrumental ones. Exiled, despised, and disabused of faith in his contemporaries, the mature Rousseau had long eschewed ordinary politics as much as Socrates had. And yet his corpus and indeed the *Reveries* itself give signs that throughout his career he attempted to educate and persuade and thereby *legislate*, if not for his contemporaries then for generations soon to come. To successfully propagate new teachings regarding the greatest things— things such as natural goodness, the question of the good life, and what (and how) to think about God—is to legislate anew for a people, since people's views on these matters necessarily shape how they conceive of and live their lives.[5] From the *First Discourse* onward, this is exactly what Rousseau attempted to do. This kind of legislating proceeds in the way implicitly suggested by Plato's Image of the Cave. It consists primarily in supplanting prior understandings of the divine, the good, the just, the beautiful, and so on with new understandings. The old puppets and puppeteers are replaced by new ones. (To be sure, *explicit* rule by philosopher-kings is proposed by Socrates only to be revealed as impracticable and undesirable. Implicit rule of the kind I've indicated is another matter.) Despite the grand scope of its ambition, philosophic legislation need not speak directly to society at large; it may suffice to educate a relative few who will proceed to educate others in turn.

The *Reveries* does not have an evident political intention. Yet the very fact that Rousseau veils the truth about the philosophic life indicates that he has written the *Reveries* mindful of certain political *concerns*. The solitary walker might want to be done with society, but he can't be, if only because society is not done with him. In fact, though, it seems to me that Rousseau does *not* want to be done with society. And his political concerns are substantial enough that perhaps they should be regarded as intentions after

4. For a fuller treatment of the centrality of political philosophy to philosophy as such and to Rousseau's embrace of this view, see Meier, *Political Philosophy and the Challenge of Revealed Religion*, 3–22 and 115–86, respectively.

5. "There is almost no human action, however particular one supposes it, that does not arise from a very general idea that men have conceived of God, of his relations with the human race, of the nature of their souls, and of their duties toward those like them. One cannot keep these ideas from being the common source from which all the rest flow." Tocqueville, *Democracy in America*, 417.

all. Two major political concerns can be discerned in the *Reveries*, though we may doubt whether Rousseau expected to succeed on either count. Neither is new, though each explores territory that was not explored in his prior works. First, he hopes to safeguard and perhaps revivify the philosophic life properly understood—which is to say Socratically understood, though with distinctively Rousseauan revisions and additions. Second, he means to promote wholesome activities and even a new and wholesome orientation to life. As far apart as these two ends are from each other and as improbable of success as they may be, the means whereby Rousseau seeks to accomplish them are one and the same: in each case he offers himself as an exemplar. To readers who are philosophically capable and inclined, he provides an introduction to the philosophic life and something like an invitation to it. I say *"something like* an invitation" because admission requires more than Rousseau's permission; it requires that one be able to find one's way to the destined place. But if the invitation is for that reason attenuated and thus less than an invitation, it may also be *more* than an invitation for those who do manage to find their way: to these readers the *Reveries* may offer an *initiation* into the philosophic life. Readers who are not philosophically inclined also receive an introduction and invitation to a certain kind of life, indeed a *good* life, though not a philosophic one. The life advertised to them is one of rustic simplicity and inner cultivation amid the beauty and fruitfulness of verdant nature. It is a life of relative naturalness and freedom, of botany and reverie, as practiced by the solitary walker. I don't mean to say that Rousseau expects that readers would want to emulate the extreme that is *his* life. He knows that the appeal of a quiet life in the country, replete with regular stretches of solitude, though it will surely register with many readers, is likely to fall short in the face of innumerable passions and desires. He himself, who had an unusual gift for solitude, still had to be forced into it (I, 1). Nor would he have *wanted* vast numbers to emulate his solitude, for this would not be consistent with society's good (VI, 21). Yet he seems to suppose that the *Reveries*, particularly the splendid Fifth and Seventh Walks, might move readers toward a quieter and more natural way of life.

The *Reveries* is not an attempt at legislation on par with the *First* and *Second Discourses*, the *Social Contract*, or *Emile*, though its promotion of a more natural life is continuous with the efforts of those earlier works. Nor does Rousseau mean to defend the legislative enterprises of his prior works by defending himself, as he had done in the *Confessions* and the *Dialogues*. But he does seem to intend that readers taken by the *Reveries* might be led to the earlier, more robustly legislative works—one in particular. In the Third Walk he refers to "The Profession of Faith of the Savoyard Vicar," which appears at the center of *Emile*, as "a work vilely prostituted and pro-faned among the present generation but which may one day *make a revolu-tion among men*, if good sense and good faith are ever reborn among them" (III, 17; emphasis added). Yet another political concern can be discerned in the *Reveries*, though this one can't really be called a political *intention*. It is to articulate the place and meaning of political activity—legislative activity—in the philosophic life, at any rate in *his* philosophic life.

That Rousseau ever meant to act the part of the Legislator might seem doubtful. In several works he voices a profound pessimism regarding the prospects of a renewed politics, let alone a new founding or legislating. In the *Second Discourse* he observes that "the same vices that make social institutions necessary, make their abuse inevitable" (*SD*, 187–88; 62). And in the *Social Contract* he insists that the doors to a free society have been closed almost everywhere, most especially in Europe (*SC*, 385–86; 157–58). But these professions of pessimism don't rule out the kind of "revolution among men" that might be made by "The Profession of Faith of the Savo-yard Vicar." Nor can they be thought to hold forever. Whatever he thought of their likelihood of success, Rousseau saw that an age of revolutions was nearing (*Emile*, 468; 343). Thus he may have written in the hope of shaping the world to follow. If peoples, like persons, sink into irreversible debility with age, don't they also like persons die and thus make way for the birth of new peoples? Any fruit that might come of Rousseau's legislative efforts would come long after his time. But that's something the Legislator knows and accepts. The Legislator is one who, "preparing for himself a future glory with the passage of time, could work in one century and enjoy the reward in another" (*SC*, 381; 154).

What is the appeal of political activity to a philosopher? A number of motives are possible and indeed seem likely. But paramount among them may be a philanthropic disposition. Such a disposition is to be expected in one who is happy and feels sufficiently powerful, which in turn is to be expected in those who have preserved or recovered their natural goodness. Amour-propre surely plays a role in this, as in all political activity, but an amour-propre answerable to the purposes of amour de soi.[6]

PREREQUISITES

Rousseau offers nothing in the *Reveries* comparable to Socrates's system-atic treatment in *Republic* 6 and 7 of the qualities of soul and the educa-

---

6. The same logic is seen in Emile, whose benevolent disposition gains depth and prudence from an extended period of political inquiry (825–68; 640–75).

tion needed to become a philosopher. He treats only his own case. We may at least note, however, that nothing he says is at odds with Socrates's teaching and that the main elements of his account are decidedly aligned with Socrates's teaching. Like his classical forebears, Rousseau regards philosophy not as an academic discipline but as a rare and comprehensive way of life that requires rare and comprehensive gifts. Apt candidates for philosophy must be intellectually adept and have an ardent passion for knowledge. They must be able to tolerate and even flourish amid uncertainty regarding fundamental questions. And they must have the resources to resist the siren song of vanity that can easily corrupt great talents and great souls.

Unlike the imagined philosophers-to-be in the *Republic*, Rousseau wasn't successfully educated in civic virtue in his youth. But he did go on to develop a passionate *love* of virtue (*Dialogues*, 822–23; 126–27). And during his philosophically formative years, by which I mean the years in which he first seriously studied the arts and sciences, he was nurtured and provided for by a devoted mistress. He didn't have much formal education in the arts and sciences, it's true; but as Plato's Academy was not an available option, that might have been just as well. In any case, the greatest minds, Rousseau tells us, must necessarily be self-taught. The paths to the heights they might scale cannot be traced in advance by teachers (*FD*, 29–30; 21; *Emile*, 266; 178).

Rousseau's irregular youth left him with an inordinately touchy and demanding amour-propre from whose control he would need to free himself. But no matter how deranged and deranging his amour-propre often was, it took its bearings from an impartial conception of justice. If his youthful understanding of justice and its role in human affairs, suffused as it was by the ordinary moral consciousness, was ultimately dubious, his passion for justice was fierce, and his conscious understanding of justice was principled and impartial, and they were kept so by his amour-propre. Even as a young man Rousseau's amour-propre was a source of a moral seriousness that, though grounded in beliefs that would be found wanting when he stood at the threshold of the philosophic life, was needed to take him to—and across—the threshold of the philosophic life in the first place. Also helping to safeguard him against the allure of various unworthy and corrupt lives, including the pseudophilosophic life, were several qualities that belong to his nature. At various places he characterizes his nature (his *naturel*) as timid, independent, ardent, and indolent (IV, 2 and 41; VI, 21; VIII, 23). He doesn't explicitly identify these phenomena as prerequisites of his (or any) philosophic life. But they square uncannily well with Socrates's articulation of the prerequisites of the philosophic life in the *Republic*. Even indolence fits the picture once one recognizes that what Rousseau means by this word is much closer to freedom than to laziness.

But how can Rousseau's account be deemed similar to Socrates's when the latter emphasizes the need for virtue, something that Rousseau admits that he lacks (VI, 7)? Can a love of virtue stand in for the thing itself? Doubtful. But it doesn't need to. For if he lacks virtue (defined in a certain way) Rousseau has *goodness*. Of course we're all naturally good, according to Rousseau. But in him natural goodness has not been suffocated by artifice and corruption. As one who has withstood the un- and antinatural pressures of civilization even as he has availed himself of civilization's inestimable gifts, he is in a position to gain, wonder at, and appreciate such clear sight of what *is* as is available to human beings. Natural goodness impedes obstructions, distortions, and perceived threats. And *consciousness* of natural goodness yields yet another reward that is at the same time a further inducement to philosophize. Those who have achieved this consciousness will recognize that in studying nature they are gaining self-knowledge and that in loving nature they are experiencing and further cultivating the most benign love of self.

GOODNESS

Throughout his corpus Rousseau had gone to great pains to suppress the attractions of philosophy and cast suspicion on it as corrupting and immiserating. Whatever he allowed onto the positive side of philosophy's ledger were presented as brief and unaccountable exceptions to the larger and darker picture. His harsh criticism of philosophy may have been exaggerated even by his own lights. But it was not fundamentally untrue by his lights; and its purpose was to serve the cause of truth. After all, most of what is called philosophy *had* been corrupting and immiserating in his view. Even truly estimable works of philosophy posed great dangers while offering only small and improbable benefits. He maintains this stance in the *Reveries*, despite the book's being, as it were, his *Apology for Philosophy*. His intention to communicate the goodness of the philosophic life to some has not weakened his resolve to veil philosophy's goodness from those for whom it would not be good—and who in turn might be bad for *it*. Indeed, Rousseau's critique of philosophy in the *Reveries* goes further than the prior critiques by denying the goodness of philosophy even for himself. As we've seen, he purports to find thinking "painful and charmless" (VII, 5). Yet this criticism, like the others, doesn't say quite what it seems to say. We'll examine this claim in part 2, but brief consideration of the matter now will be helpful preparation.

The case for the *Reveries* as an articulation and celebration of the philosophic life divides into two broad lines of argument. First is the argument from performance, as we might call it: the book recounts and indeed *demonstrates* the joyfulness of the philosophic life. Parts of the *Reveries* palpably beat with the joy attending activities and practices that most of us would consider in some way contemplative. Some of these expressions of joy are almost surely overstated: on closer examination they seem less joyful than defiant. Others, however, make sense and ring true. We encounter in the *Reveries* the joy of freedom and idleness, of one who pursues meandering thoughts during meandering walks; the joy, indeed the rapture and ecstasy, of reverie (VII, V); the joy of botany, in which Rousseau apprehends the wonders of nature and even merges with nature (VII); the joy of wholesome and sometimes tender interactions with strangers, especially children (IX); the joy of remembering those who had loved him, particularly Madame de Warens, whose own goodness had nurtured his (X); and the joys of simple rustic life in which the "solitary walker" could spend time every day eating, working, and singing with a handful of pleasant companions who also left him the privacy he needed.

If the casual reader sees all of this, the careful reader will see all of this and more. Part of what is encompassed by this "more" seems to push against reading the *Reveries* as an endorsement of the philosophic life, either by uncovering grounds on which to suspect Rousseau of exaggeration or by prompting us to ask whether some of the activities and experiences he recounts really deserve to be called contemplative. Yet even as a close reading takes some of the wind out of the sails of the interpretation of the *Reveries* as philo-philosophic, it provides new winds or even new sails that push *for* this interpretation. However much we might come to suspect Rousseau of exaggerating his "raptures" and "ecstasies," and however many of his experiences we deem on inspection not to be contemplative, we can't help but notice that whatever he might *say* about disliking reflection, the book he has written, *the book he has chosen to write for the sake of his own pleasure* (I, 15), is full of rational, scientific, and even synoptic reflection. This is evident from the opening paragraph onward—which is to say, before Rousseau purported to deny it. In the first paragraph he poses a scientific question, "What am I?"—not *who?*, but *what?*—and prepares to undertake an unprecedented scientific inquiry.[7] Probably the clearest examples of directed, rational inquiry in the *Reveries* are the meditation on truth and lying (which turns out to be a

---

7. Pierre Manent observes a "scientific tonality" in these features of the *Reveries* and in the book as a whole. See Manent, "To Walk, to Dream, to Philosophize," 220–21.

meditation on justice and injustice) in the Fourth Walk and the exploration of freedom versus obligation in the Sixth Walk. If other parts of the book are not as obviously rational, however, that's only because they are more subtly and artfully rational—and thus in a sense *more* rational. Indeed I would contend that the entirety of the *Reveries* is informed by and even consists in subtle and rigorous reflection, however much Rousseau's style and rhetoric suggest otherwise and however *un*reflective some of the experiences on which he reflects may be. His protestations notwithstanding, it is evident that Rousseau finds pleasure in reflection and in writing as well. Certainly he *expects* to find pleasure in reflection and writing. Why engage in such a project if he does not find it rewarding? The *Reveries* as a whole and even in its most unlikely parts is a performative apology for a thoughtful life.

And yet the truth is even more interesting and illuminating than that. Here we come to the second line of argument in favor of reading the *Reveries* as philo-philosophic. Not only is Rousseau's claim to dislike thinking undermined by his demonstrated embrace of the philosophic life; it is also *self*-undermining. For on close reading with attention to context—precisely the kind of reading Rousseau would expect of a philosophic reader—his claim is so qualified as to signify something very different from what it initially appears to mean. Some kind or kinds of thinking are indeed fatiguing to him, but not philosophy. Indeed, Rousseau makes the case *for* philosophy even while seeming to make the case against it.

The claim to dislike thinking appears amid a lengthy and exultant discussion of botany—that is to say, a discussion of *Rousseau's* botanizing, which is animated by a radically different spirit from that which animates others'. Whereas others practice botany instrumentally, in pursuit of drugs with which to treat our ills, Rousseau delights in the study of plants for the wonders that they *are*. His claim to dislike thinking is not discordant with the surrounding discussion of botany because he suggests that his botanizing consists not so much in thinking as in *reverie*. Here is the entirety of the Seventh Walk's fifth paragraph:

> I have sometimes thought rather deeply, but rarely with pleasure, almost always against my liking, and as though by force. Reverie relaxes and amuses me; reflection tires and saddens me; thinking always was a painful and charmless occupation for me. Sometimes my reveries end in meditation, but more often my meditations end in reverie; and during these wanderings, my soul rambles and glides through the universe on the wings of imagination, in ecstasies which surpass every other enjoyment. (VII, 5)

It does not take long, however, for the reader to realize that botany as Rousseau pursues it is rigorously scientific. It presupposes considerable knowledge and understanding, and it yields more of the same. Indeed, that which seems most *unscientific* in Rousseau's account—that is, his experience of oneness with nature—is testimony to the scientific character of the endeavor. For it is not nature simply or nature in toto but rather the *system* of nature with which Rousseau merges (VII, 9, 16); and there can have been no apprehension of this system without scientific rigor and knowledge. Nor are this rigor and knowledge left behind once one has climbed the ladder, so to speak. Rousseau's splendid sense of merging with nature requires not only that he *have* apprehended nature as a system but also that he *continue* to apprehend it that way, which is to say, that he continue to *think*, that he continue to hold in mind the *thought* of nature as system, even as he *experiences* what his thinking has revealed.

Is it not possible, though, that however wonderful its *yield*, Rousseau does not enjoy the *activity* of thinking? He seems to suggest as much, for only two paragraphs after introducing his new kind of botanizing he assigns the experience of oneness with nature to ecstatic and intoxicating *reverie* (VII, 9). But there are reveries, and there are reveries in Rousseau's book, and this one is of a different sort from those that he has given up. And sometimes what Rousseau *calls* reverie isn't.

Rousseau does find some thinking painful. In the six paragraphs separating the two accounts of his ecstatic oneness with nature (VII, 10–15) he contrasts his own botanizing with that of almost everyone else. *He* gives himself up to his senses (10). *Others* investigate plants with a practical purpose that has nothing to do with immediate enjoyment, whether sensory or otherwise. *His* eyes wander, as he himself wanders, from object to object and always light upon something captivating. *Their* eyes do their seeing through microscopes. *He* delights in "ocular recreation," drawing great pleasure from "fragrant odors, intense colors, [and] the most elegant shapes," which compete with one another to present themselves to him. *They* do not. Rousseau explains the sources of these differences:

> To give oneself up to such delicious sensations, it is necessarily only to love pleasure. And if this effect does not occur for all those who perceive these objects, with some it is due to a lack of natural sensitivity and with most it is because their mind, too preoccupied with other ideas, only furtively gives itself up to the objects which strike their senses.
>
> Yet another thing contributes to turning refined people's attention away from the vegetable realm: the habit of seeking only drugs and remedies in plants. (11–12)

Hardly anyone, ancient or modern, has taken up botany for any purpose other than to find drugs and remedies for the ills of the body. Hardly anyone, therefore, according to Rousseau's strict standard, has really been a botanist at all. Rousseau's refusal to confer the title of "botanist" on those who study plants only in pursuit of drugs is remarkable. After all, he could have referred to such people as incomplete or even bad botanists. In fact, though, he *couldn't*: those who study plants only in search of remedies are not botanists, for they do not see plants: "Medicine has taken possession of plants and transformed them into simples to such an extent that *we see in them what we do not see in them at all,* to wit, the pretended virtues it pleases just anybody to attribute to them" (12; emphasis added).

Rousseau's desire to see plants (and everything else) as they are does not mean that he endorses and practices only disinterested inquiry. He notes with pleasure that he has "often thought that the vegetable realm was a storehouse of foods given to man and animals by nature" (VII, 14); and he praises Linnaeus, one of two exceptions to his sweeping critique of prior botanists (the other is Theophrastus, about whom more later), for "somewhat tak[ing] botany out of pharmacology schools and [bringing] it back to natural history and economic uses" (12). These endorsements of interested botanical inquiry suggest an endorsement of at least some kinds of interested inquiry into nature. They even allow for, and perhaps suggest, that philosophy by its nature is not disinterested. What offends Rousseau is not the interested study of plants but rather the particular interest that has dominated the field to the exclusion of other interests— that, and the mentality from which it arises and which it in turn reinforces. It is his criticism of this mentality in which we can finally discern what kind of thinking fatigues him. The criticism culminates in paragraph 15:

> This turn of mind, which always brings everything back to our material interest, which causes us to seek profit or remedies everywhere, and which would cause us to regard all of nature with indifference if we were always well, has never been mine. With respect to that, I feel just the opposite of other men: everything which pertains to feeling my needs saddens and spoils my thoughts, and I have never found true charm in the pleasures of my mind except when concern for my body was completely lost from sight.

Feeling my needs. Concern for my body. The *needs* to which Rousseau refers bespeak our finitude and vulnerability. And the *body* is the seat of these needs. What he dislikes is not thinking as such but thinking that arises from concern for the body. This would include not only palpably bodily needs but also the needs of the self that, being vested in the body, understands itself to be separate from and vulnerable to others and thus locked in competition with them. This is the self that is constituted by amour-propre, for it is amour-propre that multiplies our needs and gives most of them the force of need in the first place.[8] But then the thinking that Rousseau finds charmless and unpleasant, though it *includes* thinking that arises from concern for the body, can be more adequately character- ized as thinking that arises from concern for the *self* in its dependence on and vulnerability to outside forces. Such thinking is unpleasant because it keeps us aware of and makes us feel our dependence, which in turn tends to intensify our dependence all the more. It is, to repeat, the thinking of an amour-propre that senses its insecurity. And amour-propre is never *not* insecure.

Finally, and perhaps most importantly, Rousseau's claim to dislike thinking is qualified *in itself*, that is, without reference to context or pecu- liarities of usage: "thinking always was a painful and charmless *occupation* for me" (VII, 5; emphasis added). The thinking that he finds wearying is thinking that he experiences as an assigned task, thinking that he feels obliged to do. Even the most gratifying activity loses its charm for Rous- seau when it becomes an obligation, even when the "obligation" consists only in someone else's expectation (VI, 4).

If some thinking tires Rousseau, other thinking enthralls him: "No, noth- ing personal, nothing which concerns my body can truly occupy my soul. I never meditate, I never dream more deliciously than when I forget my- self. I feel ecstasies and inexpressible raptures in blending, so to speak, into the system of beings and in making myself one with the whole of nature" (VII, 16). Some will doubt whether what Rousseau is describing here truly merits being called thinking. And Rousseau of course doesn't call it thinking. But let's look at what he does call it. To *meditate* (*méditer*) as Rousseau uses the word and its cognates in the *Reveries* always en- compasses reflection. And while *dreaming* (*rêver*) admittedly connotes

---

8. *The self that is constituted by amour-propre.* This formulation would seem to suggest that we have at least two selves, one constituted or governed by amour-propre and another, or others, that are not, at least if amour de soi still breathes in us at all. Wouldn't it be more accurate to speak of a single self that is constituted or governed *partly* by amour-propre and partly by amour de soi, and refer to that within us that is anxious and aggressive-defensive as the self *insofar as* it is constituted or governed by amour-propre? I don't believe so, for phenomenologically—and how else can one speak or conceive of such a thing as the self except phenomenologically?—the two variants of self-love tend to present themselves as distinct and contending beings.

something less than rigorous thinking, the connotation is often misleading in Rousseau's case, since he used this term and its cognates, especially *rêverie*, to refer to a broad array of cognitive activities that includes rigorous reflection.[9] (The complement to Rousseau's expansive use of "reverie" is his remarkably narrow use of "thinking."[10]) Indeed, we can discern that the "dreaming" referred to in this passage includes a measure of scientific analysis, since it occurs when Rousseau apprehends and loses himself in a *system*. The *Reveries* is not the first of his books in which Rousseau used the word "reverie" to stand in for rigorous, sophisticated, and philosophic reflection. In the *First Discourse* he commented on "the dangerous reveries of such men as Hobbes and Spinoza" (*FD*, 27–28; 20), and in a letter to Voltaire he referred to the *Second Discourse* as his own "sad reveries."[11] Nor was his peculiar use of the word as peculiar as all that. Others, including Montaigne, Descartes, and Diderot, had used the word to encompass philosophic reflection.[12] They too had reason to obscure the depth and seriousness of their meditations, if not from everyone then from most, including especially civil and ecclesiastical authorities. And if the language of dreaming and reverie doesn't count against the scientific basis and philosophic character of Rousseau's activity, neither does the claim that he "forgets [him]self" in undertaking it (VII, 16). For as we'll see, what is forgotten is not the self as such but rather a certain *form* of the self, namely, the self that is constituted and governed by amour-propre.

If it still seems a stretch that the self-described idler was in fact an expositor and celebrant of the philosophic life, that may be because of what one thinks one knows about the meaning and function of nature in Rousseau's thought. As I've already noted, what it means to live according to nature in Rousseau's view is to be governed by or in accordance with amour de soi. Few interpreters are apt to reject this formulation wholesale. But what underlies and gives rise to it needs to be noted, for it is there, I believe, that

---

9. Meier observes that in all three Walks in which "reverie" seems to designate an activity, the activity is one or another kind of rigorous thinking: "By means of replacement and delimitation, *rêverie* is more precisely determined to be *réflexion, méditation,* and *contemplation.*" These more rigorous activities have something in common with reverie: each "is characterized as essentially free of social constraint or any purpose external to them." In short, the word "reveries" "serves Rousseau as a signpost to the philosophic activity of the *Promeneur Solitaire* and as its abbreviation." See Meier, *On the Happiness,* 315.

10. See Gourevitch, "Provisional Reading of Rousseau's *Reveries,*" esp. 508.

11. See Gourevitch, 489–90n1. Gourevitch's brief gloss makes the central point: "The term traditionally makes what is being said appear more innocuous than it is."

12. See Raymond, introduction to the *Reveries.*

many readers miss the mark. And it is there, on the still dark terrain of nature, that the goodness of the philosophic life needs to be demonstrated.[13]

Rousseau insisted that his thought constituted a coherent philosophic system grounded on the principle of natural goodness, that is, the principle "that nature made men happy and good, but that society depraves him and makes him miserable" (*Dialogues*, 934; 212–13). Nature is the starting point and standard for all of Rousseau's thought, both critical and prescriptive. That's not to say that he endorses only what he regards as natural—indeed, he allows that the best social institutions are those that most *denature* man (*Emile*, 248; 164)—but nature and its goodness always serve as his formal standard; and often they serve as a substantive standard and goal. But what *is* natural? Here we come to what is probably the most common source of skepticism regarding Rousseau's embrace of the philosophic life. Rousseau equates the natural with the original (*le primitive*). Most readers, following his evident practice in the *Second Discourse*, understand by "original" that which was first *in time*. Yet "original" admits of a broader meaning that supersedes temporal primacy. In fact Rousseau articulates just such a meaning in the only definition of "nature" to be found in his corpus:

> We are born with the use of our senses, and from our birth we are affected in various ways by the objects surrounding us. As soon as we have, so to speak, consciousness of our sensations, we are disposed to seek or avoid the objects which produce them, at first according to whether they are pleasant or unpleasant to us, then according to the conformity or lack of it that we find between us and these objects, and finally according to the judgments we make about them on the basis of the idea of happiness or of perfection given us by reason. These dispositions are extended and strengthened as we become more capable of using our senses and more enlightened; but constrained by our habits, they are more or less corrupted by our opinions. Before this corruption they are what I call in us *nature*. (*Emile*, 247–48; 163; emphasis in the original)

What is natural? Answer: dispositions that are not corrupt. Dispositions that have *developed* but have not been corrupted. Dispositions informed by sensory and *rational* capacities ("judgments we make . . . on the

---

13. The following brief treatment of the meaning and function of nature in Rousseau's thought is based in part on more extended discussions in my earlier work. See *Rousseau, Nature, and the Problem of the Good Life*, 47–65 and *Eros in Plato*, 143–62.

basis of the idea of happiness or of perfection given us by *reason*"). Reason is part of human beings' natural endowment, and reason that remains uncorrupted contributes to the increased perfection of nature in man.[14] This is worlds away from the depiction of nature given in the *Second Discourse*. If we were to take the *Discourse*'s depiction as a limiting *definition*, "the increased perfection of nature" would be a nonsensical idea; the "natural man living in the state of society" or "savage made to inhabit cities" would be a contradiction in terms (*Emile*, 484; 355); and the philosopher would be among the *least* natural human beings imaginable.

Most readers do take the *Second Discourse*'s depiction of nature as a limiting definition—and it is no surprise that they do. Rousseau has invited this (mis)understanding. The "natural man" of the *Discourse*—the only man so described in the work—is barely distinguishable from the beasts. Why did Rousseau proceed this way? In light of what we've already discussed, we can well imagine that he was moved at least in part by practical considerations. In an age of corrupt refinement, the route to be encouraged—the only path likely to lead to a more natural life—consisted in moving toward simpler and more rustic conditions.

But Rousseau, it seems to me, also had an important theoretical and pedagogical reason for depicting nature as he did in the *Second Discourse*. Some of what *is* can be best articulated by a story that purports to tell what once *was*. Nature, as the origin of the word suggests—certainly nature for Rousseau—is bound up with and can't be understood apart from growth and development. That is why a *genetic* account of nature can illuminate things that an *eidetic* account cannot.[15]

I have borrowed these categories (genetic, eidetic) from Seth Benardete, who used them to interpret Plato, not Rousseau.[16] But perhaps the most illustrative example of the eidetic uses of a genetic account is a different book altogether, one that, though written in a language that had no word for nature, sheds a great deal of light on it all the same. Or so it seems to me—and to Rousseau. The text I'm referring to is the book of Genesis, of which the *Second Discourse*, Rousseau's own genetic account of nature,

---

14. The same point is made in the *Dialogues*, in which the Frenchman finally learns that Jean-Jacques, "this man of *nature* who lives a truly human life," "behaves uniquely according to his inclinations and his *reason*" (*Dialogues*, 935–36; 214; emphasis added).

15. Michael Davis aptly observes that "it is a regular feature of Rousseau's writing to present what seem to be logical relations as temporal movements." See Davis, *Music of Reason*, 16.

16. "'Eidetic' is short for what results from an analysis of something into its kinds[;] 'genetic' stands for the result of examining the coming into being of a genus or one genus from another." Benardete, *Plato's "Laws,"* 18n18.

is a scientific restatement. Genesis has been read by many as an earnest historical narrative, as has the *Second Discourse*. Yet chapters 1 through 11 of Genesis ask to be read not so much as an account of what *was* as an account of what *is*[17]—as, again, does the *Second Discourse*.

And yet Rousseau's genetic account of "the present nature of man" (*SD* 123; 13), whatever its virtues, is partial, for it does not recognize the naturalness of any kind of specifically human excellence. If the predominance of amour de soi in the soul were the sum and substance of naturalness in a human being, no human being, not even the philosopher, could equal the well-being of the beasts of the field. If the philosophic life is the most natural *human* life—if the life of the mind is preferable to living in *imitatio bestiarum*—it must entail the fullest development or satisfaction of that which naturally distinguishes human beings from the other animals. And so it does.

In a famous passage from the *Second Discourse* Rousseau specifies two distinctively human natural qualities: freedom and the faculty of self-perfection (*SD*, 141–42; 26). A strong case can be made for the philosopher as the human being who exercises and enjoys more freedom than anyone else. To be sure, Rousseau no sooner cites freedom as a human distinction than he acknowledges "difficulties" surrounding the claim. And yet these difficulties arguably *support* the philosopher's claim to distinctiveness: the same thinkers who have leveled the most serious challenges to free *will* have allowed that freedom of *mind* is a real if rarely realized human possibility.

Further support for the philosophic life as the most natural human life can be found in the faculty of self-perfection, the second natural human distinction—or perhaps it's the first, for later in the *Discourse*, in a note, Rousseau refers to this faculty as *the* human distinction (*SD*, 211; 208). Here too we face a difficulty. The faculty of self-perfection is only the capacity to change; and change can be, indeed most major changes have been, *away* from nature. How can such an open-ended and nonteleological capacity provide the basis for establishing that any way of life is more natural or less natural than any other? An answer emerges when we ask two questions. First, what is it that *propelled* human beings to change in the first place and that still propels us now—what lies behind the actualization of *any* unrealized possibility? The faculty of self-perfection as Rousseau presents it is an open door; by itself it doesn't account for why we would walk through the door. Second, if we are not directed toward

17. See Kass, *Beginning of Wisdom*, 10.

any particular telos, on what basis can one way of life be deemed better or more natural than another? The answer to both questions and thus the most important human distinction in Rousseau's view is *the expansiveness of human self-love*—of human self-love as such, not only amour-propre but amour de soi as well.

Human beings on Rousseau's understanding are innately characterized by a reaching-beyond-themselves, by a desire to have or rather to *be* more. He speaks of this quality only minimally and almost clinically. Where Plato had spoken memorably and evocatively of eros, Rousseau, on the rare occasions that he calls it anything, speaks of "the desire to extend our being" or "the positive or attracting action . . . of nature, which seeks to extend and reinforce the feeling of our being" (*Emile*, 429–30; 312; *Dialogues*, 804–5; 112).[18] ("Being" as Rousseau speaks of it is not metaphysical but rather psychological or metapsychological. "Being" and "the *feeling* of our being" are synonymous.) Unlike Plato's eros, the desire to extend our being has no given telos; at any rate, it does not recognize one. Moreover, it is at least as likely to lead us into activities that would stimulate desire or fear to such an extent as to constrict our being as it is to enlarge our being. Philosophy itself partakes of this ambiguity. But true philosophy undertaken by those with the requisite capacities and preparation does not. If human beings are distinct from other animals by virtue of the desire to extend our being, the philosophic life is distinct from other human lives by virtue of being the life of the *most* extended being.

How does philosophy extend one's being?

The answer is fourfold (at a minimum). First, with philosophic reflection we can disabuse ourselves of prejudices and delusions that give rise to irrational hopes and fears and thereby to fruitless and immiserating pursuits. Philosophy, that is to say, can correct thinking that undermines our well-being. This can be a deeply therapeutic process. And not only can reflection identify and refute false and harmful beliefs; it can also help us see that we haven't been living according to our professed beliefs: it can help us discover that we have been unknowingly harboring self-serving beliefs that are at odds with the truth we have claimed to know. Just such

18. The desire to extend our being, or the natural expansiveness of human self-love, which (as we've seen) is explicitly acknowledged in *Emile* and the *Dialogues*, is also implied in the *Second Discourse*, in two ways. First, it is implicit in our "natural repugnance to see any sensitive being perish or suffer, principally our fellowmen" (*SD*, 125–26; 14–15), which is a response to *our* suffering upon seeing the suffering of others, i.e., to our suffering *in* others. Second, it is implicit in the faculty of self-perfection, since this faculty, as Rousseau articulates it, is in itself only a possibility. It could not have had the enormous practical significance that it has had were there not a separate and prior expansive *impulse*.

a process of discovery is narrated in the *Reveries*. Of course such "self-serving" beliefs are not self-serving at all: they serve something *in* the self (namely, amour-propre) that has been undermining the well-being of the self as a whole.

The second way in which philosophy can enlarge one's being is by exercising capacities of the soul that would otherwise be un- or underemployed. "To live is not to breathe, it is to act; it is to make use of all our organs, our senses, our faculties, of all the parts of ourselves which give us the sentiment of existence" (*Emile*, 253; 167). We *are*, we experience *being*, by exercising our faculties. Now it may be that most of us would be well advised *not* to exercise certain faculties of mind, since the result is likely to be the incitement of unfulfillable desire or intense anxiety or some other existence-diminishing phenomenon. But those with the nature befitting a philosopher and over whom the sway of prejudices and irrational beliefs has been limited by education or good fortune will find that the exercise of even the most potentially trouble-making cognitive faculties can enliven and enlarge them. This is one reason why contemplating unpleasant realities needn't be entirely unpleasant for the philosopher. Whatever the effects of the object of contemplation—and these may be disturbing and thus constrict one's being—the *activity* of contemplation can offset some part of these effects and perhaps even outweigh them. Contemplation is indeed activity. Rousseau refers to various of his contemplative pursuits as *idle*. But "idle" (*oiseuse*) as he uses the term means only that the purpose of an activity not lie beyond enjoyment of the activity itself.[19] This is why he can describe his botanizing as an "idle occupation" despite acknowledging in the same passage that he "examines each flower with interest and curiosity" and that this examination yields pleasure precisely when he "begins to *grasp* [*saisir*] the laws of their structure" (VII, 23; emphasis added).

Third, philosophy can help one transcend narrow egoism, which, in its inherent defensiveness, entails constrictive fear, dread, and anxiety. The meaning of this transcendence will be unfolded more extensively in the chapters to come. For now I will say only that it should be understood both negatively and positively. Negatively: as freeing oneself from thralldom to amour-propre, from the sense that one's well-being depends on one's relative standing in the world. Positively: as insight into and identification with the true nature of the self. Transcendence of narrow egoism,

---

19. That an activity is undertaken for no purpose beyond itself does not mean that it is undertaken without intention. This subtle but not, in my view, trivial distinction has sometimes been elided. See, for example, Friedlander, *J. J. Rousseau*, 78–84.

it should be noted, does not mean the *dissolution* of the self or even of amour-propre.

Finally, human beings have capacities and qualities that somehow correspond to or have special affinities with various phenomena in the external world, such that contemplating those phenomena can activate or further activate these capacities and qualities. These correspondences or affinities have been recognized as important to Rousseau's aesthetics.[20] My suggestion is that they are pertinent to his conception of the philosophic life as well.

The enlargement of one's being through philosophy surely owes a great deal to the philosopher's moral transformation. Those who have recognized and digested the compelling character of the apparent good—to the *extent* that they have digested it—will have ceased believing in moral dessert in any ordinary way. Accordingly, they will have ceased believing that they deserve immortality. And having ceased believing that they deserve immortality, they will have had an easier time letting go of the *hope* for immortality. (One of the amazing features of the ordinary moral consciousness is that it effectively encourages us to suppose that what we intensely desire we also, thereby, deserve; and where we believe in dessert, we believe, or *want* to believe, that the desired thing will come to us. And so is born a most stubborn, because morally principled, *hope*.) Losing hope for immortality will surely strike many as a great misfortune. Here, though, we might think of Socrates, who seemed to suggest from his own credible experience that one who has ceased hoping for immortality will also have received great gains—not only the questionable gain of having swallowed a hard truth but also freedom from the dread of mortality and even the fulfillment of our deepest desire, the desire for eternity. For as we'll see in connection with the Fifth Walk, Rousseau, like Plato, regards the immortality for which many desperately long as a proxy for or misinterpretation of eternity, which is what the soul most deeply wants. And, again like Plato, he sees eternity as central to philosophy, which is perhaps the deepest explanation of the goodness of the philosophic life.

DANGERS

We've already seen ample evidence of Rousseau's acute consciousness of philosophy's potential to harm society. I would merely add a practical point to the earlier discussion. A healthy society needs patriots who love it viscerally and who become angry on its behalf. And anger *is* necessary, even if untutored anger is a scourge. This is Rousseau's view. He vindicates

20. Kelly, *Rousseau as Author*, 181.

anger—a certain *kind* of anger in certain kinds of circumstances—and seems to want to educate it through the example of his own righteous indignation, even as he eschews and even deprecates anger of other kinds and in other circumstances.[21] Yet even the most righteous and necessary anger will be attenuated by philosophy. Philosophers might well feel a deep debt of gratitude and a special dedication to the society into which they were born or the society in which they have found refuge; and these noble passions might well suffice to make them resolute defenders of society. The example of Socrates, who served in combat with rare bravery and distinction, suggests as much, at least if we interpret his example generously (*Symposium*, 220d–221c). But society needs more than dedicated defenders. It also needs angry partisans of justice. And such anger is *precluded* by philosophy. If the example of Socrates suggests philosophy's compatibility with dedicated defense, it also suggests philosophy's *in*compatibility with even the most righteous and salutary anger. Now perhaps it is only philosophers *as philosophers* who lack what society needs. Perhaps philosophers *can* give vent to anger and other subphilosophic passions as needed: philosophers, after all, aren't *only* philosophers; they are human beings with all the capacities and propensities adhering therein. But even in the best case, philosophers will inevitably experience these passions with less zeal than would exemplary citizens. And that's to say nothing either of the less-than-best cases or of nonphilosophers whose civic spirit has been dimmed by philosophers, whether true philosophers or pseudophilosophers it matters not. Philosophy, in short, threatens to subvert popular faith and all that "was built upon this faith, propped up by it, grown into it."[22]

The vulnerability of popular faith to subversion by philosophy will vary from one situation to another. And sometimes a little subversion, that is, a dose of chastening skepticism, can be a humanizing antidote to fanaticism and cruel moralism. Just such an effect was sought—and to a considerable extent achieved—by liberalism's philosophic progenitors. But might not even a little subversion sometimes be too much, yielding enervation and demoralization? And doesn't the opposite danger also loom, that is, that the *force* of moral passion will persist even as the grounds of the passion have crumbled under withering philosophic examination, thereby untethering the passion from reason all the more? Might not the force of

21. Regarding Rousseau's expressions of anger in his writings, see Shklar, *Men and Citizens*, 30; Coleman, *Anger, Gratitude, and the Enlightenment Writer*; and Pagani, *Man or Citizen*, 8.

22. Nietzsche, *Gay Science*, section 343.

ungrounded moral passion even *grow*, fueled by the urgently felt need to vindicate itself? And let's remember that all these scenarios presuppose philosophy that has been undertaken honestly rather than cynically or fanatically. That is a kind of tribute to philosophy, but hardly a reassuring one. However great a good philosophy might be when confined to its proper precincts, it threatens society with destruction when popularized.

Popularized philosophy also threatens philosophy itself. Indeed, Rousseau judges the threat already to have been realized. Consider his charge that philosophy is the station with the most prejudices (*Emile*, 535; 399). Could there be a more devastating critique of philosophy on its own ground? Of course philosophy that has been heavily beset by prejudices is no longer philosophy. But that's just the point. Popularization will tend to corrupt philosophy into something else—a vanity project, an ideology, a power play, anything but the disciplined love of wisdom. When that has happened, who knows whether potential philosophers will be drawn to philosophy or, if they are, whether they will be able withstand the blandishments of such corruption and resist being corrupted themselves. The philosophic life requires long preparation. Its freedom of mind requires years of discipline and refinement by a certain kind of moral faith. Its virtue, which is true virtue, requires prior steeping in vulgar or demotic virtue. To be sure, philosophy partakes of the spirit of play. But this spirit cannot be won except by way of seriousness. Philosophy's playful spirit comes about only after moral seriousness has become so serious as to question itself. The overcoming of the ordinary moral consciousness in favor of the cognitivist view of morality is in truth the *self*-overcoming of the ordinary moral consciousness.

Brief and partial though it is, our tour of philosophy's goods and evils shouldn't conclude before we've registered a complicating observation. Namely, philosophy's evils may not *only* be evils. Some of them may sometimes be necessary to philosophy's goods. Rousseau's own story suggests as much.

His exaggerations notwithstanding, Rousseau was persecuted both by the ecclesiastics of the ancien régime and by the *philosophes* who sought to supplant them. He was persecuted for publishing the fruits of his philosophic inquiry. He was persecuted, that is to say, because he spoke as a true philosopher. Might this evil, as painful and damaging as it was, have been helpful or even necessary to his continued development as a philosopher? We can't know, but we have reason to think that it might have been. Rousseau might finally have achieved a more complete and secure overcoming of the ordinary moral consciousness because he felt the *need* to do so. To suffer injustice is bad enough. To suffer injustice while falsely professing the wisdom of resignation is almost intolerable. It demands that one finally make good on one's claim.

Rousseau's Life—and Ours

If Rousseau's view of the philosophic life proves surprisingly akin to that of his Socratic or classical forebears, his articulation of it is nevertheless distinctive and distinctively illuminating. Its signal contributions to *our* understanding of the philosophic life seem to me to fall into three broad categories.

SELF-GOVERNANCE

Rousseau's struggle to take to heart the cognitivist view of morality takes him, and us, on a tortuous exploration of the soul. We see the moral consciousness at work with ferocity and beguiling cleverness. Only after cultivating a new way of seeing does Rousseau see that what had presented itself to him as a pure love of justice was in fact petty self-pride. Both the disguise and the reality, both love of justice and petty pride, are expressions of amour-propre. Thus one of Rousseau's signal contributions to our understanding of the philosophic life is his illumination of amour-propre's powerful and persistent tendency to oppose the philosophic life.

Insight into amour-propre's insidious machinations can considerably curb this opposition, but not entirely. One who has seen through amour-propre will still be subject to its furies, alas. Or maybe *not* alas: for Rousseau claims in the *Second Discourse* that amour-propre, although the source of the worst things in us, is also the source of the best (*SD*, 189; 63). Among the things we owe to amour-propre are virtue, science, and *philosophy*. It's unclear whether in the passage I'm referencing philosophy isn't listed as one of the *worst* things. Rousseau depicts philosophers as motivated far more by the desire for distinction than by love of the truth. Yet *true* philosophy, certainly the ascent to true philosophy, makes use of amour-propre. Although this ascent ultimately entails the subordination of amour-propre to amour de soi, amour-propre must be enlisted in the project of its own overcoming. Amour-propre can also help drive the further perfection of the philosophic life by one who has already embarked on it—again, not an autonomous amour-propre but an amour-propre that has been subordinated to amour de soi. Amour-propre makes possible other goods as well, goods that don't belong to philosophy per se but might still have a place in the philosophic life; for amour-propre is a source of all passionate particularism, including romantic love and "the sweetest sentiments known to men: conjugal love and paternal love" (*SD*, 168; 46).

One might doubt whether such particularism is consistent with the disposition of the true philosopher. Can the special love of one's own be squared with the philosopher's love of the good? Perhaps not. But perhaps the two can coexist all the same: perhaps *squaring* is not the question, for the philosopher remains a compound and embodied being. Perhaps even *illusion*, which Rousseau regards as an essential ingredient of romantic love (*Emile*, 743; 570–71), might find some breathing space in the philosopher. What distinguishes philosophers from others is not that they are immune from the subrational passions but that they are not possessed by them. Consider Socrates's revised and enriched model of the soul in book 9 of the *Republic* (revised and enriched vis-à-vis the better known tripartite model introduced in book 4). Within the human soul, as Socrates bids Glaucon and company to imagine it, are three distinct creatures: a great multiheaded beast, a lion, and, by far the smallest, a human being. Yet that small human being has it within his power, if the whole person has developed well, to govern the beasts. Rousseau subscribes to the same principles: he too understands the soul as an arena—or, better yet, a polity—in which numerous factions pursue their own interests while also holding with the possibility of rational governance. What Rousseau adds to Plato's account is further exploration of rational self-governance—exploration and even instruction, particularly regarding how to mitigate inflamed amour-propre.

THE RATIONALITY OF THE SEEMINGLY IRRATIONAL

The life articulated in the *Reveries* is a life of rational inquiry in pursuit of wisdom. Rousseau engages in sustained, rigorous reflection on himself, the world, and the relation between the two. Yet he also recounts avowedly ecstatic experiences that are apt to look more like the *abdication* of reason than its cultivation and exercise. Some of these experiences belong to reveries properly so called; others arise from botanizing. *Are* these experiences subrational, or is it only from within the narrow horizon of modern rationalism that they seem so? Might a more capacious conception of reason—the classical rationalism of Plato, for example—be able to accommodate and make sense of them? Plato, after all, gives us levels of cognition that are no part of discursive reasoning yet make discursive reasoning possible in the first place. Think of the uppermost segment of the Divided Line in the *Republic* (509d–511d). Think too of the *Symposium* and Socrates's remarkable habit of standing stock-still, abstracted from his immediate surroundings, on one memorable occasion for a full day and night (175a–b, 220c–d). Both of these images suggest nondiscursive contemplation. And what is the relation of Rousseau's ecstatic experiences to philosophy proper? Are they part of it? If they are not part of philosophy, do they nevertheless *serve* it in some way, as poetry ministers to Socrates's philosophizing? Or do they not serve philosophy per se but rather the philosopher—perhaps as a recreation or a restorative? Or are they *at odds* with philosophy for being inconsistent with the self-awareness that would seem to be the principle and goal of the philosophic life?

No answer to these questions can be complete until we've examined the Fifth and Seventh Walks in part 2. Even so, the outlines of a response can be sketched now—especially to the last question.

Philosophers as understood by Rousseau do indeed pursue self-awareness above all else—this notwithstanding that they spend more time studying the external world than focusing exclusively on themselves. For in studying the external world, including (especially) other human beings, philosophers study that of which they are part and whose constituent elements and energies also constitute *them*. They do not seek to lose or forget themselves, and they never willingly allow imagination to interpose itself gratuitously between themselves and what *is*. In the Seventh Walk, Rousseau reports that he has given up previously cherished reveries for fear that they would inflame his imagination and populate his mind with fearsome prospects (VII, 7). Meier carefully shows that while Rousseau did indeed give up these reveries in order to quiet his imagination, the real problem with imagination was not that it threatened to overwhelm him with dread but rather that it inhibited philosophy by interposing itself between him and the world.[23] Yet Meier seems to me to overstate Rousseau's retirement from reverie. Some of the reveries that Rousseau recalls were indeed inimical to philosophy; these are the ones he has given up. But not all reveries meet this description. Not even all reveries that Rousseau describes as *self-forgetting* interfere with philosophy; for these reveries, though they are self-forgetting in a certain sense, are not self-forgetting in the decisive sense. And the same is true of his ostensibly self-forgetting botanizing. Nowhere in the accounts of these experiences does Rousseau indicate that he has ever ceased to be aware of his experience *as his own*. He does forget something about himself—but what? In feeling himself one with nature, he ceases to experience—he forgets—only his separateness from nature. And to forget one's separateness from nature is to forget

23. Meier, *On the Happiness*, 95–97.

only a certain *form* of the self (as Plato might put it), namely, the egoic self or the self that is constituted by amour-propre. What's more, with this forgetting of one form of self comes the *recovery* of another form of self. The forgetting of the factitious self, that is, the self constituted by amour-propre, is at the same time the recovery, the remembering, of a prior, natural self, the self constituted and governed by amour de soi. The recovery of the natural self opens the way to clearer sight of nature and a more natural way of being. Thus reveries and botanizing that might have seemed suspect from the standpoint of philosophy prove to hold an important place in the philosophic life. They not only don't interfere with philosophy; they *conduce* to it.

The distinction between self-forgetting that interferes with philosophy and self-forgetting that is consistent with or even conduces to philosophy can be more clearly apprehended by examining two passages—the only two passages in the *Reveries*—in which Rousseau speaks explicitly of forgetting himself. Conveniently, one of these passages recounts a kind of self-forgetting that obstructs philosophy, while the other recounts a kind of self-forgetting that conduces to philosophy.

The account of aphilosophic or antiphilosophic self-forgetting appears in the Eighth Walk, as Rousseau recalls the effects on him of (long-ago) prosperity:

> When all was in order around me, when I was content with all that surrounded me and with the sphere in which I was to live, I filled it with my affectionate feelings. My expansive soul extended itself to other objects and, continually drawn outside myself by a thousand different kinds of fancies, by gentle attachments which continually busied my heart, *I somehow forgot even myself.* I was entirely devoted to what was alien to me; and in the continual agitation of my heart, I experienced all the vicissitudes of human things. This stormy life left me neither peace within nor rest without. (VIII, 2; emphasis added)

The account of self-forgetting that conduces to philosophy appears in the Seventh Walk, amid a description of his newly improved way of botanizing:

> I never meditate, I never dream more deliciously than when *I forget myself.* I feel ecstasies and inexpressible raptures in blending, so to speak, into the system of beings and in making myself one with the whole of nature. (VII, 16; emphasis added)

Notice the differences between this passage and the previous one. Where the passage from the Eighth Walk has Rousseau forgetting himself (a) through *attachment* to (b) *objects* that were (c) *alien* to himself, this one has him forgetting himself (a) through *identification* with (b) a *system* or *whole* (c) of which he is *part*. The self-forgetting recounted in this passage is thus self-*discovery*. Perhaps that's why the claim of self-forgetting in the Eighth Walk is qualified—"I *somehow* forgot myself"—and this one is not. The problematic kind of self-forgetting is less than fully conscious—it is, so to speak, a forgotten self-forgetting. The enriching kind of self-forgetting, by contrast, is a more conscious self-forgetting. That Rousseau views these experiences in the ways I have suggested is confirmed in two additional ways. First, whereas the self-forgetting referenced in the Eighth Walk is recounted in the past tense, that of the Seventh Walk is related in the present tense. Second, whereas the self-forgetting referenced in the Eighth Walk yielded a condition that Rousseau had *mistaken* for happiness, that of the Seventh Walk was, or rather is, joyful.

If self-forgetting can either impede or serve philosophy depending on what self is being forgotten, so too can *imagination* either impede or serve philosophy depending on its status in the polity that is the soul. Imagination *subverts* philosophy when it is effectively autonomous, as it was in the reveries that Rousseau has given up. It can *serve* philosophy in a ministerial capacity. Rousseau's view of imagination thus recalls—indeed, repeats—the *Republic*'s renewed discussion of poetry in book 10, where Socrates criticizes poetry for its distance from truth but then indicates that he would happily welcome poetry that ministers to philosophy back into the city (595a–608b).

CONTINUED PERFECTION

The most overarching of Rousseau's contributions to our understanding of the philosophic life, and at the same time perhaps the least noticed, is one we've already noted: namely, the need to continue perfecting the philosophic life even after one has taken the philosophic "turn."

The *Reveries* makes clear that Rousseau's own development, not only as a thinker but as a human being, does not end upon his becoming a philosopher. He still has a journey to take—where, exactly, he does not at first know. The destination is a higher ground than he has yet inhabited, a ground that affords a broader and less obstructed perspective as well as some protection against the inhospitable weather and other dangers that arise periodically above ground. (Human beings entered the cave in the first place for a reason.) The *path* to this destination, or Rousseau's core task upon embarking on the philosophic life, is to take to heart more fully, which means to know more fully, the insights that belong to the cognitivist view of morality. His continued journey as a philosopher is thus continuous with the journey that led him *to* the philosophic life. The philosopher is no extraterrestrial. The cave and the lands above it are separate places; they are not separate *worlds*. (See *Republic*, 508c.) This hardly means that the task is easy. We are apt to be least comprehending of what is already familiar to us, for we frequently mistake familiarity for knowledge.[24] And if we are *proud* of having climbed out of the cave, so much the worse.

Rousseau's articulation of the philosophic life, and in particular his journey to a more complete embrace of the cognitivist view of morality, should be of great interest to all who seek self-knowledge, whether or not they are drawn to the philosophic life. And his journey should be *taken*, or at least seriously explored, by all who already profess anything like the cognitivist view. For to repeat—and if anything bears repeating, it's something we think that we know but do not—professing the cognitivist view of morality doesn't prove that one really embraces it. Many of us, like Rousseau at the start of the *Reveries*, suppose that we have transcended the spirit of retribution when we have not. And *un*like Rousseau, we aren't likely to discover our delusion and correct our course on our own.

That few of us are likely to complete the journey doesn't make it any the less necessary. This notwithstanding that failing at the journey is likely to be unpleasant and may diminish our ability to act wholeheartedly. Unpleasantness doesn't excuse us from the demands of honesty and self-awareness; and the diminishment of wholeheartedness is no loss when the heart at issue is a cruel one. And cruel indeed are those who believe themselves free of punitive impulses when they are not. This is something Rousseau discerned in his persecutors, and it is one more thing we can learn from him. It is fitting that we might learn this from Rousseau, for if growing numbers of people profess something like the cognitivist view of morality, that may well be owing to Rousseau himself. Not that he intended to popularize the cognitivist view. To the contrary, he regarded it, along with much else that belongs to philosophy, as potentially enervating and subversive of morality. The teaching that he sought to popularize was

24. "What is familiar is what we are used to; and what we are used to is most difficult to 'know'—that is, to see as a problem; that is, to see as strange, as distant, as 'outside us.'" Nietzsche, *Gay Science*, section 355.

the one offered in "The Profession of Faith of the Savoyard Vicar," which propounds a gentler morality or at any rate a gentler response to sin than that which prevailed in Rousseau's day without contravening the ordinary moral consciousness. Indeed, "The Profession of Faith of the Savoyard Vicar" may offer the strongest case *for* the ordinary moral consciousness that has ever been made without recourse to Revelation. The force of its argument was sufficient to inspire the likes of Kant. In the *Reveries* Rousseau points readers to the Vicar's Profession—not only by suggesting that his own views are similar to the Vicar's (III, 17), but even more so by telling his story. Reflecting on his story might help us see that we too have fallen short of the transcendence we profess. And it would offer an honest and wholesome way of reconciling our moralism with whatever contrary philosophic insights we might hold.

CHAPTER 2

The Reveries of the Solitary Walker

An Introduction

Early in the *Reveries* Rousseau suggests that he has undertaken to write the book as a sequel to his *Confessions* (I, 12–13), thereby instructing us to read it as an autobiographical work. Scholars have taken this instruction both too literally and not literally enough. They take it too literally by failing to see that besides being autobiographical, indeed by virtue of being autobiographical, the *Reveries* is also a work of philosophy. They don't take Rousseau's suggestion literally enough because they fail to see how much of an autobiography the *Reveries* really is. The book isn't only a collection of personal reflections and recollections, let alone reveries, notwithstanding Rousseau's claim—immediately following the suggestion that the book is a sequel to the *Confessions*—that "these pages will, properly speaking, be only a shapeless diary of my reveries" (I, 13). The *Reveries* tells the story of a philosophic life, albeit in an exceedingly elusive way.

The first interpretive error, the failure to recognize the *Reveries* as a work of philosophy, should not be too surprising, given the scholarly penchant for mutually exclusive categories—in this case, mutually exclusive disciplines and genres. Not that the *Reveries* looks anything like conventional autobiography or conventional anything for that matter; but surely, one supposes, a book as personal and seemingly random as this can't be a work of philosophy in any strict sense. And so only a handful of scholars have regarded the *Reveries* as a serious philosophic work. The second interpretive error, the failure to see how much of an autobiography the *Reveries* really is, should come as even less of a surprise. Indeed, it seems almost unfair to call it a failure at all, given the intricacy and sweep of Rousseau's artistic veiling. The finest interpreters have understood that the *Reveries* speaks to the contemplative life, and a few have seen in the book something approaching a thematic arc. But a thematic arc is not a narrative arc: no one has yet interpreted the *Reveries* as the *story* of a philosophic life.[1]

That the *Reveries* is a disordered assortment of thoughts and observations is not the only false claim Rousseau makes at the outset of the book. Another is that he is writing the book only for himself (I, 14). The first reason to be skeptical of this claim is the evident care he put into the book—not only his thoughtfulness and rigor but even more so the time and effort he took to edit it. Why edit—and not only for clarity but also to ensure opacity and circumspection—if not in the expectation that the book would eventually be circulated?[2] Other reasons to doubt that Rousseau wrote the *Reveries* only for himself include his use of the second-person imperative voice (e.g., V, 11) and the employment of various scene-setting techniques. Even if Rousseau had preferred that the *Reveries* not be published, he knew that his wish would not likely avail. Short of destroying the work, he could do nothing to prevent its posthumous

---

1. The scholars who have come closest to reading the *Reveries* as the story of a philosophic life are Charles Butterworth, Michael Davis, Heinrich Meier, Pierre Manent, and Victor Gourevitch. All five recognize the *Reveries* as a philosopher's investigation of his life. But none sees the *Reveries* as the story of the coming-to-be, the being, and the further development of a philosopher. Butterworth reads the book as a philosopher's or retired philosopher's exploration of a life that in its latter stages is no longer truly contemplative or philosophic ("Interpretive Essay," esp. 151–52). Davis announces with the title of his book that he reads the *Reveries* as a kind of philosophic autobiography, but the autobiography he sees in the *Reveries*, if I understand it correctly, is the phenomenology of philosophizing rather than the story of a philosophic life (Davis, *Autobiography of Philosophy*). Meier recognizes that Rousseau's self-study is indeed the investigation of a philosophic life and that the *Reveries* depicts a number of "attempts at detachment." But he does not interpret these attempts as marking the plotline of a life, let alone a story of further perfecting the philosophic life (see Meier, *On the Happiness*, 217, 219). Manent illuminates the philosophic meaning and intention of a number of important or perplexing passages in the *Reveries* but offers no reading of the book as a story (Manent, "To Walk, to Dream, to Philosophize"). Gourevitch comes closest to my reading. He recognizes that "the dominant theme of the *Reveries* is the suffering of an innocent man, and achieving happiness in the teeth of it"; and he alone among prior interpreters speaks of the book's "*plot*," which, "broadly speaking," "may be said to consist in re-naturing—de-civil-izing—one civil man" (Gourevitch, "Provisional Reading of Rousseau's *Reveries*, 491). But Gourevitch's excellent sketch is still just that, a sketch, leaving a great deal unsaid. An interpreter who does regard the *Reveries* as a narrative is Karen Pagani; see "Living Well Is the Best Revenge." But whereas I see the *Reveries* as an account of the further perfection of the philosophic life, Pagani sees it as something closer to the opposite: "This text reveals a breakdown and revision of the ethical imperatives regarding rectificatory action and sentiment that Rousseau so laboriously forged over the course of his life." See Pagani, *Man or Citizen*, 27–28.

2. For the extent of Rousseau's editing, see Butterworth, "Preface," vii; and Butterworth, "Appendix A, Description of the Notebooks," 241–45.

circulation. But in fact there is no reason to suppose that he did wish to deprive posterity of his final insights and reflections, several of which were new and important. Thus the question is not *whether* Rousseau wrote for others but rather for *which* others he wrote. And yet in one sense Rousseau does seem to have written the *Reveries* for himself. Its core teaching, its articulation of the philosophic life, is addressed to readers that Rousseau would have regarded either as kin or as friends. A kinsman is one's *own*. And a friend, as Aristotle teaches and as Rousseau understands, is in a very deep sense another oneself.[3]

The feature of the *Reveries* that most powerfully undermines Rousseau's slighting characterization of the book and points to its true character as the story of a philosophic life is something that, to my knowledge, has gone unnoticed by scholars. The *Reveries*, as I have suggested, has a remarkably extensive relationship with another book that also tells a story about the philosophic life, indeed the premier book on the subject: Plato's *Republic*. The relationship between the *Reveries* and the *Republic* is not only thematic but also formal. Rousseau's ten numbered Walks correspond in important ways to Plato's ten numbered books. Clearly Rousseau conceived of the *Reveries* as a counterpart to the *Republic*. What *kind* of counterpart? How is the story told in the *Reveries* like and unlike the story told in the *Republic*?

The *Republic* does indeed tell a story. The entirety of the dialogue consists of Socrates recounting a conversation. The conversation has an arc—it progresses, and its participants are changed by it. The primary topic of the conversation, as everyone knows, is justice. The progress of the conversation is progress toward an improved understanding of justice. The dramatic culmination of the *Republic* is a twofold realization. The first part of the realization is negative: justice understood politically is shown to be deeply problematic with respect to both desirability and possibility. The pursuit of perfect political justice would impose costs so steep as to amount to the imposition of a nature-suppressing tyranny and therefore no justice at all. Among these costs are the permanent abolition of private attachments within the guardian class and, at the outset, the exile from the city of everyone over the age of ten. The second part of the realization is that there is a kind of justice that is *not* problematic but rather desirable and, in principle, possible. This desirable justice is justice within an individual soul, or between the various parts or forms of the soul. Justice in

3. Aristotle, *Nicomachean Ethics*, 1166a. Regarding the affinity between Rousseau's conception of friendship and Aristotle's, see Reisert, *Jean-Jacques Rousseau*, 79–85.

the soul means *health* of the soul. And the truly healthy soul turns out to be the soul of the philosopher. Through its action, the *Republic* also suggests a relationship between the negative and the positive realizations. The negative realization seems to be a prerequisite for the positive realization: to attain justice in the soul seems to require that one have understood and accepted the impossibility and undesirability of perfect political justice. The *Reveries* tells a comparable story, albeit with illuminating additions and qualifications. To lay out the full argument will require that we make our way through all ten of the *Reveries'* Walks. Here indeed Rousseau's choice of "Walks" over "chapters" is apt. It may be too much to hope that we readers can walk precisely as Rousseau walked, but perhaps we can walk *where* he walked, on paths he has delicately marked out. But before plunging into the *Reveries'* varied and demanding terrain, let me offer what I hope will serve as a helpful overview cum structural map composed of three parts and an addendum.

The Story and Its Themes

The story told by the *Reveries* is the story of Rousseau moving toward a deeper acceptance of the insuperability of injustice among human beings—a deeper acceptance of the fact that wrongs are not always made right—and then, or even thereby, toward the actualization of justice, that is, health of soul, in himself. To see this narrative arc requires that we recognize the distinction between Rousseau as the subject of the book and Rousseau as the narrator. By *Rousseau as subject* I mean the person who is at the center of the book's various recollections and meditations—the young lover of Madame de Warens, the famous author, the target of a cruel conspiracy, the amateur botanist, the philosopher who has meditated on such matters as the sentiment of being, truth and lying, and so forth. By *Rousseau as narrator* I mean the person who is speaking to us from the page *about* those prior events and meditations. Crucial to my reading is the claim that Rousseau the narrator is as much a character in the book as Rousseau the subject. Indeed Rousseau the narrator is the protagonist. It is he whose story is told in the *Reveries*. The story is told obliquely and telescopically: obliquely because it is not meant for all and telescopically because, though it is Rousseau's story, it is also in important ways the story of the philosophic life as such. Rousseau the narrator develops over the course of his narrating. He comes to understand things that he hasn't previously understood, and he achieves things that he hasn't previously achieved. Rousseau the narrator is like Socrates in the *Republic* in that he narrates "now," or in the telling, events that have already taken place, though he is *un*like Socrates in the *Republic* in that he himself demonstrably develops over the course of the narration. (The *Reveries* isn't the first book in which Rousseau doubled himself. In the *Dialogues* he had given us a character named *Jean-Jacques* discussing the philosopher *Rousseau* with an unnamed Frenchman.) The narrator's progress, his condition at any step along the way, is revealed by his selection of which experiences and insights to recount but even more so by how he interprets them. The recounted experiences and insights are not ordered chronologically. The narration, however, *is* chronological; the narrator's development is the plotline of the book.[4]

Being a narrative in no way compromises the *Reveries* as a work of philosophy—no more than the dialogue form detracts from the philosophic heft of Plato's writings. Indeed, the contrary is true. Like Plato's dialogues, the *Reveries* conducts an inquiry and makes an argument *through its action*. Given that the argument concerns activity and experience, indeed a way of being, it can be articulated more richly by literary representation than by discursive reasoning alone. Rousseau never explicitly indicates that the action of the *Reveries* constitutes an argument any more than Plato does in his dialogues. Nor should he have, any more than Plato should have. For just as Plato is not a character in his own dialogues, Rousseau the author is not a character in the *Reveries*. The protagonist of the book is Rousseau *the narrator*; and as his story is told in real time, as it were, he is in no position to explicate the argument that Rousseau the author is making, not until he has come to his final insight and *become* Rousseau the author.

At the outset of the *Reveries* and indeed for most of the book Rousseau's condition is much like that of the perfectly just man whom Glaucon imagines in book 2 of the *Republic*, that is, the just man who is perceived as *un*just and who is consequently subjected to terrible penalties.[5] That Rousseau himself was the victim of the injustice he recounts allows him to offer a vivid and intimate experiential account. He shows us the moral consciousness at work—struggling, developing, and finally overcoming itself.

That the action of the *Reveries* arises from the injustice done to a private individual by other private individuals might seem to imply that the book has little to offer in the way of *political* wisdom. In fact the opposite is true. It is because the *Reveries* is so personal a book that it is a profound book

---

4. This peculiar character of the *Reveries* surely accounts for its having been so widely misunderstood, even, or perhaps especially, upon comparison with the *Confessions*. See, for example, Kelly, *Rousseau's Exemplary Life*, 242: "The *Confessions* proceeds chronologically[;]the *Reveries* does not." Both true and untrue.

5. For an elaboration of this point, see Grace, "Justice in the Soul."

of political philosophy. By showing how he experiences and reacts to injustice, Rousseau treats one of the greatest of political themes. To be sure, philosophy is ultimately *trans*political; and the way to the philosophic life, insofar as it entails overcoming the ordinary moral consciousness in favor of the cognitivist view of morality, is a way *out* of the political, for the ordinary moral consciousness is the psychic core of the political. But philosophers are still human beings in the world. Their transcendence of politics is in thought, not the whole of life. They have attained a transpolitical *perspective* from which to view and engage the political world. It is precisely because of this transcendence—keeping in mind that to transcend is not to disown[6]—that political philosophy in general and Rousseau's political philosophy in particular can teach us about politics.

The author of the *Reveries* subscribes to the cognitivist view of morality. He is, in this way, a Socratic. Rousseau the narrator, however, begins the *Reveries* as, let's say, a semi-Socratic: Socratic insofar as he has seen the impossibility and undesirability of perfect political justice and the consequent need to accept this truth, but *semi*- because he has not yet really *accepted* what he has seen. The primary indicator of his less-than-complete Socratism is his vociferous and oft-repeated outrage at the injustice done to him. (His vociferous and oft-repeated protestations to the contrary must strike the sensitive reader as defiant to the point of being self-refuting.) But this is precisely what changes over the course of the *Reveries*. Rousseau finally achieves—he enacts for us—the acceptance that has hitherto eluded him. Resignation to injustice is a crucial step, perhaps *the* crucial step, in his becoming a true philosopher in his own view and, I believe, in the Socratic view as well. To be sure, the Platonic Socrates teaches that philosophy is learning how to accept *death*, not injustice (*Phaedo*, 64a). But this is not inconsistent with my focus on injustice, for what makes our own death so difficult to accept is that we regard it as the ultimate injustice against ourselves. We are *offended*. Life still owes us something, we think.

Rousseau's eventual acceptance of injustice isn't perfect, as indeed it never could be, for the simple reason that amour-propre can't be entirely purged from the soul. The latter fact is worth underscoring, for it bears on the limits of philosophy and what is at stake if we ignore these limits. Amour-propre is not only self-love; it is also a moral passion and the source or stuff of other moral passions. Why should this be? Why is self-love so deeply invested in morality? What does self-love have to do with

---

6. *Trans*political does not mean *a*political. To transcend is both to supersede and to include. Cf. Hegel, *Phenomenology of Spirit*, 68.

the passion for justice? The answer arises from amour-propre's character as *relative* and therefore *conditional* self-love. Relativity implies comparison and judgment, and judgment requires a standard—in this case, a standard by which to judge one's basic worth or lovability. Precisely *as* the relative form of self-love, then, amour-propre sets the conditions we must meet to *succeed* at self-love.

As a relative form of self-love, amour-propre is the desire to compare well to others and thereby (so we think) *be* well. Comparison requires metrics or criteria. The criteria may vary across epochs, cultures, and the like, but insofar as they are criteria of our lovability or basic worth they are ipso facto moral criteria. Now consider: as long as we suppose that our worth and well-being depend on meeting certain conditions—*any* conditions—our attachment to these conditions is apt to be at least as fierce as our pursuit of our own well-being. For if these conditions are called into doubt, so is the very possibility of affirming our worth. Morality, by setting the terms and conditions that must be met for us to be able to love ourselves, creates the possibility of loving ourselves.

The moral demands imposed by amour-propre are manifold and fall under a variety of names. Some belong to courage, others to moderation or generosity or love, and so on. Yet in a manner of speaking, they all belong to *justice*, for they constitute the standards by which we judge and affirm our own and others' basic worth and lovability. (It is not only Plato and Aristotle who sometimes treated justice as the sum of all virtues. In interpreting justice in this way they gave voice to a common way of thinking even among ourselves: where there is a verdict concerning basic worth, one has been tried at the bar of justice, or at any rate what claims to be the bar of justice.) And so amour-propre, besides being a form of self-love—again, precisely *as* this form of self-love—is also an attachment to and passion for justice. The attachment to and passion for justice, in turn, depend on and also fortify the *belief* in justice, that is, the belief that justice must and indeed will be done. Without the belief that justice will be vindicated in practice, one might admire and love justice, but not in the passionate way of the morally expectant and energized. Without the belief in justice, amour-propre has no wind in its sails. Perceiving this, amour-propre rebels against the thought that justice might *not* be vindicated. It resists resignation. Therefore the key to achieving internal justice or health of soul in Rousseau's reformulation of classical philosophy turns out to be the overcoming of amour-propre.

Rousseau finally does overcome amour-propre, as we'll see—though, again, not completely. None of us can overcome amour-propre entirely. He himself, the preeminent explorer of amour-propre of his age, remains subject to inflamed amour-propre even after he has become as perfect a philosopher as he will ever be (VIII, 19, 23). But by limiting the time he spends in society he can dramatically reduce his exposure to said inflammation. And—most important—even when his amour-propre *is* inflamed, he is no longer mastered by it, for he now recognizes amour-propre for what it is and knows better than to accept its judgments as true or its counsel as wise. Thus does Rousseau free himself of amour-propre's tyrannical rule. He may even assume rule over *it*, for he seems to be able to employ outrage and indignation, which are expressions of amour-propre, in selective and salutary ways. A person who knows anger and indignation to be grounded in incoherent reasoning might nevertheless choose to give them vent when doing so would be helpful in securing a worthy end.

Rousseau's view that amour-propre persists even among the freest and wisest of human beings speaks to the limits of philosophy's freeing power. Does it speak too much? Rousseau's acceptance of the insuperable limits of philosophy's reign in the soul might seem to make him an imperfect Socratic. In truth, though, it might make him a *more* perfect Socratic and, if Rousseau is right, a more perfect philosopher than Socrates in this regard—more perfect because more honest. Socrates, in Rousseau's estimation, falsely believed that he could remain indifferent to the opinions of others in all circumstances.[7] Even in his philosophizing Socrates remained captive of a certain pride, which is a form, albeit the noblest form, of amour-propre.

Or might Socrates's independence and pride have been a touch ironic? The possibility hardly seems implausible. Neither does it seem implausible, come to think of it, that Rousseau might have been onto Socrates's irony and was being ironic himself when purporting to criticize Socrates and to offer himself as a corrective example.

One might question whether the endpoint I see Rousseau as reaching in the *Reveries* is truly desirable or that it has anything to do with wisdom. Is it really a moral and intellectual *achievement* to let go of the belief that justice will always be vindicated in the end? Many would say that ceasing to believe in justice constitutes an intellectual and moral failing. And others who might regard it as a triumph of honesty would nevertheless consider it a mournful one. To be sure, the passion for justice can wreak horror—and not only when it is cynically solicited. But if moralism tends to lend itself to fanatical excess and self-serving bias, *de*-moralization can eventuate in irresolution and decay and even, paradoxically, in *moralistic*

7. Kelly, *Rousseau's Exemplary Life*, 60, 71–73.

excess. For as we've already discussed, human beings tend to be so tightly gripped by moral need and passion that the effort to disown them may result in a surreptitious and all the more dubious and fearsome moralism. Call it the return of the repressed (after Freud) or undaunted nature reentering the place from which it has just been driven (after Horace): in either case the effort to solve a problem has only obscured and complicated it. Thus a case begins to emerge for moderating moral passion rather than debunking it. And moral passion *can* be moderated, especially where certain kinds of institutions have been created and certain kinds of practices adopted. Such was the view and indeed the practical intention of the classical political philosophers.[8] Such was Rousseau's view and intention as well. Like the Athenian Stranger of Plato's *Laws* and like Aristotle in book 3 of the *Nicomachean Ethics*, Rousseau quietly communicates the dubiousness of the ordinary moral consciousness while overtly endorsing a more humane version of it.

The story told in the *Reveries* was something new in Rousseau's work and perhaps in the history of Western letters. In his prior writings Rousseau had occasionally voiced the wisdom of resignation. In the *Confessions* he had even recounted the steps whereby he had attained this wisdom in the wake of the Illumination at Vincennes.[9] But the wisdom of resignation,

8. Consider Thucydides, Plato, and Aristotle. Thucydides illuminates indignation's tendency to destructive irrationality and notes the relative goodness of a mixed regime in which the extreme moral passions of one faction are checked by those of another; see 8.97. Plato too calls attention to the excesses of moral indignation in a number of dialogues. Perhaps most telling is the *Laws*, in which the Athenian Stranger makes the case for the cognitivist view of morality (860d) but then proceeds, even though neither of his interlocutors has balked, to concede a great deal to the ordinary moral consciousness after all, as if to signify that the ordinary moral consciousness is bound to resurge in the face of injustice. Aristotle does something quite similar in his treatment of moral responsibility in book 3, chapters 1–5 of the *Nicomachean Ethics*, where he raises and then refutes objections to the ordinary moral consciousness—or rather, raises and *purports* to refute objections to the ordinary moral consciousness. For it is far from clear that these purported refutations succeed. But even as Thucydides, Plato, and Aristotle tacitly expose the incoherence of the ordinary moral perspective, their shared practical intention is not to refute but rather to *moderate* the moralism of their readers by highlighting the unendurable pressures the moral actor may sometimes face.

9. Kelly parses this process with admirable clarity in *Rousseau's Exemplary Life*, 183–238. The goal toward which Rousseau moves in the *Confessions*, both in thought and in life, is the same as that of the *Reveries*: "a firm foundation in necessity or certainty" (*Rousseau's*

like any wisdom, *is* wisdom only if one has assimilated it—if one not only proclaims it but can articulate it and live by it. And it is only in the Seventh and Eighth Walks of the *Reveries* that Rousseau, for the first time in his writings, gives real evidence of this. Of course it is possible that he *had* assimilated the wisdom of resignation prior to writing some or all of his earlier books but declined to disclose it for pedagogical or political reasons. We cannot know precisely when he reached this point. Fortunately, we don't need to know. What matters is not the *when* but the *that*, the *how*, and the *why*. And these we can know, because he gives them to us to know.

Whether the elevation Rousseau attains with his philosophic breakthrough (VII) and his penetration of amour-propre's disguise (VIII) is the highest peak available to human beings can perhaps be doubted. To do justice to that question, one would have to look beyond Rousseau, or rather look at Rousseau in the light shed on the philosophic life and soul by other thinkers. And that's to say nothing about the claims made by nonphilosophers—by poets and prophets, for example. But there can be no denying Rousseau's place among the great philosophers who have reflected deeply on the philosophic life. In *The Reveries of the Solitary Walker* he has sent us a dispatch from outside the cave. Life outside the cave turns out to be demanding, at least for the exquisitely sensitive Rousseau in eighteenth-century Europe. The terrain can be challenging and the weather rough. There are wild animals and canny tribesman to be reckoned with. Perhaps after too many hours at a time the sun itself proves oppressive. These difficulties sometimes drive Rousseau back, if not into the cave then perhaps into a shadowed hillside cleft. Not even his final insights alleviate all such difficulties, though they do ease the strain and help him maintain soundness of mind. This is in no way to discount Rousseau's final achievement or his life as a philosopher, but only to acknowledge that the philosopher never ceases to be a human being with human needs and human limits.

Rousseau's Rêveries *and Plato's* Politeia

We turn now to the *Reveries'* elaborate relationship with the dialogue known to us as the *Republic*, though we would do well to remember that the dialogue's true title is *Politeia*, which means something much more

---

Exemplary Life, 234). The chief obstacles to this goal prove to be imagination and the desire for glory—again, the same as in the *Reveries*.

like *Regime* or *Constitution*. Each of the *Reveries'* ten Walks speaks to the correspondingly numbered book of the *Republic*.

That the *Reveries* was constructed this way must seem highly unlikely, for it is hard to think of two books by great political philosophers that present themselves more differently than these two: the one seemingly a meandering collection of reveries and reflections by an aging and idle solitary, misunderstood and persecuted, seeking to understand himself and keep himself company in the short time that remains to him; the other, the founding of a city in speech by a morally charged community of ambitious young men led by a strange older man whom they have "arrested" so that he might join them in an evening of festivities but who somehow makes them forget their plans and attend instead to the deepest and most pressing questions of their lives (and to himself as the one who might provide the answers). Yet one's incredulity should at least be tempered upon recalling that the *Republic*'s city in speech is developed precisely as an analogue of the soul—and upon remembering that justice is finally said to be the good order or health of the soul (368d–369b; 443c–d). Thus the *Republic* no less than the *Reveries* is an investigation of the individual soul and its well-being. Now as it happens the city is a problematic analogue for the soul. Yet the fact that it *is* problematic—and the blindness of Socrates's interlocutors' to this problem—needn't hinder the cause of self-knowledge but rather can be made to serve it, both in the interlocutors and among readers. Both they and we are presented with the opportunity to discover something about how our political and spirited passions balk at certain truths. The construction of the city in speech, the focus of almost the entire dialogue, is indeed a path to self-knowledge.

The *Republic* also addresses the education to philosophy more directly than does the *Reveries*—and not only in book 7, with its curriculum that begins with arithmetic and ends with dialectic, but also in the moral and civic education of books 2 and 3, since those selected for philosophic education will have received that moral and civic education in childhood and youth. As we'll see, Rousseau's own development as depicted in the *Reveries* loosely parallels the education recounted in the *Republic*—not so much the education imagined for the guardians, however, as that which Socrates imparts to his interlocutors.

I do not mean to say that Rousseau simply restates Plato's view, or what he takes to be Plato's view, for a different age. But I do mean to show that there are deep affinities and to my knowledge no contradictions between Rousseau's and Plato's respective articulations of the philosophic life.

Seeing its affinities with the *Republic* can help us understand much about the *Reveries*, beginning with its character as a narrative. What's narrated in the *Republic* is of course a dialogue. The *Reveries* too is dialogical. Where Socrates converses with Glaucon and company, Rousseau converses with himself—*with* himself but *for* readers, just as Plato allows his readers to listen in on Socrates and his companions. Like any good conversation, the *Reveries* has direction, but it also dilates and meanders. And like the best of conversations, its dilation and meandering serve to move the conversation forward even as they make us forget all about progress and direction.

The parallels between the *Reveries* and the *Republic* will be examined in part 2's commentary. But to give skeptical readers reason to be open to my claim, I offer a brief preview.

The *Reveries'* First Walk performs the same introductory and foundational tasks as the *Republic's* first book. It sets the terms for the work as a whole. It explicitly raises the question that will propel the rest of the work, or what I will call the work's explicit, animating question. And it indicates the work's chief problematic, by which I mean the problem that needs to be solved if the explicit animating question is to be successfully addressed. Admittedly, such commonalities, being customary for introductory chapters and merely formal at that, aren't remarkable—or rather, they *wouldn't be*, were it not for the fact that the *Reveries'* chief problematic is the same as the *Republic's*. That problematic proves to be the overturning of the ordinary moral consciousness and its supersession by the cognitivist view of morality.

Speaking of overturning: The trajectory of the *Reveries'* Second Walk has Rousseau literally being (a) upended (by a Great Dane), finding himself thereafter in (b) a state of blissful simplicity, then descending into (c) a condition of agitation and suffering as he recovers his individuality before, finally and only with great effort, purporting to find (d) equanimity through belief in divine providence. The same trajectory is enacted in book 2 of the *Republic*, where Glaucon and Adeimantus give speeches that (a) overturn society's moral pretensions, to which Socrates responds by leading the group in constructing in speech (b) a simple and innocently happy city, which then (in response to Glaucon's objection) adds "relishes" and thus becomes (c) an agitated and feverish city, before it begins to be (d) purified by a new teaching about the gods.

The Third Walk of the *Reveries* primarily concerns religious beliefs. This is where Rousseau relates the inquiry he undertook years earlier, through which he purportedly arrived at beliefs similar to those he would later present in "The Profession of Faith of the Savoyard Vicar." He recounts having reached the consoling and edifying conclusion that the world is governed according to a moral order made possible by the existence of an afterlife. The Third Walk also contains the sole passage in the *Reveries* in which Rousseau claims to have had courage (15), which he needed in order to undertake his inquiry into God and the soul. And the *Republic*? Readers will recall that in book 3 Socrates criticizes commonly held beliefs about the soul's fate after death and proposes replacing them with edifying beliefs. (Socrates never says that these beliefs are true.) Most edifying about the proposed new beliefs is that they support courage (386a–388e).

Rousseau's Fourth Walk is an intricate meditation on truth and lying. Book 4 of the *Republic*, by contrast, centers on justice; indeed it seems to mark the culmination of the quest for justice. But the contrast between Rousseau's topic and Plato's is not nearly as great as it first seems. In fact it is no contrast at all. In addressing truth and lying Rousseau is addressing nothing other than justice and injustice. For it turns out that what determines whether something is a lie is not that it is inaccurate but that it is unjust. (A falsehood that isn't harmful is not a lie but rather a fiction.) Of course Rousseau does not fully explain in the Fourth Walk what justice is. Then again, neither, as it turns out, does Socrates. What Socrates formulates as justice in book 4 is later revealed to be only vulgar justice or a phantom of justice (443c). And just as Socrates proceeds in the remainder of book 4 to apply his definition of justice to the individual soul, thereby revealing the just man to be someone very different from and indeed less moral than the just man as conventionally understood—Socrates's just man is one who obeys the law not because he loves the common good but because, having a well-regulated soul, he desires nothing unlawful—so too does Rousseau indicate in the Fourth Walk that the justice of the just person (or the truthfulness of the truthful person) follows more from moderation or prudence than from devotion to moral principle.

In the *Reveries*' Fifth Walk Rousseau recounts his splendid exile on St. Peter's Island. As we'll see, it is no stretch to characterize his depiction of this sojourn as an ongoing experience of erotic fulfillment. In this the Fifth Walk relates to Socrates's characterization of the philosophic life as an erotic and happy life in the fifth book of the *Republic*.

The theme of the *Reveries*' Sixth Walk is freedom; more particularly, *natural* freedom; which proves to mean the *philosopher's* freedom. Rousseau investigates what this freedom is and how the philosopher maintains it amid society. And so Rousseau must treat the philosopher's relation to the larger world—just as Socrates does in book 6 of the *Republic*. And although Rousseau nowhere explicitly embraces anything like Socrates's philosopher-king and indeed presents himself more as the *plaything* of the political world than its shaper, the Sixth Walk restates the teachings that Socrates conveys in book 6. Like the true philosopher of whom Socrates speaks, Rousseau is useless to society only because society has made him so. And as Socrates excoriates vicious pretenders to philosophy, Rousseau calls attention to the viciousness of the *philosophes* if only by indicating that it is they, with their conspiracy, who have caused his misfortunes (VI, 10). He even goes so far as to make a qualified case, both in general and for himself, for rule by the true philosopher—the same case, with the same qualifications, that Socrates makes.

Rousseau's Seventh Walk is all about wisdom. It is the only place in the *Reveries* where Rousseau claims to be living as wisdom itself would have him live (1, 3). This makes the Seventh Walk in my view the peak of the *Reveries*, both thematically and dramatically. (Others regard the Fifth Walk as the peak of the book. I agree that the Fifth Walk enjoys a special status in the *Reveries*. Rather than the book's *peak*, however, it is more accurately regarded as its *center*, just as the timelessness described in the Fifth Walk is somehow the center of philosophy.) The Seventh Walk gives us (a) Rousseau's most decisive step toward being a more perfect philosopher. The step consists of nothing more, but also nothing less, than attending more consistently to what *is*. What makes this clearer sight possible is the quieting of his imagination. Besides making him a more perfect philosopher, this step also makes him a happier man. It is only in the Seventh Walk that we can finally believe Rousseau's oft-repeated but heretofore dubious claim to have resigned himself to his condition. The Seventh Walk also (b) addresses Rousseau's practice of botany, the study wherein and whereby he purportedly has taken this great step. Finally, after speaking from and about this high ground, the Seventh Walk (c) concludes with a more sober set of reflections: Rousseau finds that he is still subject to the delusions of amour-propre. Is he no wiser than before, then? He *is* wiser, as one can see in his response to the discovery of his continuing foible: rather than excoriate himself or others, he laughs gently. These three distinct discussions parallel a similar tripartition in book 7 of the *Republic*. *Republic* 7 opens with (a) the famous image that compares the ascent to philosophy—presented here as the ascent to *wisdom*—to emergence from underground imprisonment into sunlit freedom. Socrates then proceeds (b) to outline the *studies* whereby this ascent might be achieved. These studies culminate in dialectic, through which one might finally gain clear sight of what *is*. Dialectic, however, is also a perilous thing, and so book 7 concludes (c) with sober reflections on the harm to which dialectic can lead.

Early in the Seventh Walk Rousseau observes, with little fanfare and no explanation, that his newly enhanced ability to see what *is* has purified him of hatred, revenge, and indeed all irascible passions (3). Only in the Eighth Walk does he explain. In a certain sense the Eighth Walk is a kind of descent, in that Rousseau revisits and unpacks his former deficiency, that is, his former self-deception and failure to understand. Book 8 of the *Republic*, with its cascading depictions of defective regimes, is also a descent. But in each work what is a *thematic* descent is at the same time a *narrative* step *higher*. Precisely by investigating these lower phenomena from the standpoint of newly gained wisdom, both Rousseau in the *Reveries* and Socrates's interlocutors in the *Republic* deepen, or at least (in the case of Socrates's interlocutors) have the opportunity to deepen, their understanding. So too might we deepen our own understanding.

In the *Reveries*' Ninth Walk, Rousseau, who had earlier lamented his enforced solitude, indicates that he has found ways to be happily sociable after all. Following as it does the breakthroughs recounted in the previous two Walks, the Ninth Walk proves to be a kind of implicit discourse on the pleasures of the philosophic life—not the pleasures of contemplation itself, which have already been treated, but the unique pleasures available to the philosopher in more ordinary realms of experience. In this the Ninth Walk parallels book 9 of the *Republic*, in which Socrates offers three purported proofs of the superior happiness or pleasure of the just man (the philosopher) and the misery of the unjust man (the tyrant). In fact, Rousseau parallels each of the three proofs with a comparable argument of his own.

Finally, Rousseau's very brief Tenth Walk, although unique in the *Reveries* for indicating a relationship to the Bible (by being dated Palm Sunday), nevertheless also responds directly to book 10 of the *Republic*. Where *Republic* 10 culminates with Socrates relating the myth of Er, which purports to explain what determines the character of one's life on earth and the fate of one's soul after death, the Tenth Walk of the *Reveries* gives us Rousseau's explanation of what "determined my whole life." Socrates's myth is long and complex, but it is possible to state its primary teaching baldly. Most of those who live justly do so only in order to avoid punishment. At best they have been habituated to virtue; they do not know or even believe in the choiceworthiness of virtue for its own sake. Those who *philosophize*, however, will always manage to live well—not because of fear or because they have been habituated to virtue but because, as philosophers, they *know* that virtue is good in itself, meaning good for *them*selves. And so both the *Reveries* and the *Republic* conclude by explaining what has determined the choice of this most choiceworthy way of life.

Concentric Rings

So far I have posited two overarching structural features of the *Reveries*, its narrative character and its correspondence with the *Republic*. I would now like to suggest a third: The *Reveries* is constructed, with respect to themes, as a group of concentric rings centered around the Fifth Walk, with the very brief Tenth Walk serving as a kind of coda. That is to say, there is a discernible thematic link between the First and Ninth Walks, between the Second and Eighth Walks, between the Third and the Seventh, and between the Fourth and the Sixth. The two members of each respective pair have a common focus or theme. However, in each pair the later of the two Walks marks a step forward—displays deeper insight or greater wisdom—than the earlier Walk, thus expressing Rousseau's continued perfection as a philosopher. This continued perfection, however, proceeds on an unchanging basis: philosophy, though it takes place in time, is grounded in the timeless. This is what makes the Fifth Walk the appropriate center of the *Reveries*. For the focus of the Fifth Walk is the relation, the *centrality*, of eternity to philosophy. Most of Rousseau's signal contributions concern development through time, whether in *Emile* (the development of the individual according to nature), the *Second Discourse* (the development of the species), or even the *First Discourse* (the typical development of societies). The same can be said of his signal contributions concerning the philosophic life. Yet his keen awareness of development never obscures the ground on which development takes place. Timeless nature persists and is somehow the ground of history. The *study* of nature reflects this, and so does the life devoted to the study of nature. Philosophy not only investigates the timeless but also experiences it. The *Reveries* expresses this in its very structure, which depicts the development of the philosophic life over time but also, in the Fifth Walk, the timelessness that is its ground, its core, and even its end.

As I did concerning the *Reveries*' parallels with the *Republic*, here too let me preview the argument just enough to render my claim plausible.

The connection between the First and Ninth Walks is seen in their respective treatments of solitude. Rousseau begins the First Walk by describing himself as sociable by nature yet consigned to miserable solitude. The Ninth Walk by contrast, shows him better off with respect to both sociability and solitude. His insight and good cheer have helped him work around his enemies and find pleasant ways—pleasant ways that may point to even more pleasant ways—to interact with those to whom his identity is not known. As for solitude, it is only in the Ninth Walk that we find

Rousseau appreciating it for the blessing it can be: "I am my own only when I am alone" (19).[10]

The connection between the Second and Eighth Walks is found in their shared focus on Rousseau's attempts to mitigate his suffering by denying human agency. The agency that he particularly needed to deny was that of his persecutors: it is much easier to accept pain whose source we take to be accidental or impersonal than pain that we believe has been deliberately and unjustly inflicted on us. In the Second Walk Rousseau claims to find solace in the thought that his tormentors are enacting not their own will but that of God, who, knowing Rousseau to be innocent, could be counted on to end his suffering and compensate him for it. In the Eighth Walk he no longer recurs to God's (or anyone else's) will but rather to something submoral within his persecutors that renders them, in his eyes, mere automata. Some will doubt that the solution of the Eighth Walk is superior to that of the Second. What matters for now is that Rousseau considers it to be so. Twice in the *Reveries* he claims to have acted according to "what nature willed" (*ce que la nature a voulu*), by which he means that he had resigned himself to necessity. The claims appear in the Second and Eighth Walks—in the first paragraph of the Second Walk and the last paragraph of the Eighth. The *Reveries'* concentricity can be that precise.

The connection between the Third and Seventh Walks concerns the study of nature. Of course one could say that the whole of the *Reveries* is nothing but the study of nature. But it is only in the Third and Seventh Walks that Rousseau explicitly inquires into the study of nature as such. In the Third Walk he particularly highlights his desire "to know the nature and destination of [his] being," a desire whose earnestness distinguishes him from those who "studied human nature to be able to speak knowingly about it, but not in order to know themselves" (III, 3). This desire doesn't cease to be operative. Nevertheless the Seventh Walk goes beyond the Third with respect to *how* Rousseau has come to study nature (we've already noted the breakthrough recounted in the Seventh Walk). This difference accounts for the light spirit with which he now philosophizes. Where the Third Walk is singular for its reference to *courage* (III, 15), the Seventh Walk is notable for *laughter* (VII, 1, 26, 28). Rousseau has acquired a greater lightness and equanimity as he has perfected his philosophic life.

The Fourth and Sixth Walks of course flank the central Fifth Walk, and their thematic link is particularly apt to this proximity. The Fifth Walk

10. Rousseau makes a similar claim at II, 1. But that claim, unlike the one in the Ninth Walk, is not borne out by the surrounding evidence.

recounts the period of Rousseau's exile on St. Peter's Island, during which he enjoyed what he calls a "solitary life" (17). This solitude doesn't mean that he was without human contact—he spent considerable time every day interacting with others (including his wife!)—but, rather, that he was not distracted or alienated from his inclinations. It was in this condition that he could engage in solitary pursuits, most notably those reveries in which he would abstract himself from everything around him and allow himself to be filled with the timeless and sufficient experience of his own existence—which is to say, reveries in which he would intensify his solitude to the point of literally forgetting society. Detachment, however, must be achieved; and solitude must be protected. This is where the significance of the Fourth and Sixth Walks begins. In contrast with the Fifth Walk's intense interiority, the Fourth and Sixth Walks address Rousseau's relations with the external world, including the place of politics in his life and thought. The Fourth Walk concerns the question of truth and lying, which proves to resolve into the question of justice. The Sixth Walk reflects explicitly on whether it was good for Rousseau to have taken as active a public role as he did by writing the books he composed between 1749 and 1764. It is appropriate and indeed eloquent to have these discussions flank the Fifth Walk: experiences of the sort recounted in the Fifth Walk necessarily take place within a space delimited by the external world—either *allowed* by the external world, or *shaped* by it, or in *defiance* of it. The dependence of the internal on the external and the delimitation of the internal by the external is one of the chief themes of the *Reveries*. In the Fourth and Sixth Walks this theme comes to the fore and is treated differently from the way it is treated in the other Walks. In the other Walks Rousseau notes the ways in that the surrounding world impinged on him. In the Fourth and Sixth Walks he engages the question of how to respond to the surrounding world in such a way as to do *justice* (IV) and to exercise and protect his *freedom* (VI). The broad connection between the Fourth and Sixth Walks is reflected in two small details. First, these are the only two Walks in which Rousseau speaks about or even mentions *abbés*, whom he takes in both cases to be false friends (IV, 1; VI, 10). Second, in both Walks his reflections are prompted by an unpleasant but otherwise insignificant incident. (The Fourth Walk's reflections on truth and lying are said to have been prompted by a communication from the *abbé* Rosier [IV, 1]. The Sixth Walk's exploration of freedom is said to have been prompted by Rousseau's realization that he has unconsciously altered the route of his regular walk [VI, 1–2].) Thus are our inner lives impinged on by the slightest of external phenomena. But also: thus can the slightest of external phenomena offer opportunities for self-knowledge. This indicates that the Fifth Walk's abstraction from the world, even if it is central to philosophy, is not sufficient for it.

I have suggested that the Tenth Walk be regarded as a kind of coda. I will add only that I cannot imagine a better coda to the *Reveries* than this very brief chapter in which Rousseau reflects with gratitude on the years he spent as a young man at Les Charmettes, years in which his soul took flight with *love*—love for a woman, love of learning, and, perhaps as a result of these, love of life.

The concentricity of which I've spoken doesn't speak against the *Reveries'* parallelism with the *Republic*, and it doesn't mean that Rousseau necessarily regarded the *Republic* as itself concentrically structured, though it is possible that he did see the dialogue this way, as have some penetrating readers of Plato in our own time.[11] Nor do these two structural principles preclude the possibility that additional ones might be at work in the *Reveries*.[12]

Addendum: Unfinished but Complete

The foregoing structural arguments presuppose that the *Reveries* as Rousseau left it to us is complete, or very nearly so, that is, that he intended to write only ten Walks and that the Walks as we have them are, at a minimum, complete, edited drafts. The manuscript evidence supports this presupposition. The first seven Walks were fully drafted, edited, and transposed by Rousseau into a fresh notebook. The remaining three Walks were also fully drafted and edited by Rousseau, though not transposed onto fresh paper, which may mean that they never received a final review (though it also may mean no such thing, since the notebook containing the first seven Walks was too full to allow the remaining Walks).[13] Yet very few scholars seem even to have entertained the possibility that the

11. See especially Brann, *Music of the Republic*, starting at 108: "The *Republic* is composed of concentric rings encompassing a center." Also see Barney, "Ring Composition in Plato"; and Howland, *Glaucon's Fate*, 17–19.

12. Gourevitch, "Provisional Reading of Rousseau's *Reveries*," argues that "the *Reveries* quite naturally breaks into five sets of two Walks each" (491).

13. For a review of the manuscript evidence, see Butterworth, "Appendix A, Description of the Notebooks," 241–42.

Reveries as we have it is complete.[14] Their view is not senseless. The book may not break off midsentence or midparagraph, but neither does it end with an obvious conclusion. Moreover, the final Walk is markedly briefer than all its predecessors. Whereas the prior nine Walks are lengthy essays composed of anywhere from fifteen to forty-two paragraphs, the Tenth Walk consists of a single, if long, paragraph—and it is dated Palm Sunday, 1778, less than three months before Rousseau's death. Yet these facts hardly foreclose the possibility that the book as we have it is what Rousseau intended it to be. Both Plato, whom Rousseau deemed his worthy judge and master (*SD*, 133; 19), and Bacon, whom he called perhaps the greatest of philosophers (*FD*, 29; 21), composed works that appear incomplete but prove upon careful reading to have been in all likelihood completed to the author's satisfaction (the *Critias* and *New Atlantis*, respectively). And if the manuscript evidence *suggests* that the *Reveries* is complete or nearly so, the coherence of the book, especially the structural features I have already sketched, comes close to *proving* it. If any of my three claims regarding the structure of the *Reveries* has merit—if the book tells a complete and coherent story that requires all its separate parts; or if it has the relationship to the *Republic* that I have suggested; or if the other Walks are structured concentrically around the Fifth—then we must conclude that the book as we have it is close to what Rousseau intended it to be.

Does the Reveries tell a complete and coherent story that requires all its separate parts?

The manuscript evidence gives some reason to think that Rousseau originally planned only seven Walks and that he decided sometime later to add more. There exists a playing card on which appears, in Rousseau's hand, a list of seven topics that roughly correspond to the topics of the first seven Walks.[15] Meier offers several reasons for supposing that Rousseau would have regarded the *Reveries* as fittingly completed with the Seventh Walk.[16] But the first seven Walks as Rousseau ultimately wrote them go beyond and are even at variance with what is written on the playing card. And a crucial thread of the *Reveries'* narrative—on my reading, *the* crucial thread—is not fully worked through in first seven Walks. This thread is the

---

14. I am aware of only two exceptions among major interpreters. Michael Davis regards the *Reveries* as more or less complete according to Rousseau's intention. Victor Gourevitch acknowledges, and perhaps more than acknowledges, the possibility. See Davis, *Autobiography of Philosophy*, 264–66; and Gourevitch, "Provisional Reading of Rousseau's *Reveries*," 518.

15. This card is kept by the Bibliothèque publique et universitaire de Neuchâtel, custodian of the notebooks in which Rousseau composed the *Reveries*.

16. See Meier, *On the Happiness*, 47–48.

story of Rousseau's progress toward the wisdom of resignation, toward accepting the insuperability of injustice on earth. In the Seventh Walk, with his claim to have been purified of the irascible passions, Rousseau *points to* his progress. But he does not *explain* it until the Eighth Walk, with his insight into the sly machinations of his own amour-propre. And even then he has not finished. The Ninth and Tenth Walks are also important to the story: the Ninth for showing that his insight into amour-propre enables him to have a rewarding social life even amid suspicion and denigration, and the Tenth for offering a fitting reflection on the love that made his philosophic life possible in the first place—fitting because grateful. It is worth noting that with both of these points—both his ability to flourish in isolation and the birth of philosophy out of the spirit of love—Rousseau sounds a notably Socratic theme. Plato and Xenophon give us a Socrates who seems to have enjoyed a happiness untinged by bitterness amid a community that mostly regarded him with suspicion and disdain. And in his account of his own philosophic life in the *Phaedo* Socrates attributes the decisive step in his development as a philosopher, or his "second sailing," to love: love for the logos and love for humanity (*Phaedo*, 89b–91c).

Perhaps Rousseau originally considered writing the *Reveries* as a collection of only seven Walks. But the book that he wrote is far more than a collection of seven meditations to which he appended three more. The ten Walks constitute a whole unto themselves, designed according to the principle of graphical necessity. We may and indeed should take the book, and be grateful for it, just as we have it.[17]

17. *Just as we have it*: by this I mean the Pléiade version (*Œuvres complètes*, vol. 1 [Paris: Gallimard, Bibliothèque de la Pléiade, 1959]) with certain modifications made and explained by Charles Butterworth in his English translation of the book.

PART II

CHAPTER 3

"What Am I?"

First Walk

Don't you know that the beginning is the most important part of every work?

Socrates's maxim, addressed to his young interlocutors as they are about to determine the education befitting the guardians of their city in speech in book 2 of the *Republic* (377a–b), is apt instruction for us as well. A book too is a work; and it too can be an education suited to those with the greatest capacities. Surely Plato means with Socrates's statement to direct readers to revisit with special care the beginning of the *Republic*. And so should we attend with special care to the beginning of *The Reveries of the Solitary Walker*.

But what counts as the beginning of the *Reveries*? Is it the whole of the First Walk, or only the first *part* of the First Walk? And what size part would that be? A paragraph? A sentence? A word? Might *all* these firsts be of special importance?

They might indeed.

As a Whole

As noted earlier, the First Walk performs three main tasks: (a) It introduces and sets the terms for the *Reveries* as a whole. (b) It poses the book's explicit animating question. And (c) it indicates the work's chief problematic, or the problem that needs to be solved if the explicit animating question is to be successfully addressed—which makes this problematic the *truly* animating question of the work and its chief concern. Book 1 of the *Republic* performs these same major tasks—these and apparently no others. That the opening chapters of the *Reveries* and the *Republic* perform the first two tasks is hardly remarkable—what else would we expect a book of philosophy to do in its opening chapter than introduce the work and raise the question that it claims to address? That the opening chapter of each book performs the third task as well—that each indicates a crucial problematic and does this so subtly as to ensure it will go unnoticed by most readers: that *is* perhaps remarkable, if only because undertaking this task shows the books to be works of remarkable depth and refinement. That the chief problematic is the same in both books—that certainly is remarkable. It is a decisive clue to the meaning of both books and a fruitful point of access to the heart of the *Reveries*. Let us examine how each text performs the three common tasks.

Book 1 of the *Republic* (a) introduces and sets the term for the work as a whole in two important ways. First is the marvelously rich opening scene that enacts in a playful and urbane way the gravely earnest conflict to be negotiated thereafter—that is, the relation between wisdom and power. Second is the scene that immediately follows. Socrates, although he has just been (so to speak) arrested by Polemarchus and company, quickly ascends to a position of rule by stimulating the young men's intense interest in what soon emerges as (b) the explicit animating question of the *Republic*, the question of justice: what is justice, and is justice good for the just man? The *Reveries*, by contrast, (a) begins with the lament of a philosopher who hasn't been playfully arrested but rather all too truly exiled ("proscribed from society by a unanimous agreement" [I, 1]), which prompts Rousseau to state (b) *his* animating question: "But I, detached from them and from everything, what am I? That is what remains for me to seek." It gradually becomes apparent, however, that the fruitful investigation of the two works' respective animating questions (*What is justice? What am I?*) requires something else—the *same* something else, or the same problematic: namely, (c) the overcoming of the ordinary moral consciousness and its replacement by the cognitivist view of morality. Overcoming the ordinary moral consciousness becomes the deep focus of both works because it becomes the focus of the *action* of both works. Both the *Republic* and the *Reveries* teach the overcoming of the ordinary moral consciousness. They teach *about* it, and they teach to the way *to* it. Let us consider this matter first as it emerges in the *Republic* and then, more extensively, as it comes to light and is developed in the *Reveries*.

Readers will recall that Socrates devotes the bulk of *Republic* 1 to refuting—and, in the central case, transfiguring—the conceptions of justice extracted from or volunteered by Cephalus, Polemarchus, and Thrasymachus, respectively. The primary teaching that comes out of this discussion is the priority of the good to the just. This teaching emerges almost immediately once Socrates raises the question of justice. Cephalus, who has implicitly voiced an understanding according to which justice demands giving back to others what belongs to them, agrees that it would be *un*just to follow this rule if the item at issue were a weapon and the one seeking its return were a friend overtaken by a fit of madness (331c–d). The just *is* just only if it is good: whatever purports to be an act of justice or a rule of justice or the art of justice can be no such thing in any instance in which it would produce a bad result. More precisely, what we learn from the Socrates-Cephalus exchange is that what one *takes* to be good determines what one conceives to be justice. Socrates doesn't explicitly state the priority of the good to the just; he elicits it from Cephalus and thus allows the others (including us) to make the discovery on their own. Already, then, Socrates has begun to uncover the compelling character of the apparent good, not only with respect to what we desire and what we do but also with respect to what we consider just or moral—which is to say, not only in our desiring and pursuing but even in our *denying* ourselves what we want. With that Plato has begun to direct us to the overcoming of the ordinary moral consciousness. He directs us further with Socrates's subsequent exchanges with Polemarchus and Thrasymachus—the former by establishing that justice could not be harmful to anyone, the latter by further illuminating the incoherence of the ordinary moral consciousness. Even the immoralist (Thrasymachus) turns out to be a moralist of a kind, and his moralism is no more resistant to the logic of the cognitivist view of morality than are more conventional moralisms. Socrates never explicitly rejects the ordinary moral consciousness in the *Republic*. But by the end of book 1 he has launched a powerful critique.

As the first book of the *Republic* obliquely indicates the need to overcome the ordinary moral consciousness, so too does the First Walk of the *Reveries*. In the latter case this problematic does not arise in connection with the quest for justice. Rousseau is already a philosopher; he already knows, or thinks he knows, something about what justice and indeed wisdom demand of him. His quest, rather, is to know himself more deeply. And his *challenge*, which is the proximate source of the problematic he shares with Socrates and company, is to live by the wisdom he already (thinks he) has. He doesn't yet understand this to be his challenge, however. That is to say, Rousseau *the narrator* doesn't understand this to be his challenge. But the author of the *Reveries* does; and he shows the reader with eyes to see that the narrator still lacks an important part of what Socrates called "human wisdom" (*Apology*, 20d). Rousseau never speaks of the ordinary moral consciousness or the cognitivist view of morality by these or any other names. Nevertheless the overcoming of the ordinary moral consciousness, or rather the story that culminates in it, begins where it ought to begin, in the First Walk.

The First Walk treats the moral consciousness in a most deceptive

way—deceptive to the reader because *self*-deceptive. Rousseau the narrator has not attained the resignation to necessity and the consequent
equanimity that he claims. It takes some time for readers to be able to
see that they are in the hands of an unreliable narrator. And it takes much
longer to see—indeed, it seems to me that few readers ever do see—that
narrator and author are distinct from one another, that the author has
made himself, his *prior* self, into a character in his book.

Almost from the beginning of the First Walk Rousseau the narrator lays
claim to the wisdom of resignation. Yet he also gives us, just as early, several reasons to doubt the veracity of his claim, beginning with the defiance
with which he states the claim. (It is not the sincerity of the claim that we
must doubt, only its veracity.) He acknowledges that he underwent fifteen
or more years of unjust proscription from society (1–2), including "no less
than ten years" of "delirium" against which he struggled in vain, before,
"finally, feeling that all my efforts were useless and that I was tormenting
myself to no avail, I took the only course which remained—that of submitting to my fate without railing against necessity any longer. I have found
compensation for all my hurts in this resignation through the tranquility
it provides me" (4). If Rousseau did conclude that resignation was the
only remaining course, that was because his persecutors forced him to
do so. In their artless totalism, his tormentors had left him nothing more
to fear—which also means nothing more to *hope*, since the realization of
one's final fear is also the extinguishing of one's final hope (5–7). Rousseau acknowledges that he had indeed clung to a final hope. Even after he
had despaired of ever being treated justly by his contemporaries, he had
maintained a slender hope that future generations might read his works
and judge them (and him) without prejudice. But a recent event "as sad
as it was unforeseen has finally just erased this weak ray of hope from my
heart and has made me see my fate forever and irreversibly fastened here-
below" (7). The event to which he refers is presumably his failed effort to
elicit sympathetic interest in his plight or, barring that, to place his newly
completed, unpublished *Dialogues* into safekeeping.[1] Only by letting go
of this final hope—only by becoming indifferent to the fate of his writings and reputation in the future as in the present (15)—could he achieve
resignation. Such is the power of even the slenderest hope. Feeble though
it was, Rousseau's last ray of hope had been "a hold by which a thousand
diverse passions incessantly perturbed me" (7). "Since then," however,

1. See "History of the Preceding Writing," which Rousseau appended to the *Dialogues*
(977–92; 246–57).

meaning, since that final hope was extinguished, "I have become unreservedly resigned, and I have found peace again" (7).

Rousseau depicts his progress toward acceptance as the realization of agency. At first he was the victim of his enemies: they were the active ones. Or, if one prefers, it is they whose actions had efficacy. When recounting this state of affairs, Rousseau speaks of himself in the passive voice. He "has *been proscribed* from society" (1) and "*cast into* an incomprehensible chaos" (2). He was "*taken as* a monster, a poisoner, an assassin" and "was at first overwhelmed by" "this strange revolution" (3). When he describes his subsequent liberation, however, he adopts the active voice. "*I took* the only course that remained" (4). "*I have found* peace again" (7). Admittedly, his agency was severely qualified: he took "*the only course that remained.*" And he found peace only after his enemies "*made [him] see*" that his fate had been fixed: his only "action" was to submit to what he couldn't change. But this hardly diminishes his accomplishment: however clear the logical imperative to do so, accepting what one cannot change is often excruciatingly difficult and nothing less than an act of wisdom. And yet Rousseau's accomplishment *is* diminished, or at any rate deeply compromised, by his dependence on forces beyond his control. Should his persecutors in any way slacken, or should he come to doubt that they had done all the harm to him that they could, fear and hope would arise anew. (And is it really plausible that his persecutors *had* done all the harm that was in their power to do?) Active voice or not, Rousseau has not yet exercised the agency required to achieve and sustain the acceptance that he claims to have achieved. He has not yet discovered the nature and limits of his agency, or what he can and cannot do. Nevertheless he has made progress. If he hasn't yet seen and done all that he needs to see and do, he has come to understand in principle that wisdom and freedom, not to mention tranquility and whatever happiness might be available to him, require the willing acceptance of necessity.

Another indication that Rousseau has not achieved the resignation that he professes appears in the twelfth paragraph. Having concluded the eleventh paragraph by pronouncing himself "tranquil at the bottom of the abyss, a poor unfortunate mortal, but unperturbed, like God Himself," he concedes that he can't "cast [his] eyes on what touches and surrounds" him without indignation or distress. His response to this distress, he says, has been to turn inward. Yet among the rewards of his inward turn are not only consolation and peace but also hope (12)—this despite his earlier claim to have been "delivered" from hope (7). Now to be sure, Rousseau's new hope is categorically different from his former hopes. In the past, he had placed his hopes in other men. Now, by contrast, he places hope only in himself, which is to say, in his own innocence: "I find consolation, hope, and peace only in myself—I no longer ought nor want to concern myself with anything but me." But consider: although his hope is "*in*" himself, it rests on a God who will right the wrongs that he has suffered. This becomes evident in the very next lines: "It is in this state that I again take up the sequel to the severe and sincere examination I formerly called my *Confessions*. I consecrate my last days to studying myself and to preparing in advance the account I will give of myself before long" (12). To whom other than God would Rousseau be planning to give an account of himself before long? Hope for divine justice is perhaps a sturdier thing than hope for just treatment by men—but only for one who has a firm faith in God as vindicator of the just. Rousseau's agitation suggests that he does not have such a faith. (In the Second Walk he will speak explicitly about his faith in God. But given his continued distress, not to mention the evident eclipse of faith as the *Reveries* proceeds, the reader cannot easily believe that his professed faith has moved him any closer to resignation and peace of mind.)

Even Rousseau's plans for his remaining days presuppose faith in a vindicating God. He tells us that he plans to set down in writing the "charming periods of contemplation" that he regularly experiences, especially on his walks, so that he might relive them with pleasure in the future. These recollections are to make up the "Walks" of which the *Reveries* is to be constituted. But notice one of the pleasures he anticipates: "each time I reread them I will enjoy them anew. I will forget my misfortunes, my persecutors, my disgrace, while dreaming of *the prize my heart deserved* (6; emphasis added). If Rousseau's faith in a just and providential God should prove less than solid, this pleasure would give way to agitated distress. And the evidence indicates that his faith *is* less than solid if indeed it was ever real at all. Perhaps, as one in whom a philosophic nature had been activated, he could not securely hold *any* faith. Rousseau has some part of the wisdom of resignation, perhaps the larger part. He can recite the main outlines of this wisdom. He knows what's needed, and why. What he doesn't yet know is the how, and what *that* requires is a deeper self-awareness than he has yet achieved.

Three Sections

In addition to the thematic and functional resonance between the First Walk of the *Reveries* and book 1 of the *Republic*, there are also remarkable structural parallels. Each divides into three narratively discrete sections;

and in each case, the second of the three sections is by far the longest and itself divides into three subsections. Broadly speaking, the sections and subsections of the *Reveries* do the same things—they address the same themes and propel the *Reveries'* First Walk in the same ways—as the corresponding sections and subsections of *Republic* 1.

The first section of *Republic* 1 (327a–328b) constitutes the dialogue's opening tableau. Socrates recounts how he and Glaucon, having visited the Piraeus to pray and to observe a new religious festival, had just set out for home when they were accosted by a party of young men led by Polemarchus, who prevailed on the two to return with them to Polemarchus's home (really the house of Polemarchus's father, Cephalus), where, Polemarchus promised, they would dine together before going out for an evening of festivities beginning with a dramatic torch race on horseback. Socrates and Glaucon have little choice but to accept the invitation, as is made clear by a playful but portentous exchange:

> Polemarchus said, "Socrates, I guess you two are hurrying to get away to town."
> "That's not a bad guess," I said.
> "Well," he said, "do you see how many of us there are?"
> "Of course."
> "Well, then," he said, "either prove stronger than these men or stay here."
> "Isn't there still one other possibility . . . ," I said, "our persuading you that you must let us go?"
> "Could you really persuade," he said, "if we don't listen?" (327c)

I have already identified the question of justice as the animating question of the *Republic*. The question put by Socrates to Polemarchus that I have just quoted, regarding the relation between wisdom and power, or the *plight* of wisdom in the face of the power of the multitude, is a version of the question of justice, indeed the decisive version, if we pose the question of justice with an eye to political justice in particular. Both thematically and dramatically, this section is a proper introduction to the *Republic* as a whole.

Socrates manages in no time to stimulate in his young interlocutors a keen desire to understand justice and its relation to happiness. All thoughts of the torch race and even dinner are forgotten. Here begins the second section of *Republic* 1 (328b–354a), in which Socrates examines three successive conceptions of justice: first, the brief discussion of the conception of justice that Socrates infers from something Cephalus has said; then a longer discussion of Polemarchus's conception of justice;

and, finally, the much longer discussion of Thrasymachus's conception of justice. It is important to note that whereas Socrates simply refutes or at least purports to refute Cephalus's and Thrasymachus's conceptions of justice, he challenges only *parts* of, and then *revises*, Polemarchus's conception. The revised definition—namely, justice as doing good for one's friends who themselves are good and doing harm to no one—is criticized by Thrasymachus but refuted by no one. It seems to me that this revised conception of justice is the one to which Socrates himself adheres both in the *Republic* and elsewhere.

The third and final section of *Republic* 1 (354a–c) consists of Socrates's concluding reflection on the inadequacies of the preceding discussion. Though brief, this reflection is decisive, for it prompts all that is to follow in the subsequent books, beginning with Glaucon and Adeimantus's challenge to Socrates that he vindicate justice as good in itself for the just person.

The First Walk of Rousseau's *Reveries* is structured comparably. Its first section consists of the first paragraph alone, in which Rousseau declares that he has been exiled from society and then poses the question that he means to pursue in the rest of the book: "But I, detached from them and from everything, what am I?" "Unfortunately," however, "that inquiry must be preceded by a glance at [his] position."

This "glance" is the work of the First Walk's second section, which consists of paragraphs 2 through 11, though Rousseau's glance is remarkably steady and unblinking and his "position" turns out to mean not only his enforced solitude but also how it came about and, most especially, how he has experienced and ultimately come to terms with it. Like *Republic* 1's second section, the second section of the First Walk is itself tripartite. In each of the subsections, moreover, Rousseau seems to me to speak to the same theme that is addressed in the *Republic*'s corresponding subsection.

The First Walk's third and final section, consisting of paragraphs 12 through 15, lays out Rousseau's intention in the chapters to come—that is, to pursue the question he has already posed, *what am I?*—and the reasons for doing so. Rousseau, a most unusual man suffering through a most unusual plight, perhaps seems to be preparing an idiosyncratic inquiry into his idiosyncratic self. Yet we soon come to see that his question is a question for all of us and that by putting the question to himself alone he inquires into the human soul and human being as such. To ask *What am I?* is not to ask what *kind* of a human being one is but rather what it is to be human. Our peculiarities are the gateway to the universal. This is especially true of Rousseau, whose paramount distinction, as I've already suggested, is the strength with which nature still makes itself heard in him, the same nature that in most of us has been largely muffled. And Rousseau's peculiar *situation*, his involuntary solitude, lets nature's voice resonate all the more by muting the din of the world.

In the third section Rousseau states the intention of the *Reveries* as a whole. In this he seems to suspend the parallels with *Republic* 1, which contains no comparable statement. Yet this suspension is more apparent than real, for Rousseau's statement of intention proves to be quite misleading. The section does set up and in some ways determine the course of the work as a whole, but only obliquely, which is to say, no more so than the corresponding section of *Republic* 1 sets up and determines the course of *that* work. Nor is the question that Rousseau poses in this section (*what am I?*) any less universal or consequential than the question of justice that Socrates implicitly poses in the corresponding section of *Republic* 1.

FIRST SECTION: PARAGRAPH 1

In performing the tasks that it does, the whole of the First Walk serves as a discrete and fitting introduction to the *Reveries*, just as the whole of book 1 serves as a discrete and fitting introduction to the *Republic*. So too, however, does the *Reveries'* opening paragraph alone serve as a discrete and fitting introduction, as does the opening tableau of the *Republic*. And the same is true of the opening sentence of each work, and even the opening word. Let's examine the paragraph in full.

Me voici donc seul sur la terre, n'ayant plus de frère, de prochain, d'ami, de société que moi-même.—

"So here I am, alone on the earth, no longer having any brother, neighbor, friend, or society other than myself." "Here *I* am": this is a translator's necessary concession to the demands of idiomatic English. The first word in the French original is not "I" (*je*) but rather a first-person pronoun in the objective case, more like the English *me*, as in "Look at me," the better to convey the involuntariness of Rousseau's aloneness. Compare this to the *Republic*'s opening: "Socrates: 'I went down to the Piraeus yesterday . . .'" Socrates speaks of himself as one with agency, though here too idiomatic English obscures the force of the original: Socrates's first word in the Greek original is *Down* (*katarun*). The *Reveries* opens with the unconnected and hence unprotected, passive, and solitary *I*. And yet Rousseau does not say that he has no brother, neighbor, friend, or society at all but rather that he has none *other than himself*. Although alone, he is not lonely. He has himself for company. He will tell us in paragraph 12 that he is writing this book for his future self. We readily understand that one who reads is not altogether alone. The same is true for one who writes, especially if writing for a particular person whom the writer knows will read the writing with interest, and most especially if the writer cares for or loves that person and trusts that that person cares for or loves the writer. These conditions are clearly met in Rousseau's case. He anticipates that in writing for himself he will give himself up entirely to the *sweetness* of conversing with his own soul. (*Livrons-nous tout entier à la douceur de converser avec mon âme.*)

> Le plus sociable et le plus aimant des humains en a été proscrit. Par un accord unanime ils ont cherché dans les raffinements de leur haine quel tourment pouvait être le plus cruel à mon âme sensible, et ils ont brisé violemment tous les liens qui m'attachaient à eux.—

"The most sociable and the most loving of humans has been proscribed" from, has been *written out of*, society (*proscrire*: to proscribe; from the Latin *prōscrībere*, literally to write in front of). Proscribed by whom? By everyone: "By a unanimous agreement they have sought in the refinements of their hatred for what torment could be the cruelest to my sensitive soul, and they have violently broken all the ties that attached me to them." But consider: wasn't Rousseau also a member of society? If so, how can his proscription have been unanimous? If we insist on taking him literally (admittedly we risk becoming pedantic, but it seems a risk worth taking with so careful a writer), there are only two possible answers: either Rousseau, the most sociable and loving of humans, was not a member of society even prior to his proscription, or else he was a member of society and joined in the decision to proscribe himself. The first possibility seems plausible, since he had made such a point of his Genevan citizenship while living in France. And yet he doesn't quite say that he was proscribed from *French* society. He doesn't even say that he was proscribed from *society*. He was simply proscribed. Was he proscribed from the human community? Perhaps he was. But the second alternative, that is, that he signed on to his own banishment, is also plausible, if paradoxical. The *unanimity* with which he was forced into exile puts one in mind of the unanimity of the social contract as he had famously articulated it,[2] and that same account had made proscription a necessary and fitting fate for the one who has formed or re-formed a people. That person is the Legislator. Although he proposes and persuades with the ostensible backing of divine authority,

2. Regarding the unanimity of Rousseau's proscription as a mirroring or reversal of the unanimity of the social contract, see Gans, "Victim as Subject"; and Bloom, *Jean-Jacques Rousseau*.

the Legislator must wield no political authority and must not even remain among the people for which he has legislated: "When Lycurgus gave his homeland laws, he began by abdicating the throne. It was the custom of most Greek cities to entrust the establishment of their laws to foreigners. The republic of Geneva did so too, with good results" (*SC*, 382; 155). So too did Rome uphold this principle, in word if not always in deed. Banishment does not deprive the Legislator of the fruits of his labor. That fruit won't ripen for a long time, and the Legislator is the rare person who "could work in one century and enjoy the reward in another." Banishment deprives him only of the as yet *unripe* fruit of his labor. And unripe fruit is not only bitter; it can be downright sickening. They for whom Rousseau has attempted to legislate is the same *they* who "have sought in the refinements of their hatred for what torment could be the cruelest to [his] sensitive soul." And yet—

J'aurais aimé les hommes en dépit d'eux-mêmes—

"I would have loved men in spite of themselves." Such, it seems to me, must be the attitude of the Legislator with respect to those for whom he legislates. One who loves a population *blindly*, without taking note of its flaws, will be hostile to the presuppositions, let alone the revolutionary character, of any founding. One who loves blindly does not love well. At the other extreme, one who sees *only* flaws and who can love people only for what they might yet become—for what one might yet make them into—is no lover at all: such a one is a misanthrope, not a Legislator, and least of all a Philosopher-Legislator. Legislators, it would seem, love those for whom they would legislate in something like the way that good parents love their children or good teachers love their students: they love them as they are but also want to guide them toward what they might yet be. (Those who would object on the grounds that a Legislator's love is bound to be selfish while proper parental love is the very paradigm of selfless devotion should consult Aristotle's treatment of friendship in the *Nicomachean Ethics*, wherein maternal love, though initially put forward as the very paradigm of selfless devotion [1159a], gradually comes to sight as a paradigm of noble *self*-love: the mother loves her child as fiercely as she does because she recognizes the child as a part of herself [1161b] and labored so hard in giving birth [1168a].) Of course Rousseau's work as a Legislator is behind him now. The *Reveries* is at most the memoir of a retired Legislator. But that needn't keep it from speaking to future generations and from educating those who, by virtue of their affinity to Rousseau and his teaching, show themselves to be his descendants.

Ils n'ont pu qu'en cessant de l'être se dérober à mon affection. Les voilà
donc étrangers, inconnus, nuls enfin pour moi puisqu'ils l'ont voulu.—

"Only by ceasing to *be* have they been able to slip away from my affection. They are thus strangers, unknowns, finally nothings to me, because
that is what they wanted." Here at the story's beginning Rousseau already
understands that in order to rescue oneself from the tyranny of inflamed
amour-propre and thus attain a certain acceptance and calm, one must
regard one's enemies in a certain way—as distant beings ("strangers")
with no claim, certainly no moral claim, to one's respect ("nothings").
He understands that it is necessary to regard them impersonally. But he
does not behave accordingly. He does *not* regard them as "nothings." If
he did, he wouldn't defensively attribute his estrangement from society
exclusively to *their* choice ("that is what they wanted"). Indeed, by pinning
responsibility on them Rousseau seems to betray a felt need to justify his
own actions, which is further evidence that he has not yet attained the insight necessary to (so to speak) operationalize the wisdom of resignation.

In truth, an alternative reading cannot be discounted. On that reading,
the opening paragraph of the First Walk is a *preface* to the *Reveries*, whose
narrative proper begins in the *second* paragraph. Both readings are consistent with my overall interpretation of the *Reveries* as a philosopher's autobiographical bildungsroman. A good story requires time and suspense,
and self-knowledge requires time and training. Readers' attention must
be focused and their passions engaged if they are to follow the Solitary
Walker on his long path:

Mais moi, détaché d'eux et de tout, que suis-je moi-même? Voilà ce
qui me reste à chercher. Malheureusement cette recherche doit être
précédée d'un coup d'œil sur ma position. C'est une idée par laquelle
il faut nécessairement que je passe pour arriver d'eux à moi—

"But I, detached from them and from everything, what am I?" The question speaks for itself. In fact it speaks for the book to come. But its formulation is interesting. In the first six sentences of the book, Rousseau has
presented himself as the target or object of other people's actions. Here in
the seventh sentence, as he is ready to embark on something that is truly
and necessarily his own, his idiom becomes more complex: *I*—or rather,
more literally if less idiomatic in English, *me—what am I myself?* The focus
of his inquiry, Rousseau tells us, is both me and I, both himself as object and
himself as subject. The *I* or the self as subject may be the essential thing—it

certainly seems to be Rousseau's quarry—but it cannot be reached except by way of the *me* or the self as object, that is, the self that has been conditioned by outside forces. And the self as object cannot be reached except by working through these very outside forces: "Unfortunately, this inquiry must be preceded by a glance at my position. This is an idea that I must necessarily follow in order to get from them to me." Rousseau can't get to the solitude in which he hopes to encounter his deepest and truest self except by going through those who, by imposing solitude on him in the first place, created the crucible through which he must pass in order to reach himself. Passing through an externally imposed solitude is an apt description both of what Rousseau did in the years prior to writing the *Reveries* and of what he does, or the path that he traverses, in the *Reveries* itself.

SECOND SECTION: PARAGRAPHS 2–11

The First Walk's second section begins with a claim that is both precise and imprecise: "Although I have been in this curious position for fifteen years and more, it still seems like a dream to me" (2). Why fifteen years *and more*? Is the number actually larger than fifteen? But then why not say sixteen or seventeen or whatever number it might be? Or does Rousseau have something more in mind that makes him want to pronounce the number fifteen? The question might not be worth raising if it weren't for some other curious appearances of fifteen in the *Reveries*. One of these other appearances is already before us: fifteen is the number of paragraphs constituting the First Walk. What could be the significance of fifteen? The answer is suggested throughout paragraph 2, beginning with its first sentence, the one I've just quoted, which, as the opening line of the First Walk's second section, is also the opening line of the *Reveries'* main narrative. The "curious position" in which Rousseau spent fifteen years "still seems like a dream" to him, a bad dream amid a bad sleep: "No doubt about it, I must have unwittingly made a jump from wakefulness to sleep or rather from life to death. Dragged, I know not how, out of the order of things, I have seen myself cast into an incomprehensible chaos where I distinguish nothing at all." What does this depiction call to mind if not being forcefully cast from sunlight into the darkness of a cave? Here is Socrates describing for Glaucon what such an experience would be like:

"If such a man were to come down again and sit in the same seat, on coming suddenly from the sun, wouldn't his eyes get infected with darkness?"
"Very much so," he said.

"And if he once more had to compete with those perpetual prisoners in forming judgments about those shadows while his vision was still dim, before his eyes had recovered, and if the time needed for getting accustomed were not at all short, wouldn't he be the source of laughter, and wouldn't it be said of him that he went up and came back with his eyes corrupted, and that it's not even worth trying to go up? And if they were somehow able to get their hands on and kill the man who attempts to release and lead up wouldn't they kill him?"

"No doubt about it." (516e–517a)

Socrates's scenario is hypothetical: "*If* such a man were to come down again." Does anyone who has left the cave really return to it? In fact a whole cohort does, is *compelled* to do so—namely, the guardians-in-training, upon completing their education in the liberal arts up to and including dialectic (539c). "Now, after this [education], they'll *have to* go down into that cave again for you, and they must be *compelled* to rule in the affairs of war and all the offices suitable for young men, so that they won't be behind the others in experience" (539e–540a; emphasis added). "How much time do you assign to this?" Glaucon inquires. Socrates's answer: *fifteen years*. Only those who perform these fifteen years of duty and in the process confirm their excellence are released from the cave, whereupon they are compelled to ascend and look toward the good and to "use it as a pattern for ordering city, private men, and themselves for the rest of their lives." Now to be sure, Rousseau's enemies did not consign him to darkness fifteen years prior to writing the *Reveries* so that he might rule in war or any other affairs. Yet his activity and experience during these years were comparable to the guardians' fifteen-year consignment to the cave in several senses. His work during these years was the *political* work of self-defense (the *Letter to Beaumont*, the *Confessions*, the *Dialogues*), which, if successful, would benefit both himself and society. His experience during these years was the *darkness* of bewilderment and disorientation. And he most surely experienced both his need to engage in apologetics and his consignment to darkness as having been *compelled*: "*Dragged* I know not how."

What brought these fifteen years to an end? Has Rousseau emerged from the cave to look on the good? Indeed he has, though this moment in his story won't be narrated until the Seventh Walk, where he attains his clearest and most comprehensive sight of what *is*. He won't speak of the good *as such*, let alone *in itself*, but the clearer and more comprehensive sight of what *is* to which he attains in the Seventh Walk includes clearer and more comprehensive sight of nature's goodness, including the natural goodness of man. And this apprehension of goodness is clearly good for him.

The second section as a whole explores Rousseau's enforced solitude. But "this strange position," as he calls it, was not static. His experience of solitude over the course of fifteen years unfolded in three stages that are treated respectively in three subsections (i.e., three subdivisions of the First Walk's second section). Each subsection offers its own discrete teaching on the relation between justice and happiness, thereby paralleling the subdivision of *Republic* 1's second section into three discrete explorations of the same (i.e., Socrates's successive exchanges with Cephalus, Polemarchus, and Thrasymachus).

Paragraphs 2 and 3 (the first subsection of section 2) recount how Rousseau initially experienced his abrupt banishment. We've already noted paragraph 2's account of his thorough dismay and disorientation. Paragraph 3 provides the particulars. Rousseau, the same man that he has always been, is suddenly regarded as "a monster, a poisoner, an assassin . . . the horror of the human race, the plaything of the rabble." Here begin the great agitation and indignation that would rage in him, if not constantly then chronically, for many years. Beneath the agitation and indignation was bewilderment. So unprepared was he for the "strange revolution" that beset him, and so bewildered was he by the mendacity of the conspirators, that he felt as if he had fallen into a bad dream. He suffered from the sense of having fallen unawares into an unreality. We've already noted his sense of unreality, but we haven't yet seen in it all that is worth seeing. If my reading of the *Reveries* is on the mark, we should be able to discern an important affinity between this part of Rousseau's story (again, the first subsection of the First Walk's second section, or paragraphs 2 and 3) and *Republic* 1's exchange between Socrates and Cephalus. And so we do.

Rousseau's sense of unreality, which he likens to troubled sleep and even death, recalls the stories about the afterlife that have come to nag at Cephalus in his old age and have given rise to his new or newly intensified concern about justice. Cephalus has begun to worry because the afflictions that are said to be dealt out in Hades are *just*. Thus he now spends time sacrificing to the gods, lest he leave any debts unpaid on earth. On first consideration Rousseau does not seem troubled in any comparable way. He makes no mention of any misdeeds of his own; his response to the "strange revolution" in his life is not guilt or even doubt or defensiveness but rather bewilderment and pain. Yet might it not be—does it not seem *likely*—that Rousseau's agitation and indignation indicate nagging doubt or suspicion regarding his own innocence? Machiavelli observes that we tend to impute justice to the successful *because* of their success.[3] We implicitly presume that the world is so constructed that those who realize their ambitions must have deserved to do so. This way of thinking not only empowers the clever and ruthless; it also undermines innocent victims of injustice. Protestations of innocence, even when true, will be suspected of exaggeration if not outright falsehood—and not only by others, but by the innocent victims themselves: they too have a stake, indeed a higher stake, in the moral worldview discerned by Machiavelli. One who is undergoing severe and protracted suffering, as Rousseau was, might wonder whether he doesn't *deserve* to suffer. If he loudly professes his innocence, that might be an effort to shout down an inner voice vested with the authority of the Ordinary Moral Consciousness.

In paragraphs 4 through 6 (the second subsection of section 2) Rousseau recounts his purported achievement of resignation and tranquility. We already know the main lines of the story: After struggling violently and vainly, he "took the only course which remained—that of submitting to [his] fate without railing against necessity any longer" (4). He was able to take this course only when he was finally shorn of *hope*—which also means, when he was finally rid of *fear*, for the *effectual truth* of fear is the same as that of hope, and the effectual truth of being *delivered* from fear is the same as that of being delivered from hope: "What do I still have to fear from them, since everything is over? No longer able to make my condition worse, they can no longer alarm me" (6). Both fear and hope (except when hope is firmly grounded in faith in a just and providential God) push against the possibility of acceptance and resignation. Or more precisely, fear and hope open a door through which imagination may enter and capture our minds. It is imagination that punishes us with dreadful prospects or sets us up for later disappointment. Nor does imagination hinder resignation only by shaping our consciousness of what is yet to come. It can also hinder resignation by distorting our view of the present, as it is doing to Rousseau even "now," while he tells his story.

Rousseau claims that by depriving him of hope, his enemies have enabled him to achieve complete resignation and tranquility. Yet he calls these claims into question even as he makes them. One way in which he does so is by professing his resignation and tranquility in so strikingly

---

3. "In the actions of all men, and especially of princes, where there is no court to appeal to, one looks to the end. So let a prince win and maintain his state: the means will always be judged honorable, and will be praised by everyone." Machiavelli, *Prince*, 71; also see 34–35.

unresigned and untranquil a manner. Another way involves imagination. Here I am referring to his marked tendency to exaggerate the depredations of his position. Such exaggeration is the obverse of bluster. Let's accept that Rousseau has suffered terribly in just the ways and for just the reasons he says. Let's even concede that the suffering of such a sensitive soul is greater than any suffering the rest of us have known. But is it credible that "all the tricks of Hell could add nothing more to it," and that "physical suffering itself, instead of increasing my torments, would bring diversion from them"? Is Rousseau really enduring "a situation which nothing can make worse" (6)? Surely he knows better. And if he doesn't, if he can't imagine that things could be worse, this lack of imagination arises from an *excess* of imagination in the service of amour-propre.

Yet another way in which Rousseau undermines his claim to have attained resignation and tranquility is found in the concluding line of paragraph 6: "They have deprived themselves of all mastery over me, and henceforth *I can laugh at them*" (emphasis added). Not that there is anything false or untoward in such laughter—if it is honest. But in this context Rousseau's laughter almost certainly bespeaks the gratification of a needy, which is to say an inflamed, amour-propre.

As the second of the three subsections, this one should correspond to the Socrates-Polemarchus exchange—as indeed it does. For one thing it is longer than the previous subsection, just as the treatment of Polemarchus's conception of justice is longer than the treatment of Cephalus's conception. A more substantive affinity between the corresponding subsections is that each leaves us, as none of the other subsections does, with a wise principle to live by—if we can. And in both cases the principle entails eschewing harm. Just before it ends with Thrasymachus's belligerent entrance into the discussion, the Socrates-Polemarchus exchange yields a formula for the just treatment of others that is never refuted and that seems to describe Socrates's conduct toward others. It is to do good for friends who themselves are good and to do harm to no one. Rousseau's corresponding subsection teaches that the way to tranquility is through the overcoming of hope and fear. Overcoming hope and fear, as it happens, will not only alleviate one's exposure to harm, but also, in consequence of that easing of mind, diminish the inclination to harm others. Rousseau, in other words, effectively embraces the same principle that emerges from the Socrates-Polemarchus exchange. He had formulated this principle in the *Second Discourse* as the two principles of *natural right*, "of which one interests us ardently in our well-being and our self-preservation, and the other inspires in us a natural repugnance to see any sensitive being perish or suffer, principally our fellowmen" (*SD*, 125–26; 14–15). There is no knowing whether these principles have ever been broadly upheld, let alone enforced, by human beings, for there is no knowing whether human beings have ever lived in anything like the original natural state depicted in the *Second Discourse*. But that is a secondary concern. The important thing is that these principles animate any and all human beings to the extent that they are natural. Or to state it from a different perspective, these principles must animate any and all natural human beings to the extent that such human beings exist. A natural man who *does* exist, at least on his own telling, is Rousseau. Thus Rousseau indicates that, in his dealings with others, he lives by the same principle that Socrates articulates with Polemarchus and seems to live by. (In principle, less natural human beings could also be governed by the rules of natural right, for reason—the same reason that "has succeeded in stifling nature"—has reestablished them "on other foundations" [*SD*, 126; 15].)

Paragraphs 7 to 11 (the third subsection of section 2) pick up the preceding subsection's tendency to overstatement and melodrama. This is where Rousseau recounts overcoming his final "weak ray of hope" (7), that is, that his works might one day be accorded a fair hearing. Here the object of overstatement is less Rousseau's suffering, though that does occur ("Everything is finished for me on earth. People can no longer do good or evil to me here"), than his purportedly categorical triumph over his suffering. Here is the entirety of paragraph 7 (all emphasis has been added):

> Not quite two months ago, *complete* calm was reestablished in my heart. For a long time I no longer feared anything, but I still hoped; and this hope, deluded one moment and frustrated another, was a hold by which a thousand diverse passions incessantly perturbed me. An event as sad as it was unforeseen has finally just erased this weak ray of hope from my heart and has made me see my fate *forever* and *irreversibly* fastened here-below. Since then I have become *unreservedly resigned*, and I have found peace again.

Pathetic and self-indulgent as he can be, our narrator can also burst with triumphalism. He can even strike both notes in the same line: "here I am, tranquil at the bottom of the abyss, a poor unfortunate mortal, but unperturbed, like God Himself" (11). It is this line, the concluding line of the First Walk's second section, that sets up his decision at the start of the third section to sever himself even more completely from society.

The third subsection, of course, should—and yes, does—correspond to the exchange between Socrates and Thrasymachus. Like the Socrates-Thrasymachus exchange, Rousseau's third subsection is the longest of the three. But that's a small thing. The matter of real interest is that the discovery that supposedly allowed him to let go of the last faint ray of hope and thus truly free himself and attain tranquility was *his discovery of the truth of Thrasymachus's teaching about human nature.* Rousseau has already given us to understand that he has been reconciled to the enmity of his contemporaries for some time now. But during most of that time he maintained a faint hope that future generations might come to see him and his work differently. What dashed this final hope were the events following his completion of the *Dialogues.* After failing to safeguard his newly completed manuscript by depositing it on the great altar at Notre Dame, he turned in desperation to the public, to which he tried to distribute copies of a pamphlet. But, alas, he found no takers. Those to whom he offered the pamphlet couldn't have known its content, let alone the character of the pamphleteer. But they could read at a glance the title: *To All Frenchmen Who Still Love Justice and Truth.* Thus by declining to accept the pamphlet, they conceded that they did not love justice and truth. Thrasymachus's contemporaries would at least have disguised their unjust characters. So severely have things deteriorated by Rousseau's time that passersby felt no need even to pay hypocrisy's tribute to virtue. So, at any rate, has Rousseau interpreted their response. What a dismal discovery! And yet according to Rousseau it was also a liberating discovery, for it completed his disenchantment with society and allowed him finally to resign himself to his fate and attain tranquility. (That Rousseau attained tranquility at this moment is of course *his* view, that is, *the narrator's* view. In my view, which I take to be the author's view, the step recounted in this subsection is a step forward, and an important one at that; but, practically speaking, it isn't the decisive step that the narrator says it is.)

THIRD SECTION: PARAGRAPHS 12–15

The First Walk's second section concludes with a summary statement of Rousseau's condition both external and internal, both his isolation and its interior result—in that order: "Everything is finished for me on earth. People can no longer do good or evil to me here. I have nothing more to hope for or to fear in this world; and here I am, tranquil at the bottom of the abyss, a poor unfortunate mortal, but unperturbed, like God Himself" (11). The next paragraph, which begins the third section, seems to continue in the same vein. It begins with Rousseau restating the isolation he has just described, only this time from a subjective perspective, with phrasing that recalls the opening of the *Reveries*: "Everything external is henceforth foreign to me. I no longer have neighbors, fellow creatures, or brothers in this world. I am on earth as though on a foreign planet onto which I have fallen from the one I inhabited" (12). Yet in the very next line Rousseau reveals that he is *not* at peace, certainly not consistently: "If I recognize anything around me, it is only objects which *distress me* and *tear my heart asunder*; and I cannot cast my eyes on what touches and surrounds me without forever finding some disdainful object which makes me *indignant* or a painful one which *distresses* me" (emphasis added). If Rousseau is "unperturbed, like God," he must be so only within a narrow compass of experience—either that, or else God Himself is much more perturbed than is commonly believed. Clearly Rousseau has *not* attained resignation and tranquility; and this time he knows he hasn't, and he responds accordingly. He decides to withdraw from the world, though perhaps the more accurate formulation would be that he decides to orchestrate the world's withdrawal from him—"So let me remove from my mind all the troublesome objects"—and to consecrate his last days to studying himself (12). With this Rousseau has begun to lay out his plan and purpose in writing the *Reveries*. One who has been reading closely even just to this point might already suspect that the Walks to come will not accord with what our narrator projects here, as indeed they will not. Rousseau will not make good on his intention to give himself up entirely to the sweetness of conversing with his soul and to "set down in writing" "charming periods of contemplation" such as those that have often filled "the leisurely moments" of his daily walks (12); and the resulting book will not be "only a shapeless diary of [his] reveries" (13).

An even greater duplicity than his false promise regarding the Walks to come, however, is Rousseau's renewed insistence that he has achieved resignation and tranquility (renewed upon his decision to disregard "troublesome objects" and devote himself to self-study). This insistence is the greater duplicity because it is an enormous, multidimensional *self-deception*. This self-deception has hitherto undisclosed spatial and temporal dimensions. The spatial revelation: Rousseau's peaceful solitude isn't just compressed by moral suffering, meaning inflamed amour-propre; it's invaded by it. The temporal dimension: he suffers not only in the present, but also, so to speak, in the future. Although he purports to and perhaps does dream of joy in the years ahead, the character of these dreams betrays their origin in injured amour-propre. Rousseau dreams problematic dreams—problematic dreams of justice: "I will forget my misfortunes, my persecutors, my disgrace, while *dreaming of the prize my heart deserved*" (12). Such dreams are undoubtedly pleasant. In themselves they are not problematic. But they reflect something that *is* problematic. That he dreams of compensation means that he is still in thrall to hope, to a faith that he can neither discard nor wholeheartedly embrace, and to the ordinary moral consciousness he falsely supposes he has overcome.

The main correspondence between the third section of the *Reveries'* First Walk and the third section of book 1 of the *Republic* is functional. Each, on the basis of the respective foregoing sections, determines in a broad way all that is to follow in their respective works; and each intensifies the reader's interest in what's to come. But this general point needs some unpacking.

In paragraph 13 Rousseau describes his position in the world a bit differently than he has yet done, casting it this time in terms of body and soul:

> No longer able to do any good which does not turn to evil, no longer able to act without harming another or myself, to abstain has become my sole duty and I fulfill it as much as it is in me to do so. But *despite this desuetude of my body, my soul is still active*; it still produces feelings and thoughts; and its internal and moral life seems to have grown even more with the death of every earthly and temporal interest. *My body is no longer anything to me but an encumbrance, an obstacle, and I disengage myself from it beforehand as much as I can.* (13; emphasis added)

With this characterization Rousseau has effectively adopted what may be the chief conceit of the *Republic*. The *Republic* as a whole is characterized by a forgetting of or an abstraction from the body. This conceit is brought to a peak in book 5, with Socrates's proposal that private erotic and familial relations among members of the guardian class be abolished in favor of communism of women and children. But it is present throughout the dialogue and is key to its teaching.[4] The forgetting of the body is not only evident in what Socrates says; it is also evident in the dialogue's *action*— beginning, as it happens, in the third section of book 1. The action of which I speak, though perhaps it would be better described as a conspicuous *non*action, is the dinner that the interlocutors at Cephalus's house never eat. Their plan, we recall, had been to dine and then go out for the evening to watch the torch race and other festivities. In the event, however, the young men's burning desire to understand justice and happiness makes them forget all about dinner—this despite the swirling aroma of roasting meats (Cephalus is in the courtyard performing sacrifices). The body has ceased to make its needs felt, and it will remain quiescent—or be ignored—through the whole of the long night's conversation. That

---

4. See Strauss, *City and Man*, 50–138.

the body's needs could be suppressed or sublimated is entirely plausible. How long such a state could plausibly be maintained, however, is another question. And whether Socrates's severe proposals would be so happily endorsed by these young men once their thrilling ascetic state has given way, as surely it must, to the body's resurgent demands, is a question that answers itself. Are we to conclude, then, that Rousseau's discounting of his own body is utopian, that his brave talk of his soul's vigor and his body's decline is just that—brave talk? I hardly think so. Rather, he is depicting the circumstances and the ways in which the soul really can flourish even as, perhaps *because*, the body is quiet. These circumstances and ways are those that belong to the philosophic life. Nor does Rousseau depart from Plato in this: Socrates's discounting of the body is utopian in politics, and the critique of political utopianism is an important teaching of the *Republic*. But what is utopian and thus to be eschewed in politics may be precisely what's called for in the soul. This is also an important teaching of the *Republic*. Plato doesn't mean to dampen spirits but to direct them where they would find their greatest satisfaction and do the greatest good. He means to have us understand our highest aspirations as the nonpolitical phenomena that they are and to help us see that their satisfaction is to be found, accordingly, in nonpolitical, indeed transpolitical, domains.

Near the end of book 1, Thrasymachus, having been forced by Socrates to concede that "injustice is never more profitable than justice," references the dinner that has not been eaten: "Let that be the fill of your banquet at the festival of Bendis, Socrates" (354a). To which Socrates replies by confessing his *gluttony*: "I owe it to you, Thrasymachus, since you have grown gentle and have left off being hard on me. However, I have not had a fine banquet, but it's my own fault, not yours. For in my opinion, I am just like the gluttons who grab at whatever is set before them to get a taste of it, before they have in proper measure enjoyed what went before" (354a–b). And off Socrates goes, chronicling his gluttony course by course, until he concludes with a line that surely whets the spiritual appetites of his interlocutors even further: "now as a result of the discussion I know nothing. So long as I do not know what the just is, I shall hardly know whether it is a virtue or not and whether the one who has it is unhappy or happy" (354b–c). And Rousseau? He of course has no need to whet any interlocutors' appetites, "now that the desire to be better understood by men has been extinguished in [his] heart" (15). Yet somehow this very claim seems as likely to intensify the reader's interest as to diminish it. Nor is this the only appetite enhancer with which Rousseau has spiced the First Walk's third section.

Another enticement—a particularly artful one—is Rousseau's invocation of Montaigne in paragraph 14. As he had in the *Confessions* (516; 433), here too he contrasts his work with that of his illustrious predecessor:

> I will perform on myself, to a certain extent, the measurements natural scientists perform on the air in order to know its daily condition. I will apply the barometer to my soul, and these measurements, carefully executed and repeated over a long period of time, may furnish me results as certain as theirs. But I do not extend my enterprise that far. I will be content to keep a record of the measurements without seeking to reduce them to a system. My enterprise is the same as Montaigne's, but my goal is the complete opposite of his: he wrote his *Essays* only for others, and I write my reveries only for myself. (14)

The artfulness of this passage is its elaborate deception. What appears to be a contrast is in fact a kinship—and not only a substantive kinship but also a kinship in artistry. Rousseau claims to be writing only for himself while in fact writing for others. Montaigne, he says, wrote only for others, which is true enough; but for *which* others? Montaigne claimed to write only for a few friends while in fact writing for a broader readership with a public, indeed a political, purpose. So the evidence strongly suggests. Montaigne explored great questions regarding how to live well. He purported to show that the great theological and metaphysical issues that were roiling Europe were incendiary and insoluble and hence better left aside. He modeled a distinctive mentality and way of life that aimed at—and *promised to deliver*—"present enjoyment." What does all of this add up to if not the basic elements of a political project?[5] In ways large and small, the *Essays* are an advertisement for something like what we now know as secular, liberal society. Montaigne's grand ambition influenced later thinkers of the first rank, even if prudence often kept these successors from openly acknowledging their debt to him.[6]

Was Rousseau among those who regarded Montaigne as attempting a political project? It seems likely that he was. Rousseau had a keen appreciation of the ways in which a compelling portrait (including a self-portrait) can be a powerful political act,[7] indeed a legislative act. He could hardly have failed to see the power of Montaigne's self-portraiture and therewith a likely political intention in the *Essays*.

5. See Schaefer, *Political Philosophy of Montaigne*; and Levine, *Sensual Philosophy*.
6. Lampert, *Nietzsche and Modern Times*.
7. Kelly, *Rousseau's Exemplary Life*.

Might Rousseau have been indicating his own political intention by covertly likening himself to Montaigne even while seeming to distance himself from him? (Montaigne himself practiced a similarly duplicitous method of indicating his kinship with seemingly alien predecessors.) Montaigne pretended to write for his intimates while in fact attempting to prepare the ground for a new kind of society, offering, in the process, insight into the type of person (himself, the philosopher) capable of such a project. Rousseau does the same thing, though across two books rather than one—unless we follow his suggestion that the *Reveries* be regarded as an additional volume of the *Confessions* (12),[8] which would make of the *Reveries* and *Confessions* together a single work of three volumes, just like Montaigne's *Essays*. Like Montaigne, Rousseau puts himself forward as an exemplar of a new way of life, even if the character of Rousseau's exemplary life, or the content of his legislation, departs in some ways from Montaigne's. Rousseau advertises a life that is whole by virtue of being grounded in natural sentiment. Like Montaigne, Rousseau explores the person (himself, the philosopher) capable of such a project. This latter task he performs extensively in the *Confessions* but perhaps more deeply in the *Reveries*, where he not only explores his soul and his experience but also indicates how and why he has undertaken such a grand political project and its place in his philosophic life.

---

8. "It is in this state that I again take up the sequel to the severe and sincere examination I formerly called my *Confessions*" (I, 12).

CHAPTER 4

"A Faithful Record"
Second Walk

The Second Walk is memorable for its drama—for a dramatic accident and a dramatic transformation. The accident is Rousseau's being violently upended by a downhill-barreling Great Dane (7–9). The transformation is the radical alteration of his consciousness in the accident's wake: he finds himself in an extraordinary condition of bliss (10–12). The transformation doesn't hold, which casts a grievous pall over the second half of the Walk. But to make sense of these events requires that we begin by considering with care the paragraphs that precede them.

Prelude: Paragraphs 1–6

The Second Walk picks up where the First Walk left off, with a further elaboration of Rousseau's plans both for the *Reveries* and for his life. The two sets of plans are one and the same:

> Having, then, formed the project of describing the habitual state of my soul in the strangest position in which a mortal could ever find himself, I saw no simpler and surer way to carry out this enterprise than to keep a faithful record of my solitary walks and of the reveries which fill them when I leave my head entirely free and let my ideas follow their bent without resistance or constraint. These hours of solitude and meditation are the only ones in the day during which I am fully myself and for myself, without diversion, without obstacle and during which I can truly claim to be what nature willed. (1)

This introductory paragraph, quoted here in its entirety, begins with Rousseau characterizing his involuntary exile as the *strangest position* in which a mortal could ever find himself and ends with the observation that it is only during his solitary walks—only during the most solitary hours of the day—that he is fully himself and *what nature willed*. So strange is Rousseau's position—so strange is the *human* condition—that to be what nature willed is to radically depart from the ways of one's fellows. His departure from the ways of others has consisted less in his solitude than in what he has done in solitude, that is, what he has done when being what nature willed. His solitary doings consist of two main activities: walking, and the mental activity that attends it. What is this mental activity? Or is there more than one? In the first of the paragraph's two sentences Rousseau speaks of the *reveries* that fill his walks. In the second sentence, although he is speaking of the same activity, reverie is replaced by *meditation*. This renaming can be read in two ways. Either Rousseau uses the two words interchangeably, or the substitution of "meditation" for "reverie" is a correction or refinement. The first alternative would be a way of continuing to veil the philosophic character of the activity. The second would be a way of inviting careful and determined readers to see the veil for what it is and thus discover that it is the philosophic character of his activity wherein Rousseau is able to be "fully [him]self and for [him] self" and what nature willed.

The same rhetorical policy is at work in the second paragraph, with even greater artfulness and stringency. Rousseau had no sooner set out to execute his plan than he made a most problematic discovery. Having decided to record his reveries, he found that his power to generate them had much diminished: "I soon felt I had too long delayed carrying out this project. Already less lively, my imagination no longer bursts into flame the way it used to in contemplating the object which stimulates it. I delight less in the delirium of reverie. Henceforth there is more reminiscence than creation in what it produces." Surely a lament. Or is it? Notice that Rousseau does not report a decline in his power to see or to understand but rather a less lively *imagination* and less delight in the *delirium* of reverie. Is this really a misfortune? For some it surely would be; and perhaps it is, or rather once would have been, for Rousseau. But as we've already noted, an imagination that bursts into the flames of delirium is an obstacle to philosophy and for this reason ultimately undesirable to Rousseau. This point is explicated in the Seventh Walk. Does it find support here in the Second Walk? It does, though whether the narrator understands this yet is not clear. Notice, to begin with, the curious alteration of verb tenses in paragraphs 1 and 2. Almost the entirety of the Second Walk is written in the past tense. Rousseau shifts into the present tense—he speaks in real time—in only three places: in the final paragraph (24), where he speaks of the consolation delivered by his reasoning about God, and in the first two paragraphs, where he speaks of being fully himself only during hours of solitude and meditation (1) and of the diminishment of his imagination (2). He shifts into the present tense, that is to say, *when he speaks about his activity as a philosopher.*[1] Notice too his observation that, having lost some of its power, his imagination henceforth produces more reminiscence than creation. Perhaps the eclipse of creation by reminiscence signifies a loss. Rousseau seems to present it as one. Immediately after relating the eclipse of creation by reminiscence he suggests that this is owing to a general organismic decline: "A tepid languor enervates all my faculties. The spirit of life is gradually dying out in me" (2). But what looks like enervation and gradual death may look that way only from an unphilosophic standpoint. The matter may look very different from the standpoint of philosophy. Indeed, an increase in *reminiscence* strikes me as a nicely Platonic way of indicating a *gain* with respect to the philosophic life. That Rousseau may mean to suggest as much is confirmed later in the paragraph, when he identifies pious hope as the only thing checking his complete slide into a life of reminiscence. Pitting piety against reminiscence may not seem to speak well of reminiscence. But it's a different story when the piety concerned is pious *hope.* So even as he laments imagination's decline, he qualifies the lamentation to the point of subverting it.

Fortunately, the diminished liveliness of his imagination need not keep Rousseau from recording his walks and reveries. For if new reveries are no longer possible, he can summon up old ones and relive them with all the immediacy of the original and even with certain advantages over the original occasions. The advantages arise from his ability to select only the reveries he wants and to have them abide, or rather abide within them himself, for periods longer than their original duration. This too is related in the second paragraph. In the third paragraph, he expands on the fruits of this recollection. He reports that recollecting his past reveries compensated him for his troubles and almost completely made him forget them. In reflecting on this compensation and forgetfulness, moreover, he made a monumental discovery: he "learned that the source of true happiness is within us and that it is not within the power of men to make anyone who can will to be happy truly miserable." It was only

---

1. The final section of the First Walk, wherein Rousseau laid out his plan for the *Reveries,* were also written in real time, i.e., in the present and future tenses: "I consecrate my last days to studying myself" (12); "These pages will, properly speaking, be only a shapeless diary of my reveries" (13); "I will perform on myself, to a certain extent, the measurements natural scientists perform on the air" (14); "they will not prevent me from enjoying my innocence" (15).

because of his persecutors' intention to make him miserable that he was able to make this discovery: "Without them I would never have found or become cognizant of the treasures I carried within myself." And yet reliving the rapturous reveries of the past posed its own challenges to his plan to record them. "In the midst of so many riches, how could a faithful record of them be kept? In wanting to recall so many sweet reveries, instead of describing them, I fell back into them." Rousseau tells us, in effect, that recording his reveries—even *wanting* to record them—would require that the anticipated joy of reflecting and meditating on them be greater than the joy of simply experiencing and remaining within them. The progress of the text will suggest that this is exactly what has occurred. The fruits of reverie are undeniably sweet, but the fruits of reflection and writing are sweeter still.

Perhaps this explains the puzzle of the fourth paragraph, which reads in its entirety as follows: "I fully experienced this effect [i.e., falling back into reveries instead of describing them, or perhaps, more generally, finding pleasure in recalling old reveries] during the walks which followed my plans to write the sequel to my *Confessions*, especially during the one I am going to speak of and during which an unforeseen accident came to interrupt the thread of my ideas and give them another direction for some time." *The one I am going to speak of*—. Rousseau gives us to understand that he is about to provide an example of recollecting a reverie from the past. But he doesn't: the example that he proceeds to give in paragraphs 5 and 6 is of recent vintage. Such confusion is rare in the *Reveries*; it is seen only in the Second Walk, which includes several instances of confusion.[2] What accounts for the unique confusion in the Second Walk? The likeliest explanation would seem to lie in the Second Walk's *thematic* uniqueness. Far more than any other Walk, the Second recounts a period of crippling anxiety and despondency and consequent confusion. These ills occurred in the past. With the passing of time, they have been mitigated. But they have not been dispelled; they seem to resurge to some degree merely upon being recollected. They *can't* be dispelled as long as Rousseau remains beholden to the presuppositions, the *sources*, of a distressed amour-propre. Let's examine these sources.

What triggers Rousseau's anxiety and despondency is the strange accident he recounts in the seventh paragraph—or, rather, the accident and the subsequent interlude of blissful self-forgetting, which must have made the fall from that state all the more anguished. But this proximate

---

2. For a fuller account of these multiple confusions, see Butterworth, "Interpretive Essay," 162.

cause would have been no such thing were not a prior source already in place. Rousseau's anxiety and despondency, which are noticeable as early as paragraph 4 even though they're not explicitly noted until paragraph 13, can have arisen only from *imagination*. No doubt other factors had a share in these difficulties, but imagination is the *faculty* that, by producing worrisome thoughts and scenarios, makes anxiety and despondency possible. Rousseau doesn't explicitly identify imagination as the faculty at work here—his critique of imagination won't become explicit until the Seventh Walk—but one can recognize its workings in the litany of distressing phenomena that he lists in paragraphs 13 through 22: his lifelong hatred and dread of the dark (13); the "troubling and sad conjectures" to which he abandoned himself and "the delirium of fever" that filled his mind in the period that followed his accident (14); his inference from the admittedly suspect gestures of Madame d'Ormoy that she intended to harm his reputation (15–19); and, finally, his purported discovery that his enemies intended, following his death, to defame him all the more by passing off a collection of fabricated writings as his work (20, 21). The last of these is perhaps the most telling. Recall that in the First Walk Rousseau had presented as his culminating step toward resignation and tranquility the surrender of the hope that he and his work might one day be given a fair reading. The anxiety and despondency regarding his posthumous reputation that are on display in the Second Walk show that he has remained an uneasy hostage to fortune. Imagination has once again inflamed his amour-propre and made it the driving force in his soul.

Because he does not see that all these fretful thoughts are the products of his imagination, Rousseau cannot but regard them as the judgments of "a sensible man" who knows from fifteen years of hard experience that a more benign reading of the evidence would be folly (21). When imagination is finally referenced, in paragraph 22, it is presented not as the source of his anxious thoughts but as their victim, though Rousseau does acknowledge that, once imagination has been agitated by anxiety, it becomes cause as well as effect. Referring to what he believed he had discerned about his persecutors' plans upon his death, he recalls that

> these observations made one after the other and followed by many others which were scarcely less astonishing, caused my imagination, which I had believed to be calmed down, to become alarmed all over again. And this black darkness with which they relentlessly surrounded me rekindled all the dread it naturally inspires in me. I wore myself out making a thousand commentaries on it all and trying to understand the mysteries they rendered inexplicable for me. (22)

Rousseau does not seem to consider the possibility that imagination, besides *amplifying* false beliefs and suffering, might in this case be their *originator*. That kind of realization won't come until the Seventh Walk.

Let it be noted that Rousseau did have clever and determined enemies. The historic record shows as much.[3] But what he believes he has understood about his enemies' intention to impute fabricated writings to him is unsupported by any concrete evidence. It is the work of his imagination. Besides putting the worst construction on uncertain facts, his imagination also discounts the elements of good fortune that he enjoys even now. One would never know from the First and Second Walks that the solitary walker, besides having determined enemies, also has a coterie of devoted friends, not to mention a considerable number of admirers throughout Europe. Evidently Rousseau the narrator either doesn't remember these friends or, more likely, doesn't put much stock in them. Perhaps he doubts their sincerity. Almost certainly he doubts the depth of their loyalty. But Rousseau the author is cognizant of these friends and knows that readers of the *Reveries*—certainly the book's *first* readers—will know about his friends as well, since it is only through the efforts of those friends that the *Reveries* will have made its way into print. If the narrator's amour-propre can't find vindication in triumph, it can at least find compensation in imagined martyrdom.

Thus our protagonist, for all his sensitivity and acuity, still falls short of the resignation he earlier purported to have attained. If anything, he has fallen further away from resignation. And yet he has shown a sign of progress, or at least promise. He has noted imagination's power to distort perception and judgment and thus subvert resignation and tranquility; and in doing so, he has begun to illuminate the ways in which imagination can bear, for good or for ill, on philosophy, self-awareness, and freedom of mind. More specifically, he has begun to see that *autonomous* imagination, imagination that is not answerable to reason, is inimical to philosophy, self-awareness, and freedom of mind. Autonomous imagination mistakes *images* of what *might be* for *sight* of what *is*. And if imagination that is unanswerable to reason is inimical to philosophy, imagination that is altogether unaccompanied by reflection is the renunciation of philosophy.

Being aware of the sometimes vexed relationship between imagination and philosophy can help us answer the question that sent us into the terrain of imagination in the first place, namely, why Rousseau announces

3. Butterworth investigates the historic record and finds that there "are strong indications that other people really did want to damage his reputation or otherwise cause trouble for him." Butterworth, "Interpretive Essay," 167–68.

the recollection of an old reverie in paragraph 4 only to a recount a recent reverie in paragraphs 5 and 6, a recent reverie, moreover, that he is recollecting only now, in the telling. The answer is encrypted, as it were, in the final sentence of paragraph 3. Let's have a look.

In paragraph 2 Rousseau had reported that he can compensate for his fading imagination by recalling past reveries. In paragraph 3, immediately prior to the sentence at issue, he relates a difficulty: "In wanting to recall so many sweet reveries, instead of describing them, I fell back into them." Now the paragraph's final sentence itself: "This is a state which is brought back by being remembered and of which we would soon cease to be aware, if we completely ceased feeling it [*C'est un état que son souvenir ramène, et qu'on cesserait bientôt de connaître en cessant tout à fait de le sentir*]." "This *is* a state"—Rousseau has abruptly shifted to the present tense: he is no longer speaking of particular past experiences but of a certain kind of mental state as such. What he observes of this state is that awareness of it depends on feeling it. Or, to put it more precisely, *knowing* (*connaître*) this state depends on feeling (*sentir*) it. Isn't this true of every mental state? It may be, but evidently there is something about reverie that leads Rousseau to think he needs to make the point. What might that something be? My suggestion: any mental state that is completely unfelt is apt to be unknown. Unfelt reverie, however, will not only be unknown; it will also be an *obstacle to self-knowledge*. Those who are truly lost in a reverie not only will lack self-awareness; they will be overtaken by *false* self-awareness. More than any other mental state, reverie puts compelling images before us; and if we don't feel and thus don't know that we're lost in reverie, we'll mistake these images for what *is*. But what does this have to do with the question at hand: why has Rousseau chosen to recollect a new reverie after announcing that he would summon up an old one?

The answer is that—he doesn't. If close attention reveals that paragraphs 5 and 6 recount a recent reverie where we had been led to expect an older one, *very* close attention reveals that this recent reverie is less a reverie at all than a *reflection*. Here is how Rousseau records the events of that recent afternoon. First he recounts that he "enjoyed that pleasure and interest which charming places have always given [him] and stopped from time to time to look at plants in the vegetation" (5). Then he proceeds to specify some of these plants by name—by their *Latin* names, which already indicates a scientific consciousness at work, as do other observations he makes about these plants. Finally, after reporting that he "looked *thoroughly* at several other plants," he recalls that he "gradually turned away from these minute observations so as to give [him]self up to the no less charming, but more moving, impression which the whole scene made on

[him]" (6). What made the scene so moving to him was its late-autumnal character, which prompted him to look on his life from *its* late-autumnal vantage point. This was reflection, not reverie. Rousseau even refers to it as such ("these reflections" [*ces réflexions*]) at one point in paragraph 6.

What Rousseau has recounted in this purported reverie that is actually reflection are successive stages of studying nature. He has enacted something akin to the ascent toward philosophy (not *to* philosophy, but toward it). The process has three stages. First, he leads us to expect an old reverie. But, second, careful reading reveals that he does not provide an old reverie, but rather a new one. But wait—*very* careful reading discloses that, third, he has not provided *any* reverie, neither old nor new, but rather reflection. Where careless readers will see nothing to remark on, careful readers will see confusion; but for very careful readers this apparent confusion will reveal itself as sleight of hand. To what end? It seems to me that Rousseau is elegantly communicating two things. One is that reflection is more central and integral to his life, to the philosophic life, than is reverie. The other is the questionable character of reverie as a class of activity. Insofar as it is the product of autonomous imagination, reverie is an obstacle to philosophy; and at this point in the book it isn't clear that reverie as reverie can be anything *but* the product of autonomous imagination. And even if reverie *isn't* always the product of autonomous imagination, one needs to remain alert to the possibility that it might become so.[4] Is this a book of reveries at all? Or has Rousseau simply masked what he more truthfully could have called *The Reflections of the Solitary Walker*?

And yet the book does speak about reveries. And if my reading is correct, certain kinds of reveries are compatible with and even conducive to the philosophic life. But that hardly seems to vindicate the title Rousseau has chosen. *Is* there a sense in which the book as a whole really is, in some decisive way, the *reveries* of the solitary walker? In fact there is. The core tenet of my interpretation is that the *Reveries* tells the story of the development of the philosophic life, that is, the rise to the philosophic life and then its ongoing perfection. We can think of the perfection of the philosophic life as progress in knowledge, or as the attainment of greater

4. Why then does Rousseau depict reverie in such an attractive light? Isn't it potentially perilous not only for philosophers but for thoughtful and responsible nonphilosophers as well? Wouldn't they too be undermined by surrendering to autonomous imagination? Perhaps not, at least not if the terms of the surrender have been determined by Rousseau. For in truth the imaginations of such acolytes would *not* be autonomous, no more so than is the conscience of the citizen vaunted in Rousseau's political works. In both cases a benign governance is at work behind the scenes, the governance of the Legislator—in this case, Rousseau.

clarity, or as ever-expanding freedom of mind. But perhaps the best way to think of it is as a process of awakening—as awakening *from reverie*. Now consider: it is the dreamers themselves who must do the awakening; they must wake themselves up. They must wake themselves up from reverie *by way of* reverie; for unless one is fully awake, even one's most rational reflections are in some sense reveries or occur within reveries. And who among us is fully awake? Thus Rousseau's chosen title is correct after all.

None of this makes Rousseau less of a philosopher or his life less of a philosophic life. It seems to do so only when philosophy is understood—is *mis*understood—as wisdom. Neither does it mark a disagreement with Plato. If Rousseau's awakening from a dream can never be complete, neither can the ascent from the cave.[5] One must continue to examine oneself and the innumerable assumptions and beliefs, conscious or merely implicit, by which we have been and continue to be formed, including, at bottom, what Rousseau in the *Second Discourse* felicitously calls "principles of soul" (*SD*, 125–26; 14–15). One must subject these assumptions and beliefs to critical scrutiny so that one might achieve clarity, the humbling of self-conceit, and perhaps the opening of higher pathways. What is this process of uncovering and examining our formative assumptions and beliefs if not *recollection*? And what is waking up if not recollecting one's self and one's life? For Rousseau as for Plato, recollection belongs to the very heart of philosophy—recollection understood not in the highly dubious way that Socrates sometimes seems to teach in the dialogues but as the discernment and assembly of what has always been implicit in our experience. Plato's careful readers have always understood that Socrates's dubious accounts of recollection admit of alternative interpretations that shed light on philosophy and the philosophic life properly understood. Rousseau was among these readers.

Among the dreams from which Rousseau has yet to be awakened is the tenacious dream of justice. His amour-propre continues to be chronically inflamed. Unlike many, he does not live under amour-propre's constant despotic sway. But the inconstancy of amour-propre's hold over him may be one reason he becomes so agitated when he does fall prey to it. The workings of amour-propre and the ordinary moral consciousness are particularly evident in paragraphs 5 and 6, where he recounts reflecting on the course of his life from the standpoint of what it might and *should have* been, that is, from the standpoint of justice in the ordinary sense.

5. Seth Benardete puts it beautifully. For Plato, wisdom is "an idol of the cave." See Benardete, *Socrates' Second Sailing*, 179.

These reflections prompted sadness and regret—and *apologetics*. As if in response to a moral challenge, Rousseau proceeded to offer a moral defense of himself:

> Sighing, I said to myself: "What have I done here-below? At least it has not been my fault, and I will carry to the author·of my being, if not an offering of good works which I have not been permitted to perform, at least a tribute of frustrated good intentions, of healthy feelings rendered ineffectual, and of a patience impervious to the scorn of men." I was moved by these reflections; I went back over the movements of my soul from the time of my youth.. . . . I mulled over all the affections of my heart with satisfaction. (6)

This is hardly an expression of the ordinary moral consciousness at its most irrational or debilitating. Rousseau successfully met the challenge of his internal or imagined critic without doing violence to others or to the truth. He did not simmer with resentment and was not plagued by guilt. It seems likely that this kind of happy experience of the ordinary moral consciousness is helpful to finally *overcoming* the ordinary moral consciousness. And one *would* want to overcome it if one understood, as Rousseau the narrator already understands, that it inhibits freedom of mind and keeps one vulnerable to extreme agitation and despondency. This vulnerability will be shown all too vividly in the section to come.

Accident and Necessity: Paragraphs 7–22

Here begin the happenings for which the Second Walk is most memorable: Rousseau's accident (7–9), followed by the blissful condition in which he found himself (or rather *didn't* find himself—that's just the point) (10–12), and then by a period of physical and moral fever (13–22). The Second Walk had begun with Rousseau determining to record his "solitary walks" and "the reveries which fill them" (1), but walking gives way to being flattened and then to feverish pacing; and pleasant contemplation gives way to unselfconscious bliss and then to anxious and obsessive stewing. Finally, as in the First Walk, the extremity of Rousseau's situation drives him to profess resignation—this time, however, on explicitly theological grounds (23–24). This extraordinary sequence of events shines a bright light on the problems of self-awareness and selfhood.

On the afternoon of October 24, 1776, Rousseau was enjoying the "peaceful meditations" that we have just noted (6) when he was violently upended by a Great Dane running ahead of a carriage (paragraphs 7–9).

Seeing the dog bearing down on him and that he had no time to lose, he attempted to save himself by overleaping the heedless animal. Unfortunately he did not achieve the necessary elevation, and his attempt to spare himself only succeeded in causing him to be flipped and land hard on his jaw when the dog caught him by the legs. (Whether a full-on collision would have been even worse is unclear. One does wonder, though, why he didn't think to leap aside rather than upward.) Although badly injured, he at first felt no pain. To the contrary, he experienced an extended period of profound calm and deliverance from all his troubles:

> Night was coming on. I perceived the sky, some stars, and a little greenery. This first sensation was a delicious moment. I still had no feeling of myself except as "there" [*Je ne me sentais encore que par là*]. I was born into life at that instant, and it seemed to me that I filled all the objects I perceived with my frail existence. Entirely absorbed in the present moment, I remembered nothing; I had no distinct notion of my person nor the least idea of what had just happened to me; I knew neither who I was nor where I was; I felt neither injury, fear, nor worry. I watched my blood flow as I would have watched a brook flow, without even suspecting that this blood belonged to me in any way. I felt a rapturous calm in my whole being; and each time I remember it, I find nothing comparable to it in all the activity of known pleasures. (10)

Rousseau' bliss arose, it would seem, from losing the sense of separation between himself and the world. We might say that he ceased to be a *me* while remaining an *I*. He didn't cease to exist but rather existed in everything. And yet if his existence expanded in space, filling all the objects that he perceived, it narrowed in time, as he became entirely absorbed in the present moment. His accident transported him to the realm of the nondual and eternal. Was this transport an ascent or a descent? Or both? Or neither? The narrator clearly takes a positive view, as is made most evident in the fifth sentence of the passage: "I was born into life at that instant." Aside from the striking substance of this remark, notice as well an interesting formal feature. Whereas the surrounding sentences recount subjective experiences *as* experiences—"I had no *feeling* of myself as there," "it *seemed* to me that I filled all the objects I perceived with my frail existence," and so on—this particular is related as an objective fact: I *was born* into life at that instant. Rousseau the narrator thus suggests that life begins in nonpersonal extension and immediacy. Does Rousseau the author take the same view? That is harder to know. But I would suggest at a minimum that the author would see no need to repudiate the narrator's judgment on the grounds that it bespeaks a romantic longing to escape selfhood or opposes philosophy in some other way. It doesn't. One could hold that life begins in transpersonal extension and immediacy while still holding that a *full* life becomes possible only with the emergence of a more discrete self. For with this emergence come the capacities for self-awareness and reflection that can immeasurably deepen life and one's appreciation of it. Of course these same capacities also make possible a slew of miseries unique to human beings, including the anxiety and despondency that would soon descend on Rousseau.

Our hero eventually recovered himself enough to set out for home, but even then he continued to be light of heart and felt no pain, this despite shivering with cold and spitting out a lot of blood (11). From his wife's cries upon his arrival, he learned that he had been more badly injured than he'd known. Yet he didn't learn the extent of his injuries, or even feel them, until the next day (12), whereupon the full sense of separate selfhood returned and bliss dissolved—with a vengeance (13–22). Not only did Rousseau finally feel the effects of his considerable physical injuries; he plunged into mental anguish. The former amplified the latter. In the days to follow, very little "was needed to alarm me, especially given the state of agitation my head was in from my accident and the resultant fever. I abandoned myself to a thousand troubling and sad conjectures and made commentaries on everything which went on around me, commentaries which were more a sign of the delirium of fever than of the composure of a man who no longer takes interest in anything" (14). This was the period in which Rousseau's imagination, which he "had believed to be calmed down," overpowered him by seizing hold of a series of admittedly suspicious phenomena— the mysterious solicitousness of M. Lenoir's secretary (14), the dubious obsequiousness of Madame d'Ormoy (15–19), and finally the supposed discovery that *they* (an unspecified they) were planning to publish "fabricated writings" that would seal his bad reputation forever (20–21)—and tormenting him with the thought that neither he nor his reputation would ever escape the clutches of his enemies (22). The latter point especially should give us pause. Rousseau was tormented by what he perceived to be the hopelessness of his situation—this despite having supposedly given up hope. So much for the triumph of the First Walk.

Resignation, Again: Paragraphs 23–24

The basis of Rousseau's purported embrace of resignation in the First Walk was entirely pragmatic. Recognizing that he would remain distressed so long as he maintained hope, he seized the opportunity for resignation when his enemies seemed to extinguish his last frail hope and even the possibility of future hope (the hope for hope, as it were). He took this step, or thought he did, because he saw resignation as needful and advantageous. Need and advantage are sufficient reasons to adopt a doctrine—for a political actor. For a philosopher, however, they have little standing. Perhaps that's why Rousseau, upon discovering that he requires a sturdier basis for resignation, follows the lead not of the philosopher but of the Legislator—of the Legislator precisely as he had described him the *Social Contract* (381–84; 154–57)

Rousseau's remarkable treatment of the Legislator is primarily a political teaching. But it is also an important point of access to his self-understanding, for there are politics within the self or soul that must be understood and negotiated. In the writings he published from 1750 through 1764 (i.e., from the *First Discourse* through *Letters Written from the Mountain*), Rousseau acted the part of the Legislator. Like other Philosopher-Legislators, he sought to influence the world less by overtly proposing new institutions and regimes than by trying to persuade people to accept new views of goodness, justice, nature, and the divine. In the *Reveries* he performs the same task *for himself*, except that in legislating for himself there can be no "persuad[ing] without convincing" (*SC*, 383; 156).

Rousseau as self-legislator bears an uncanny similarity to the Legislator he describes in the *Social Contract*. The one who legislates for a people understands those for whom he legislates—not only (a) their nature as human beings but (b) this particular multitude and how it might become a people. He propounds (c) a compelling teaching about justice and social order. And he has (d) such greatness of soul that people believe him when he declares that the laws he bears were vouchsafed to him by God. This last asset is crucial, for not even the most rational and beneficent laws will command sufficient assent on their own authority. Such are human beings that something—some*one*—is needed to supplement reason. Rousseau as self-legislator displays the same qualities. He has (a) a coherent and, he supposes, true understanding of human nature as well as (b) a deep understanding of himself. He sees (c) the goodness and healthfulness, the *justice*, of resignation. The one thing he lacks is (d) a divine basis for his self-legislation. Does he need such a basis? He seems to suppose that he does. His conviction concerning the healthfulness or justice of resignation has not sufficed. If he is truly to achieve resignation, reason needs to be supplemented by divine sanction. Accordingly, he concludes the Second Walk (23–24) by working out a theological-providential understanding of his situation.

In two places in his corpus Rousseau attempts to legislate by propounding a religious teaching. One, as we've already noted, is "The Profession of Faith of the Savoyard Vicar," in *Emile*. The other is the chapter "On Civil Religion" in the *Social Contract* (459–69; 216–24). Both of these teachings appeal to God's rectificatory justice as the grounds for consolation and confidence. Rousseau's profession here in the *Reveries'* Second Walk does the same. But there is an important difference between his self-legislation and the legislation he undertook for others. The difference concerns human freedom; and when thought through, it must ultimately *call into question* God's rectificatory justice. Let's begin by examining the route by which Rousseau purports to have come to his newfound faith. Whereas the Vicar's "Profession" and the *Social Contract*'s chapter on civil religion accord to God only the most minimal involvement in earthly affairs, Rousseau's profession in the Second Walk of the *Reveries* appeals to special providence:

> The accumulation of so many fortuitous circumstances, the elevation of all of my cruelest enemies favored, so to speak, by fortune; all those who govern the state, all those who direct public opinion, all the people in official positions, all the men of influence, picked and culled as it were from among those who have some secret animosity against me in order to concur in the common plot; this universal agreement is too extraordinary to be purely fortuitous. If there had been a single man who had refused to be an accomplice to it, a single event which had gone against it, a single unforeseen circumstance which had been an obstacle to it, any of that would have been enough to make it fail. But all the acts of will, all the unlucky events, fortune and all its revolutions have made firm the work of men. And such a striking concurrence, which borders on the prodigious, cannot let me doubt that its complete success is written among the eternal decrees. Swarms of individual observations, either in the past or in the present, so confirm me in this opinion that I cannot prevent myself from henceforth considering as one of those secrets of Heaven impenetrable to human reason the same work that until now I looked upon as only a fruit of the wickedness of men. (23)

So insidious and efficacious is the conspiracy against Rousseau, so far beyond credible human capacity, that it cannot be a human contrivance. It must be *God's* will. Rousseau entertains no thought of a third type of agent: nothing like Satan or Descartes's evil demon is considered. Most of us would not find comfort in believing that God has willed our suffering. But Rousseau is not like most people: "this idea, far from being cruel and rending to me, consoles me, calms me, and helps me to resign myself" (24). How does one take comfort from the conviction that God has willed one's suffering? The most pious of human beings might pronounce themselves consoled simply by belief that God's will is being done, even if it were God's will that their suffering go on forever. But such piety— *Augustinian* piety, as he depicts it—has no footing in Rousseau. Rather, Rousseau is comforted by the belief that God wills his suffering because he trusts both in God's justice and in his own innocence: "God is just; He wills that I suffer; and He knows that I am innocent. That is the cause of my confidence; my heart and my reason cry out to me that I will not be deceived by it" (24). Yet Rousseau does not provide grounds for his belief in God's justice—not here where he asserts it, and not in the Third Walk where he purports to recount his mature religious views and the process whereby he arrived at them. Compare this to the Eighth Walk, in which he offers different grounds for resignation and *argues* for them.

There is another lacuna in Rousseau's account of his purported faith. In the passage just quoted, he claims that his faith in God's justice has given him confidence. But he never says what he is confident *of*. The reader might naturally assume that he is referring to the afterlife, but it is notable that he never specifies the afterlife as the locus of his confidence. Perhaps his confidence in God's justice is simply confidence in the necessity of all that happens, by which I mean acceptance of the compelling character of the apparent good, that is, the conviction that people do all that they do, that they *must* do all that they do, because it seems good to them to do it. Those who accept this kind of necessity will be confident that their misfortunes are not the product of divine retribution or the dictate of moral dessert. That confidence is no small thing, for it delivers those who have it from the part of their suffering that stems from the *reaction* to pain and misfortune. Most of us, lacking this confidence, tend to moralize our suffering. We will tend to suppose that wherever there is suffering, an injustice has been done, that is, that someone has freely and intentionally done harm where no harm was warranted. Either (or both) of two outcomes are likely. When we believe or fear that *we ourselves* have committed an injustice, the likely outcome is guilt. When we believe that *someone else* is at fault, especially when the injustice has been committed against ourselves or someone (or something) dear to us, the likely outcome is anger or resentment. Those who are convinced of the compelling character of the apparent good deny the cognitive grounds of both of these reactions, both guilt and resentment.

To accept the compelling character of the apparent good is not to deny human freedom, as one might suppose, but rather to reconceive it. Human freedom arises from the capacity to reflect on the nature of things, including the good. Even if we are subject to the compelling character of the apparent good, we have it within our power to recognize that the apparent good may or may not *be* good: we can examine the merits and deficiencies of what has heretofore seemed good; we can consider other candidates for the good; and we can, indeed we are compelled to, replace the prior apparent good with the one that now seems best. We may even discover the compelling character of the apparent good and find that this discovery, as the acceptance of necessity—to the extent that we *have* accepted necessity—frees us from vulnerability to moral suffering. This finding might be what accounts for Rousseau's claim that his *reason* together with his heart "cry out" that he will not be deceived by his confidence in God's justice (24), even if he doesn't yet know how to sustain resignation and even though one might wonder whether his reason, by crying out, doesn't show itself to be less than entirely reasonable.

Does Rousseau the narrator really believe that God both knows him to be innocent and wills that he suffer? Perhaps he does; or perhaps, given his ongoing distress, he is *trying* to believe it. But even if he's confident *now*, as he writes the concluding paragraph of the Second Walk, he soon won't be. In the Third Walk, where he gives a much more thorough account of his purported religious opinions and how he came to them, he doesn't so much as allude to God's having willed the injustices perpetrated against him. And however we interpret the narrator's stance, Rousseau the *author* gives no sign that he believes his persecution and suffering to have been willed by God. When the question of how to attain resignation recurs in the Eighth Walk, God is absent from the account. In the Eighth Walk, *natural Necessity* is sovereign. From the standpoint of the Second Walk, it might seem as if natural necessity will have *usurped* God's sovereignty, just as it seems to Aristophanes's Strepsiades that Vortex has overthrown Zeus (*Clouds*, 380–81 and 825–29). But what looks to the ordinary moral consciousness like usurpation will later be recognized as *maturation*.

Rousseau will step into his fullest philosophic maturity in the Seventh and Eighth Walks. Before he can take that step, he will need to take several intervening steps in the intervening Walks. The most crucial of these steps will consist in him assuming powers that might seem to belong exclusively to God. In the Fourth Walk he exercises what one might regard as divine prerogative by defending deception when it's necessary for the good of those deceived. In the Fifth Walk, upon finding perfect happiness in the timeless experience of his own being, he claims divine self-sufficiency (V, 15). The assumption and exercise of powers normally thought to belong exclusively to God will train him in spiritual strength. Strength will indeed be needed: the step Rousseau will take in the Seventh and Eighth Walks is more difficult and daunting than any prior step. Not even the claim of self-sufficiency (V, 15), which offends piety by effectively displacing God, is as difficult or daunting as that step: in realizing one's own sufficiency there is no outright declaration against God, only a rising sense of Godlike strength and well-being that need not prevent one from recurring to God after one's exaltation has ended, at which point one might even interpret the exaltation not as the displacement of God but as God-intoxication. The step into his fullest philosophic maturity, by contrast—the step that is recounted in the Seventh Walk and whose implications for the moral consciousness are articulated in the Eighth—must be taken in the teeth of terrifying opposition. For this is the step whereby one transcends the ordinary moral consciousness—if not perfectly, decisively all the same. And however rational the transcendence of the ordinary consciousness may be—however much one might understand the transcendence of the ordinary moral consciousness as morality's *fulfillment*, that is, as that to-ward which the ordinary moral consciousness itself points—the ordinary moral consciousness and its agents will view this transcendence as noth-ing short of the repudiation of all that is good in the world.[6] *Its agents*: the most powerful of these will lie within oneself, for it seems unlikely that one will have completely expunged from oneself fear of what one had hitherto taken to be the voice of morality or even the voice of God, a voice that threatens condemnation and damnation, whether literally or figuratively may not matter much. Almost certainly a vestige of that younger self will have remained within the self. One who awaits the disappearance or whole-sale surrender of this self may wait forever. But one need not await such a capitulation. The step into philosophic maturity is possible without it, though it does require the greatest kind of statesmanship within the self: the subrational self or (more likely) *selves* must be governed by the thing within us that, though it lacks loudness and blunt force, can nevertheless hold sway because it knows, as perhaps even those lower selves know, that it is the true self.[7] This thing within us is reason, understanding by that word something more substantive and capacious than what it typically signifies today. And not only more capacious but more *loving* as well, in two ways:

6. The ordinary moral consciousness readily allows for goods that are not moral in character—health and beauty, for example. But it regards itself as the *warrant* of all goods: nothing is good if life has been devalued by the supposed repudiation of morality.

7. "As far as possible one ought to be immortal and to do all things with a view toward living in accord with the most powerful thing in oneself, for even if it is small in bulk, it rises much more above everything else in power and worth. And *each person would even seem to be this part*, if it is the governing and better part." This from Aristotle, *Nicomachean Ethics*, 1177b–d; emphasis added.

more erotic toward the truth, and more compassionate toward one's fellows (and oneself), the latter at least partly in consequence of the former.[8]

A Tale of Two Cities: The Second Walk and Republic 2

Let's not depart from the Second Walk without noting how it travels the same trajectory as book 2 of the *Republic*. In the Second Walk, as we've now seen, Rousseau (a) determines his project (i.e., decides to record his walks and reveries) and then, after some modification, launches it; after which he is (b) violently upended; whereupon he (c) finds himself in state of blissful simplicity before (d) descending into a condition of agitation and suffering as he recovers his individuality; until, finally, he (e) checks this descent with a new understanding of God's just governance of the world. Now consider book 2 of the *Republic*, which begins with Glaucon demanding of Socrates that he declare what kind of good justice is and then defend its goodness for the just actor under any and all circumstances (357a–358e). With this demand, Glaucon (a) *determines the project* that will occupy the group for the rest of the long night's conversation. He and Adeimantus (b) level powerful challenges to the intrinsic goodness of justice (358e–367e)—challenges that *upend* justice, as it were. Socrates responds by inviting his interlocutors to join with him in constructing a city in speech. The city is conceived with reference only to true need. The result, called by Socrates (c) the "true city" or the "city of utmost necessity" (372e, 369d), is small in population and extent. Its citizens live very simply and, through trade and specialization of labor, easily provide for themselves all that they need and indeed all that they *want*, so moderate are their desires and so careful are they to manage the size of the city's population. The true city is content and harmonious (372a–b). All of this—the city's self-sufficiency, the moderation and contentment of its inhabitants, the absence of conflict—arises from what seems an utter lack of spiritedness (*thymos*) or amour-propre. The citizens show no desire for distinction, either as individuals or as a community. Content with their lot, they give no indication of virtue or aspiration.[9] They show no passion to shine in the eyes of others, let alone *out*shine them. All of which is to say that the true city and its citizens enjoy a kind of civic analogue

8. *The latter at least partly in consequence of the former*: the satisfaction of philosophic eros brings gratitude, which in turn generates benevolence.

9. For an impressive dissenting view, which holds that the athymotic "true city" is nevertheless a virtuous city, see Fendt, *Comic Cure for Delusional Democracy*.

to Rousseau's postaccident bliss. And the source of the city's bliss is the same as the source of Rousseau's—namely, the absence of self-concern.

As Rousseau's bliss gives way to something else, so too does the true city's. Glaucon complains that this city is fit only for pigs. He wants a city with "relishes," a city in which individual desires—not only for luxury but also, even more so, for distinction—are given free play. Socrates accommodates Glaucon by (d) introducing all manner of superfluities into the city until, before long, the city of utmost necessity has become a city of immoderate appetite, a *feverish* city (372d) marked by agitation and disorder. As the simple and blissful simple city had paralleled Rousseau's postaccident simplicity and bliss, so this civic descent parallels Rousseau's descent. Recall that Rousseau highlighted the fever he suffered during this dark time. The term (*la fièvre*) appears twice in the brief passage quoted above from paragraph 14. Can Rousseau's literal, physical feverishness really be likened to the metaphorical feverishness of Socrates's city? Indeed it can. Bodily though it is, Rousseau's fever infects his moral and mental being. The return of bodily consciousness and individual personhood leads to moral and mental anguish. This is exactly what Socrates seems to have in mind in calling his second city feverish: civic ease and oneness give way to feverishness precisely as the desires of the body and the aspirations for individual distinction make themselves felt.

Finally, in response to the city's immoderation and its consequent need for guardians, Socrates shows that (e) the guardians must be educated—educated about many things but most of all about the *gods* and their involvement in human affairs. The future guardians' education centers on two theological principles. First, the gods are the source of good things only. Second, the gods do not lie. Socrates claims that these principles are true. Yet he makes no real effort to establish their truth, choosing instead to make the case that they are salutary. Rousseau's theological reasoning in paragraphs 23 and 24 eventuates in the same theological principles that Socrates teaches. His affirmation of trust in God's justice is also an affirmation of trust in God's *goodness*. The evils done him, though willed by God, will not in the end prove to be evil. As for Socrates's second principle, that the gods don't deceive, Rousseau holds that although people are routinely deceived about God's governance of the world—indeed, he himself had been deceived until just now—these deceptions are our own doing, and it is within our power to gain clearer sight. And like Socrates, he focuses his disquisition much more on the salubriousness of his argument than on its truth.

His newfound faith in God's special providence, Rousseau tells us, "consoles me, calms me, and helps me to resign myself" (24). This is the most credible claim of resignation that we have encountered thus far in the *Reveries*. Nevertheless resignation grounded on religious faith is only as deep and stable as the faith itself. Many have found great calm and consolation in their faith. Whether Rousseau was ever among the ranks of such believers is something we have reason to doubt. Moreover, there is something quite unusual if not outrageous about the Second Walk's affirmation of special providence even if it *was* sincere. Rousseau serenely professes that God knows him to be innocent. From the standpoint of traditional piety, this is only slightly less presumptuous than the piety that prompted Socrates to seek to refute the Delphic Oracle after hearing that the Oracle had affirmed that there was no man wiser than he (*Apology*, 21a–e). At least Rousseau doesn't seek to refute God; and although he insists on his own goodness whereas Socrates ostensibly denied his own virtue, surely Socrates's irony makes up that distance, and then some. And yet perhaps Rousseau *is* fully as brash as Socrates, or even more so. Like Socrates in the *Apology*, Rousseau in the *Reveries* denies that he is an atheist. He even inveighs against atheism (III, 11–12). But the divine providence of the Second Walk quickly recedes from view and even from memory. It has no part in the Third Walk's religious profession; and by the time we reach the Fifth Walk, Rousseau imputes to *himself* a goodness and sufficiency that conventional piety regards as properties of God alone. Rather than push God aside, Rousseau will find God within.[10] If anything could be more provocative to conventional piety than atheism, it is surely a human being's self-deification.

10. See my "Nearer My True Self to Thee."

CHAPTER 5

Becoming a Philosopher
Third Walk

The turn to God at the end of the Second Walk proves to have been a prelude to the more extensive religious profession that constitutes the bulk of the Third Walk. Here Rousseau describes undertaking at age forty a rigorous and resolute inquiry that yielded the religious opinions—opinions about God, the soul, and the order of things—to which he claims to have held fast, or at least *tried* to hold fast, ever since. These opinions are of special import to us. More precisely, Rousseau's *account* of these opinions is of special import. I emphasize presentation because he says strangely little about the opinions themselves, preferring instead to discuss their benefits as well as the process—the "severe examination" (8) and "great review" (9)—whereby he purportedly adopted them. His account is clearly intended to offer readers what he considers a more reasonable and tolerant faith than anything else on offer, whether from the church (meaning in this instance all major Christian denominations in Europe) or from the no less dogmatic philosophes seeking to supplant the church. He points readers to something like the uplifting and humane faith of the Savoyard Vicar: uplifting for recognizing the naturalness of human goodness, humane for meeting deep-seated needs without fomenting intolerance of other faiths. Even skeptics might find in Rousseau's profession a powerful and affirmative teaching so long as their skepticism isn't absolute. But what about those readers who cannot be satisfied by a probabilistic faith, or indeed by any faith at all—particularly those whose dissatisfaction with faith is animated less by prideful aversion than by eagerness to think about great questions even when, perhaps especially when, conclusive answers are unlikely to be available? What, in short, does the Third Walk offer to the philosophically disposed? This question is perhaps best approached by way of another question—as it happens, *our* question: What does the Third Walk teach about the philosophic life? How does it advance the narrative of the *Reveries* as a whole?

The answer begins to emerge when we notice several signals, oblique but strong, that Rousseau may not believe all that he says he believes. The strongest signal is that he has less to say, and less convincing things to say, on behalf of the truth or credibility of key elements of his profession than on behalf of their being salutary.

Exhibit number one is Rousseau's provocatively imprecise statement that the opinions yielded by his inquiry were *approximately* (*à peu près*) those related in "The Profession of Faith of the Savoyard Vicar." In fact, though, the Vicar doesn't speak of *opinions* at all but rather of *dogmas* and *articles of faith*. Rousseau's own terminology changes over the course of the Third Walk. In the early paragraphs of his account he refers to his religious views as "opinions" (8, 13). But he drops that word once the narrative moves from his *intention* to undertake a review to its *results*. What he has just called "opinions" he now refers to as the *sentiments* that he determined (15) or adopted (16), the *principles* that he embraced (17, 18), the *body of doctrine* that they constituted (18), and the *conclusion* he drew from them (19). With these new terms Rousseau signifies his public endorsement of important elements of the Vicar's teaching and his incorporation of these elements into his own teaching—in particular the legitimacy of consulting one's inner sentiment in order to determine what one will regard as religious truth. His embrace of parts of the Vicar's teaching is also evident when he characterizes the process whereby he supposedly arrived at his religious views not as inquiry but as *deliberation* (*délibération*): "Do not this deliberation and the conclusion I drew from it seem to have been dictated by Heaven itself to prepare me for the fate which awaited me and to enable me to endure it?" (19). Properly speaking, deliberation concerns practical affairs. We deliberate in order to determine what to *do*, not what *is*. Deliberation, moreover, concerns only means, not ends. The ends and their choiceworthiness are presupposed; they are the starting point from which deliberation proceeds. Rousseau's characterization of his inquiry as deliberation is thus a flare that illuminates what is problematic about his whole account. It indicates that what otherwise purports to have been theoretical inquiry was in fact practical reasoning aimed at providing a practical good for himself. Yet the flare is barely lit before it is extinguished. For why *wouldn't* we take for granted goods that "seem to have been dictated by Heaven itself"? And why *not* approach God and the soul as matters for deliberation rather than inquiry, if Heaven itself has told us to do so? With his brief-burning flare Rousseau indicates to philosophically attuned readers that if they mean to pursue the truth as rigorously as possible, they ought to pursue a different course from the one he is describing, just as he has.

His intention to speak this way to philosophically attuned readers may also explain why Rousseau would have chosen to refer to his ostensible views as *opinions* at all, even if only early on. After all, he could have spoken from the outset in terms of *sentiments*, *doctrines*, and *principles*. By first couching his views as opinions and then switching to a different terminology he prompts us to reflect on these terms. Opinion is a more humble term than *doctrine* or *principle*. It is also a more honest term by virtue of acknowledging that it falls short of knowledge. By first speaking of opinion Rousseau thus calls to mind the humble-bold enterprise of philosophy, its acknowledgment of how little it knows, and its determination to replace opinion with knowledge. By then *ceasing* to speak of opinion and speaking instead of doctrines and principles he signals that to adopt the faith he professes would have been a *departure* from the philosophic path.[1] It seems likely that he would have expected casual readers to miss this signal and its import. It seems just as likely that he would have expected his more philosophically adept readers to see this signal for what it is and to read the profession of faith accordingly. But what about the readers in between, that is, those who read with intelligence and care but who are not directed toward, and whom Rousseau would not want to direct toward, the philosophic life? Surely some such readers would catch on to his indication that the faith that he professes is somehow subphilosophic. Has Rousseau not undermined his own purpose, then? He hasn't, and this is where the matter becomes most interesting. Readers such as these have been prepared by Rousseau—and surely many in the Age of Enlightenment will have needed to be prepared—to find the Savoyard Vicar's natural religion reassuring and indeed reasonable. It may be subphilosophic, but it is no less reasonable for that; it might even be more reasonable for that. To be dependent on philosophy for the answers to questions of great practical import is not a happy condition for most of us, including, I would guess, most who study philosophy. If even Socrates remained ignorant about the greatest things, how likely are we to reason our way to satisfying answers? So when Rousseau ceases to speak of opinion and instead speaks of sentiments, principles, and doctrine, we're apt to feel relief. And all the

---

1. The Third Walk includes five mentions of opinion. The first appears at the end of the passage in which Rousseau most clearly avows that he is a philosopher: this is the passage in which he recounts his lifelong quest "to know the nature and the destination of [his] being" (III, 5). Once he recounts the outcome of his inquiry, the word "opinion" is used only to refer to views that *contradict* his ostensible new views: "there could be no solid reason for me to prefer *opinions* which tempted me in a moment of overwhelming despair but which would only augment my misery to *feelings* adopted in the vigor of age" (III, 22; emphasis added).

more so if we've been persuaded by him that the monumental questions at hand are not so much intractable theoretical questions of great practical import as practical questions in need of practical answers—and that the needed answers are *available* to us in "The Profession of Faith of the Savoyard Vicar."

Rousseau's willingness to concede what he must to the unphilosophic spirit—a concession as necessary for philosophy's sake as for society's—may account for another interesting imprecision in the Third Walk: namely, its extremely minimal account of the *contents* of the views he claims to have adopted and lived by. Rousseau says a great deal about the *need* that impelled him to undertake his inquiry and about needs that would arise later in life to which his newfound opinions would minister. Regarding content, however, all he offers is a brief reference to the existence of a moral order—and even here the emphasis is less on the moral order itself, let alone its basis, than on its benefits and his resolve to maintain belief in it:

> vain arguments will never destroy the congruity I perceive between my immortal nature, the constitution of this world, and the physical order I see reigning in it. In the corresponding moral order, whose arrangement I discovered by my seeking, I find the supports I need to endure the miseries of my life. In any other arrangement I would live without resource and die without hope. I would be the most unhappy of creatures. Let me hold then to this one, which alone suffices to render me happy in spite of fortune and men. (18)

As if to explain the lack of content, Rousseau proceeds to claim that he no longer commands the intellectual vigor with which he had conducted his original inquiry. He is intent on trusting his original reasoning (22–23). Why he would so confidently trust reasoning that he can't replicate isn't entirely clear, unless it's because his reasons were and still are reasons of the *heart*, which in fact they are: to adopt new views that depart from the ones he purportedly adopted long ago would be to deprive himself of consolation, compensation, happiness, and hope.

The reader might be forgiven for doubting that Rousseau lacks the vigor to think through the matters he's been discussing. In fact he demonstrates considerable intellectual vigor throughout the *Reveries*. Probably the most obvious example is the Fourth Walk's meditation on truth and lying. The intellectual vigor of the other Walks is often harder to see, but only because it is better disguised by his literary artistry, which is in itself an indication of intellectual rigor. (Not that the Fourth Walk too isn't exceedingly artful. But apparently Rousseau deemed it important to make his rigor more evident when speaking on truthfulness and lying.) Now let's consider an implication of the foregoing. If we have reason to suspect Rousseau of disingenuousness regarding his intellectual vigor, then we have reason to doubt that his profession is or ever was sincere. Why *doesn't* he state the content of his beliefs, particularly in light of his express intent to live according to them until the end of his days (23)? Why does he instead stress the needs that his beliefs satisfy? And why make repeated mention of doubts and "insoluble objections" (23), insoluble not only now but even while he was in his prime?[2] Additional cause for skepticism appears in other Walks, especially the Fifth and the Seventh, in which he suggests that he has found the answer to his moral and spiritual needs within himself, that is, without recourse to natural or any other kind of religion.

Neither the religious beliefs that Rousseau professes nor the process whereby he purportedly came to them are philosophic. Yet it would be a mistake to regard them as irrelevant to those suited to the philosophic life. Precisely by virtue of their nonphilosophic character these beliefs and their bases form the starting point of Rousseau's reflection on the theological-political problem and thus the starting point of his political philosophy. The content and the effects of these beliefs—their promise of meaning and consolation and thus personal virtue and social order—is the starting point of his political theory. Not embracing these beliefs *for himself* is perhaps the starting point of his philosophizing. And the "great inquiry" whereby he purportedly arrived at these beliefs marks the starting point of his philosophic *life*. The latter is the true subject of the Third Walk.[3]

The Third Book, the Third Walk, and Their Shared Threeness

"The beginning is the most important part of every work" (*Republic*, 377a–b). As Socrates's maxim directed us to pay special attention to the beginning of the *Reveries*, so too it should direct us to pay special attention to the beginning the philosophic life. Socrates's special relevance to the Third Walk doesn't end with this. The parallel between the *Reveries*

2. For a more comprehensive case for skepticism toward Rousseau's profession of faith, see Butterworth, "Interpretive Essay," 173–81.

3. I am indebted to Meier's reading of the Third Walk as an account of the beginning of the philosophic life, though he does not, as I do, treat this moment as the start of a continuous narrative of the philosophic life (Meier, *On the Happiness*, 48–56).

and the *Republic* seems to me especially revealing in their respective third divisions—so much so that the most fruitful approach to the Third Walk may be by way of a prior and closer than usual examination of its counterpart in the *Republic*.

Book 3 of the *Republic* can be divided into two major sections. The first and by far the longer section completes the guardians' moral and civic education, that is, their education in music and gymnastic (386a–412a). Topics include the kind of music and speech favorable to inculcating courage; various matters of poetic style; why music and musical education are so important, indeed, "most sovereign" (401d); music's role in promoting "the naturally right kind of love," which is "to love in a moderate and musical way what's orderly and fine" (403a); and the tempering of spiritedness. Book 3's second section treats the question of rule: who should rule, and why; what's needed to lend legitimacy to their rule, including the "noble lie"; and the rulers' (guardians') austere way of life (412a–417b).

Book 3 could be divided differently, of course. We could regard the respective treatments of the guardians' musical and gymnastic educations as constituting separate sections (386a–403c; 403c–412a) and thus see book 3 as having not two but three major sections. After all, musical and gymnastic education are each given longer treatment than the discussion of rule that I've recognized as a major section. Doesn't the substantive difference between music and gymnastic warrant that we regard their respective treatments as separate major divisions? It would—*if music and gymnastic were treated as we might have expected them to be treated*. But they aren't. The two educations are one, and that *one* is entirely directed to the soul. What is called gymnastic education is in fact a continuation of the education of the passions. It concerns the body, yes, but only secondarily: its overarching aim is to temper spiritedness. It takes its bearings entirely from the musical education and can be seen as nothing more or less than the culmination of musical education. The professed aim of the entire education, of musical and gymnastic education working together, is not harmony between soul and body but rather harmony within the soul.

And yet the bipartite appearance of *Republic* 3 *is* misleading. Closer investigation reveals that book 3 divides into three sections after all, though in a different way from the one we've just considered. A tripartition comes to light that describes real divisions while also revealing a hitherto submerged continuity. The continuity concerns the uneasy relation between moral and civic health on the one hand and truth and truthfulness on the other. We find a reflection on this theme at the precise center of each of

the three sections. The very same theme also predominates in the Third
Walk of the *Reveries*.

Republic 3 opens with a one-sentence summary and affirmation of the
teaching about the gods with which book 2 has just ended. Then comes
a treatment of what the guardians should be taught about the afterlife
if they are to be courageous. After this comes an explication of which
teachings are favorable and which are unfavorable to moderation. Then
comes a shift: Socrates continues to address the inculcation of courage
and moderation in the guardians, but he turns from "speeches," or the
content of poetry, to various questions of style and form: narrative versus
imitative poetry, harmonic mode, melody, and rhythm. It is here, with the
turn from speeches to style, that I locate the separation between discrete
major sections, for speech and its significance stand apart from matters
of style of form—in two ways. First, speeches are uniquely important in
Socrates's treatment of musical education. They are the thing with which
all else must be aligned. Second, the relation between truth and life is
seen differently depending on whether one examines it from the standpoint of speeches or from the standpoint of style and form. Socrates's
treatment of speeches illuminates with considerable directness and clarity the practical ambiguity of truth. What determines whether speeches
are fit for the guardians' education to virtue is not that they are true but
that they conduce to virtue. To be sure, Socrates at several points claims
that the speeches to be taught to the guardians are true. But he makes no
arguments for their truth—unless we are to understand that their utility in
inculcating virtue is itself an argument for their truth: in either case truth
proves to be secondary to moral utility if it matters at all. After the turn
from speeches to style, the relation between truth and life is treated much
more indirectly. For these reasons I judge that we should regard the part
of book 3 that treats the content of speeches, this part alone, as book 3's
first section (386a–392c).

Of particular interest is the way that this section ends. Having made
the case that the guardians must be taught courage and moderation,
Socrates concludes by soliciting agreement that the guardians should be
taught that justice is profitable and that only the just man can be happy.
This teaching might be regarded as both the capstone and the core of the
whole Socratic moral and civic education—the capstone because it treats
justice, the core because it makes happiness dependent on virtue. Yet no
sooner has Socrates secured agreement on this teaching than he reminds
his interlocutors that they haven't yet found out "what sort of a thing justice is and how it by nature profits the man who possesses it, whether he

seems to be just or not" (392b–c). Thus book 3's first section ends with an admission of incompleteness. Of even greater importance than how the section ends, however, is what we find at the center. I noted above that we find at the center of each of *Republic* 3's three sections a reflection on the vexed relation between truth and life. At the center of *Republic* 3's first section we find Socrates explaining that although "private men" must tell the truth, rulers are permitted to lie if, or rather when, it would benefit the city (389b).

The second section of *Republic* 3 (392c–412a) comprises the remainder of the guardians' moral and civic (or musical and gymnastic) education. Here are included not only Socrates's treatment of poetic style and form, but also his argument that the fine and decorative arts should be governed along the same lines as music and his treatment of what he presents as gymnastic education, with accompanying discourses on law and medicine. It's at the center of all this—which is to say, at the center of book 3's central section—that Socrates explains "why the rearing in music is most sovereign" (401d–402d). Let's consider the meaning and implication of this claim. Music forms the soul from the beginning of life—that is, prior to the awakening and development of the soul's rational capacity. This cannot but be the case. The rational capacity will naturally develop in everyone, but not to the same degree of perfection: in the well-formed soul, the rational capacity is sovereign. But the well-formed soul, in order to *become* a well-formed soul, had to be prepared for reason during the years that it was not reasonable. It had to be fitted with a kind of protorational disposition. At the heart of this disposition is a deep sense that the world is orderly, indeed that the world is governed according to a benign moral order—that the world is not essentially tragic but rather can be trusted to return good for good. The sense that the world is governed according to a benign moral order promotes calm and confidence, which in turn are favorable to the flowering of reason, whereas the sense that the world is tragic or governed by arbitrary will is apt to incite irascible passions that are antagonistic to reason. The chief means of producing the more benign, protorational sense of the world is the musical education adumbrated by Socrates. Particularly important to note is that this education must falsify reality: it must shield the young from important truths and replace them with edifying fictions. The music required for the eventual love of truth must be untruthful. This is the case even if the world is in fact governed according to a benign moral order: for if the world *is* so governed, it takes great strength of soul and depth of insight to discern this governance behind the tragic and strifeful surface of things. One who is not protected against the blunt force of the sight of tragedy and strife while young—one who sees gratuitous suffering abounding and injustice triumphing and isn't taught that these evils are evanescent—such a one will very likely be disordered by roiling passion forever after. Reason can become sovereign in a person's soul, but only after a long regency during which the person has been rationally governed and educated to reason by someone else. That someone else is ultimately the Legislator, whose reason is embodied in the laws, particularly laws concerning music. That is why "the rearing in music is most sovereign."

The right musical education brought to bear on the best nature would produce a person in whom spiritedness and the philosophic nature are harmonized. Book 3's final section (412a–417b) begins with Socrates asking: "Won't we always need some such man as overseer in the city, Glaucon, if the city is going to be saved?" (412). Glaucon, a politically minded man who can't imagine that there is any serious discrepancy between human excellence as such and political excellence, naturally agrees. Socrates, who knows that human excellence *can* be at variance with political excellence, now leads Glaucon through a discussion of what particular qualities make a man, or rather *men*, fit to rule. (Immediately after Glaucon agrees that the city needs a certain kind of *man* as overseer, Socrates shifts to the plural.) Those who are fit to guard the city, Socrates says, must satisfy three criteria: they must be prudent, they must be powerful, and they must care for the city (412c). The third criterion is the most difficult to assess—less because care for the city can more easily be faked than the other two criteria than because it is more vulnerable to decay or subversion, being subject to "wizardry" or "bewitchment" perpetrated by pain and pleasure. Guardians-in-training will therefore be watched and put to the test at every age. Only those whose devotion to the city passes muster will become what are now called *complete* guardians. The rest, that is, those whose devotion to the city has been deemed less certain, will from hereon be called auxiliaries (414b).

Socrates vindicates the distinction between complete guardians (who are hereafter referred to again simply as guardians) and auxiliaries with a story that he introduces as a noble or nobly born (*gennaios*) lie. The first part of the lie holds that citizens were fashioned and reared under the earth and only then brought out from the land, which is thus their common mother. The second part of the lie is that "the god" placed a metal in each citizen's soul—either gold, silver, iron, or bronze—thereby designating to which of the city's classes he or she is to be assigned (414d–415c). What makes the first part of the lie noble is that it promotes love of the city as one's motherland and thus love of one's fellow citizens as kinsmen. What makes it a lie is that it imputes to nature something that is artificial. The

second part of the lie is noble by virtue of reconciling citizens to their respective classes. What makes *it* a lie is that it imputes to the god a merely
natural fact. Human beings, it would seem, have difficulty reconciling
themselves to natural inequality and natural limits. The point common
to both parts of the lie, though, and the primary teaching of the noble lie
as such, is that civic virtue and thus the city's well-being require belief in
falsehoods. In this the noble lie is a sober commentary on the weak natural
grounding of civic virtue and well-being. Thus do we find at the center
of book 3's third section, as at the center of its first two sections, a teaching about the practical problem of truth—about the vexed relation, even
antagonism, between moral and political virtue and well-being on the
one hand and truth or enlightenment on the other. The problem will find
its fullest expression with Socrates's indication in book 6 that *true* virtue
begins with love of truth (485a–b) but that one can attain this virtue only
by overcoming, even while relying on, moral and civic virtue.

Like book 3 of the *Republic*, the Third Walk of the *Reveries* explores the
relation of truth to life in three successive sections. In the first section, or
paragraphs 1 through 3, Rousseau raises the question of truth's utility for
life quite explicitly. In the second section, or paragraphs 4 through 24,
he treats this question extensively though no longer quite so openly by
giving an account of his purported religious opinions and how he came
to adopt them. Finally, in a section consisting entirely of paragraph 25, he
again raises the question explicitly and offers a different response from the
one he had offered in the first section.[4] The difference, we may provisionally assume, is owing to what has been disclosed in the long, intervening
second section.

FIRST SECTION: PARAGRAPHS 1–3

In *Republic* 3 the question of truth's relation to life is everywhere present
but nowhere explicitly raised. In the *Reveries'* Third Walk the question is
explicitly raised at the outset and again in the conclusion, so that the Walk
is framed by nothing but this question, yet Rousseau addresses the question even more indirectly than Socrates does. Rousseau opens the Third
Walk with an epigraph from Solon: "I continue to learn while growing
old."[5] Rousseau says that Solon's line speaks for him too, but in an un-

4. I follow Butterworth's formal tripartition; see "Interpretive Essay," 170–81. I depart
from Butterworth, however, with respect to interpretation—most especially with respect
to the how the Third Walk's sections relate to the *Reveries'* narrative character.

5. Actually Rousseau slightly misquotes Solon. What Plutarch has Solon say is that

happy way. Unlike Solon's learning, his own has been a source of misery
(1–2). Most of his learning in the prior twenty years has consisted in two
discoveries: first, that those he had once loved and trusted as friends had
been conspiring against him; second, that there is no remedy for the misfortune the conspirators have inflicted on him. Following this sorrowful
report about himself, he speaks briefly about the relation between knowledge and well-being not only in his own life but for all human beings as
they grow old (3). Here too the tone is sorrowful, indeed pitiful. Learning
is futile for those who are nearing life's end. The time for learning is youth,
so that one might apply and benefit from it in one's maturity. Yet there is
one "study still appropriate for an old man," Rousseau tells us—namely,
"to learn to die" (3). To most ears this is apt to sound like bitter wisdom.
Others, however, will recall that learning to die was Socrates's final description of *philosophy*. What Rousseau here suggests as a palliative for
the elderly is said—and shown—by Socrates to be the way to the utmost
freedom and well-being for a human being.[6] Whatever he may be saying
about the elderly, there can be no doubt that Rousseau is deliberately
invoking Socrates's teaching.

Does his invoking signify *embracing*? Here too, it seems to me, there
can be little doubt. To be sure, as we've seen many times, Rousseau de-
rides most who have claimed the mantle of philosophy; and that which he
explicitly lauds as "true philosophy" would seem to most of us anything
but.[7] But to those awake to and moved by the invocation of Socrates—to
those imbued with intellectual eros and strength of soul—to them, as one
of them, Rousseau commends the Socratic way.

To learn to die is to accept one's mortality and thereby in a certain
sense *to* die: it is to undergo the death of the fearful, egoic self, the self
that, dominated by thymos or amour-propre, will not or cannot accept
its mortality. To accept one's mortality and to undergo the death of the
egoic self is to gain freedom from the enormous dread that haunts most
human beings, whether consciously or, as is more typically the case, on the

---

he continued to "learn *many things* while growing old." Rousseau's misquotation does not
appear to have been intentional, for it occurs in the translation on which he likely relied.
See Butterworth, trans., *Reveries of the Solitary Walker*, by Rousseau, translator's note 1.

6. *Phaedo*, 64a.

7. What Rousseau explicitly refers to as "true philosophy" is so far from signifying
intellectual eros as to come close to the opposite: "O virtue! sublime science of simple
souls, are so many efforts and so much equipment really required to know you? Are not
your principles engraved in all hearts, and is it not enough in order to learn your laws
to return into oneself and to listen to the voice of one's conscience in the silence of the
passions? That is true philosophy, let us know how to be content with it" (*FD*, 30; 22).

periphery of our mental vision, elusive enough to avoid being confronted (most of the time) but close enough to haunt us. "To learn to die" will not be heard by amour-propre as the promise of freedom or well-being. At best it will be taken as a challenge to one's pride and courage; and those who meet that challenge, though they will have won a noble victory, will still have found nothing more than a palliative in the face of mortality. To the philosopher, however, and perhaps to those with an intimation of philosophy, learning to die is far more than a palliative. Or if it *is* a palliative, it's a palliative that enables the patient to see that there is no need for a cure and never has been.

Recognizing that "learning to die" is an allusion to Socratic philosophy casts paragraph 3 in a dramatically different light from that in which it initially appeared. So too do paragraphs 1 and 2 take on a very different meaning if reread with sufficient attention and awareness. Here is the entire first paragraph—which, we recall, had been immediately preceded by the epigraph from Solon:

> Solon frequently repeated this line in his old age. There is a sense in which I could also say it in mine, but what experience has made me acquire these past twenty years is a very sad bit of knowledge: ignorance is still preferable. Adversity is undoubtedly a great teacher, but it charges dearly for its lessons; and the profit we draw from them is frequently not worth the price they have cost. Besides, before we have obtained all this learning by such tardy lessons, the occasion to use it passes. Youth is the time to study wisdom; old age is the time to put it into practice. Experience always instructs, I admit; but it is profitable only for the time we have left to live. Is the moment when we have to die the time to learn how we should have lived?

Rousseau proceeds in paragraph 2 to compare the bitterness of the lessons he has learned with the "sweet illusions" under which he had previously labored and still *would* labor if only he could. He concludes: "The sad truth that time and reason have unveiled to me by making me sense my misfortune has made me see that there was no remedy for it and that all that was left was for me to resign myself to it. Thus all the experience proper to my age is useless for me now in this condition and of no benefit for the future."

Somber passages. Yet not a line in either of these two paragraphs quite says what it seems to say. Consider, first, the claim in paragraph 1 that "ignorance is still preferable." Appearing as it does only two paragraphs prior to the passage about learning how to die, might not the ignorance that is preferable to the knowledge Rousseau has acquired be *Socratic* ignorance?

If so, his preference for ignorance would be anything but a desire to remain unaware. He gives two reasons for preferring ignorance to sad knowledge. The first reason is that although adversity is a great teacher, the price it charges often exceeds the profit we draw from it. Taken as a statement about human beings in the aggregate, this may be true. But doesn't it seem likely that the magnitude of the profit will vary according to the lesson that is learned and according to who is doing the learning? Rousseau does not say that he is among those for whom the price of learning has exceeded its profit.

Rousseau's second reason for preferring ignorance pertains to those nearing the end of life. Experience instructs us, yes, "but it is profitable only for the time we have left to live. Is the moment when we have to die the time to learn how we should have lived?" But this point is compelling only with regard to those who haven't yet begun to learn. What about old people who have already learned something about how to live? They may have learned, or made progress toward learning, to die. For them it *is* beneficial to continuing learning, so long as by "learning" we mean not the absorption of new material useful in the marketplace but rather the continued perfection of one's way of being. Admittedly even this can sound more than a touch pitiful: few things bespeak futility more than lifelong inquirers plodding forward, hopeful that the knowledge that eluded them under the bright summer sun will somehow come their way as the shadows lengthen and the snow begins to fall. But this is an unfair reading based on a distorted premise. The value of philosophic inquiry is not chiefly instrumental. Prior to any instrumental benefit is the intrinsic benefit of further realizing one's nature and thus further perfecting one's being. Here it might help to notice that those who embrace philosophy as a way of life typically describe it not only as a life of searching but also as a life of contemplation: of looking *at*, not just looking *for*. Contemplation or looking *at* has no built-in end in the way that pursuing or looking *for* does. Contemplation takes place in time, but time, so to speak, doesn't take place in *it*: time is not internal to it. Aristotle called such activity *energeia*. Another word for this kind of activity, at once both narrower and more expansive, is *eternal*, or timeless, or, as Aristotle puts it, being in the *now*.[8]

We needn't doubt that Rousseau has paid greatly for his wisdom. But for the reasons we've just examined we certainly *may* question whether the price has exceeded the profit. In what has the profit consisted? Rousseau provides an answer: "The sad truth that time and reason have unveiled to me by making me sense my misfortune has made me see that there was

8. See Aristotle, *Nicomachean Ethics*, 1174b.

no remedy for it and that all that was left was for me to resign myself to it" (2). Sad truth? Yes, that was the price. And yes, all that was left was to resign himself to it. But as we know by now, resignation needn't be grim accommodation. It can be the path to freedom and well-being. It is the path of philosophy. The Third Walk's introductory section seems to argue for ignorance over learning. And so it does. But the ignorance that it champions and indeed exemplifies is Socratic ignorance.

SECOND SECTION: PARAGRAPHS 4–24

The second section of the Third Walk, like the second section of *Republic* 3, simultaneously performs two tasks: it develops a new theology, and it outlines the education and culture needed to render the soul amenable to reason. (Alternatively, these two tasks can be seen as one, with the theology constituting a part, indeed the foundation, of a single overarching educational and cultural project.) The bulk of this section consists of Rousseau's purported account of his beliefs about God and the soul and how he came to them. Implicit in this *how* is also a *why*, or the needs that his beliefs fulfill and the benefits they bring. Rousseau makes sure never to say that he adopted his beliefs *because* of their benefits. And he certainly never says that he adopted them against the counsel of reason. Yet the reasoning whereby he was purportedly led to adopt them, like the reasoning in "The Profession of Faith of the Savoyard Vicar," accorded considerable weight to sentiment: if a proposition rang true, if it satisfied the needs of one's soul, that in itself carried weight. In emphasizing utility over truth and in veiling the disjunction between the two, Rousseau replicates Socrates's approach in *Republic* 3. But perhaps *veiling* is the wrong word. For if Rousseau does use a veil, it's a pretty sheer one. The disjunction between truth and utility, or even between truth and life, isn't so much veiled as it is contested. That is the meaning of Rousseau's according truth value to sentiment. Nor should we balk at this practice as dressed-up wishful thinking, for its defenders could pointedly counter that there is no way to resolve questions about God and the soul, even provisionally, *without* consulting sentiment. Not that these questions are easily answered even when one does consult sentiment. There is no position that is not subject to insuperable objections. But sentiment at least provides suggestive evidence, and we do need to decide these questions as best we can.

Unless we don't. Some people claim not to need any more certainty on these matters than that which unaided reason can provide. If reason can't settle a question conclusively, then there is nothing to do but rest content with, or at any rate accommodate, inconclusiveness. But as I suggested earlier, professions of dispassion and skepticism don't always hold up under scrutiny. Rousseau, like Socrates, might agree that there are some who can live well and honestly as skeptics; but he also, again like Socrates, sees this ability as exceedingly rare. It requires an unlikely constellation of personal traits, or what we might call a philosophic nature, as well as education and experience that develop rather than subvert this nature. If the *Reveries*, as I've been arguing, narrates a philosopher's life, then it is here, in the central section of the Third Walk, that the philosophic life proper begins.

The second section of the Third Walk can itself be usefully divided into three subsections.[9] In paragraphs 4 through 6, Rousseau speaks of the qualities that have always set him apart from the surrounding society. Then, in paragraphs 7 through 16, he recounts his project of personal reform. Most of this account (all but paragraph 7) concerns his "great review" (9), the inquiry whereby he set out to determine what to believe about God and the soul. Finally, in paragraphs 17 through 24, he speaks about the effects of this inquiry in subsequent years. Chief among these effects has been to satisfy certain of his needs and thereby protect him against despondency in the face of life's inevitable difficulties—difficulties that, in his case, would prove especially severe. Interestingly, Rousseau makes a point of noting more than once that although his new beliefs have sustained him, he has still been subject to painful doubts owing to insuperable objections.

In the first subsection (paragraphs 4–6) Rousseau attests to what can best be described as his philosophic nature: *nature*, because it has been decisive in determining his experience of life from the start; *philosophic*, because its core feature is a passion for self-knowledge. As we might expect, Rousseau does not explicitly lay claim to a philosophic nature. He begins, instead, by speaking of a feeling he has had since childhood that he was not made to live in "the whirlwind of the world" (4). He seems to say that he has believed himself made to live in another place. In fact, though, it is not another place but rather another *time* to which he is drawn: "my ardent imagination readily jumped beyond the interval of my life which had barely begun—as though from a terrain which was foreign to me—to settle down in a quiet resting place where I could anchor myself." The resting place was beyond the "*interval*" of his life, not beyond the place in which he lived. (Where he uses the language of place, he specifically indicates that he is employing a simile: "*as though* from a terrain which was foreign to me.") Yet that other time for which he longed was in fact *no*-time, or eternity. And what he sought "there" was not an escape from the world but rather a condition from which he could observe and engage

9. This too is pointed out by Butterworth; see "Interpretive Essay," 171–80.

it without being swept up in its "whirlwind." If the "quiet resting place" he sought had been apart from the world altogether and not just its whirlwind, he would not have needed to *anchor* himself. Notice too that it was his ardent *imagination* that expressed itself thus. It seems doubtful that imagination could have done what it did, that it would have known to step out of time rather than go to a new place, had it not been informed by philosophic reflection. Yet it also seems questionable whether philosophic reflection could have known what was wanted without the eagle eyes—and wings—of imagination. Philosophic insight and awareness, beginning with awareness of the philosophic life, would seem to require both reflection and imagination. But even this is too clumsy a formulation. In philosophy, reflection and imagination require one another in order to be what they each, independently, *are*.

The feeling that one was not made to live in the whirlwind of the world bespeaks a defect or lack, but a *fruitful* lack that one might even describe (though Rousseau himself does not) as intellectual *eros*: "This feeling, nourished by education from the time of my childhood and reinforced during my whole life by this long web of miseries and misfortunes which has filled it, *has at all times made me seek to know the nature and the destination of my being* in a more interested and careful manner than I have found any other man seek to do" (5; emphasis added). If this passage doesn't bespeak a philosophic nature or disposition, it's hard to imagine what does. But Rousseau has no interest in laying claim to a title that has been claimed by less honest sorts than himself: "I have seen many who philosophized much more learnedly than I, but their philosophy was, so to speak, foreign to them. Wanting to be more knowledgeable than others, they studied the universe in order to know how it was ordered, just as they would have studied some machine they might have perceived—through pure curiosity. They studied human nature to be able to speak knowingly about it, but not in order to know themselves" (5). When Rousseau himself desired to learn, by contrast, "it was in order to know and not in order to teach." Neither Rousseau nor the philosophers of whom he speaks claim to be dispassionate. Nor does Rousseau claim that the object of his passion differs from theirs: they seek to know, and so does he. Yet the difference between them and him *is* the difference between opposing passions, and clearly so. This goes to show that what most determines the nature or the *what* of a passion is its *why*, or the need from which it arises. Testimony to the difference between Rousseau's desire for knowledge and that of his counterparts—proof that he does not learn in order to appear learned—is his concession at the end of paragraph 5 that his inquiry hasn't been very successful: "I have sought frequently and for a long time to know the true end of my life in order to direct its use, and I soon became consoled about being so inept at skillfully handling myself in this world when I sensed that this end should not be sought in it." Those who engage in study in order to impress others are not likely to admit failure. Nor would they be consoled, as Rousseau *was*, by sensing that the knowledge they have sought should not be sought in this world.

This passage, which reads as a concession by Rousseau or as an acknowledgment of the human mind's limits in the face of its deepest need, admits of alternative readings. These alternative readings, however, don't close the gap between Rousseau and the *philosophes* but rather redefine and possibly even deepen it. Rousseau soon determined that the true end of his life should not be sought in this world. The most obvious reading of this line would be that Rousseau quickly came to deem such inquiry futile. But if that was the case, why did he continue to inquire? Why does he perhaps continue to inquire even now? (Written in the *passé composé* [*j'ai cherché souvent et longtemps*], the line allows that Rousseau's inquiring has not ceased.) But what else *could* this line mean? Consider again: Rousseau sensed that he should not seek for the true end of his life *in this world*. Might "this world" refer only to *his* world, that is, not to earth and its lifeworld but to Rousseau's own civilization, with all its conceits? Or might Rousseau be making the Socratic point that we should not expect *knowledge* of our true end in this world but that we might attain better and more comprehensive *opinions*—and that those who do so are better and even happier for the effort? On none of these readings has the choiceworthiness of the philosophic life been refuted. Quite the contrary. And those who continue to engage in philosophic inquiry and reflection after having recognized and come to grips with all that is implied in the foregoing alternative readings underline all the more the distance between Rousseau or the Rousseauan philosopher and the *philosophes*.

In paragraph 6 Rousseau sketches his religious autobiography to the age of forty. He recalls the "morals and piety" of the family into which he was born and then the "wisdom and religion" of his uncle, a minister, in whose home he was subsequently raised. Then came a period during which, he says, having passed too soon into his own keeping, he was led by "caresses," "vanity," "hope," and "necessity" to become a Catholic. This was a period of some disorder, as readers will recall from the *Confessions*. After this come the years spent in the household of Madame de Warens, where he became firmer in his Catholicism and more elevated in his religiosity, "devout almost in the manner of Fénelon. Secluded meditation, the study of nature, and contemplation of the universe force a solitary person to lift himself up incessantly to the author of things, to search with tender concern for the purpose in everything he sees and the cause of everything he feels." Rousseau reports that he emerged from this idyll with sufficient resources to keep from succumbing to the world's false promises come the time, which certainly *would* come, when "fate [would throw him] back into the torrent of the world." About to recount his great project of self-reform in paragraphs 7 through 16, he concludes paragraph 6 with the following description of his condition as he stood at the threshold of that enterprise: "I reached the age of forty, wavering between indigence and good fortune, between wisdom and aberration, full of vices induced by habit but without any bad propensity in my heart, living according to chance without any principles determined by my reason, and inadvertent about my duties without scorning them, yet often without being fully cognizant of them." There is no element of virtue in this portrait, at least not according to Rousseau's conception of virtue. But there is considerable goodness in it, which in turn implies a rare degree of strength of soul, for nothing else could account for the persistence and liveliness of that natural endowment amid the suffocating pressures of the unnatural. This same strength of soul would also see Rousseau onto the path of the philosophic life. In viewing strength of soul as the sine qua non of the philosophic life, Rousseau is at one with his classical predecessors. Unlike him, they depicted the philosophic life as the most *virtuous* life. We might wonder, however, whether Rousseau doesn't in fact share that view, not in name—in his usage "virtue" is at odds with nature—but in substance.

What I have described as a brief spiritual autobiography in paragraph 6 is presented by Rousseau as a prelude to, perhaps a preparation for, a more serious religiosity to follow. But not even the most credulous reader would deny that what Rousseau recounts here is also or instead a prelude to and preparation for the philosophic life. The same things that he presents as having nurtured him religiously can just as plausibly be understood to have nurtured him philosophically. The "morals and piety" of the family into which he was born and the "wisdom and religion" of his uncle's household help explain how it is that Rousseau developed a sense of apartness from the world and the sense that he would not find happiness in property and position but rather in more contemplative pursuits. This sense of apartness that safeguarded his religious sensibility would also have safeguarded his philosophic nature and natural goodness. Here we see Rousseau's modification—his extension and elaboration—of the Socratic teaching concerning the reliance of the philosophic life on a prior moral and spiritual foundation. We've already noted that whereas Socrates speaks of moral virtue as a prophylactic against the false and corrupting promises of the world, Rousseau speaks instead of *goodness*. In the passage that we've been examining, the meaning of this goodness—in particular, that goodness is not an essentially moral thing—is more vividly indicated than is often the case. Goodness as understood by Rousseau is not moral because it is prior to both reason and choice. Goodness signifies a wholeness, meaning psychic unity and balance, which is expressed in one's *inclinations*.[10] These inclinations are always benign, if not always in their effects then certainly in their aim. But this benignity, as admirable as it may be, is incidental. It is the effect of self-love.

The goodness of the primordial natural human being is expressed as an inarticulate "repugnance to seeing any sensitive being, and especially any being like ourselves, perish or suffer" (*SD*, 125–26; 14–15). The goodness of a social and moral human being, if it can make itself heard, expresses itself more articulately, not only in sentiment but also in the form of rules and principles. These rules and principles, which have been established by reason, constitute the moral foundation, the prephilosophic foundation, of the philosophic life. Yet the philosophic life can begin only when this foundation is itself subjected to the most rigorous and serious questioning. One must subject all one's prior beliefs and commitments to the most searching scrutiny and be willing to let go of them if they should prove rationally indefensible, no matter how cherished they may have been and no matter how painful it would be to let them go. To live the philosophic life requires that the mind free itself from, and then assume governance of, the heart. As important as *being* free, it seems, is that philosophers have *won* their freedom, if only because freedom is not available in any other way. One even wonders whether a prior *lack* of strong beliefs and commitments (whether owing to indifference, ecumenicalism, or "enlightenment") wouldn't prove an *obstacle* to philosophic education, and all the more so for appearing otherwise. Yet if the philosopher-to-be is well served by holding his or her prior beliefs firmly, it might be best if this philosopher-to-be not hold them either too comfortably on the one hand or too desperately on the other—at least if we take our bearings from Rousseau's own case. For it seems quite plausible that the irregular and sad circumstances of his childhood might have been helpful to his eventually attaining to the philosophic life even as they might also have exacerbated the challenges to perfecting his philosophic life. As a native

10. For a fuller articulation of the meaning of goodness to Rousseau, see my *Rousseau, Nature, and the Problem of the Good Life*, 19–29, and Melzer, *Natural Goodness of Man*, 15–23.

Genevan, Rousseau would have experienced what it meant to belong to a real religious and political community. But by joining his uncle's household as late as he did, by being a nephew and not a son, and by being made to leave the household for a grueling apprenticeship after only a few years, his sense of belonging would likely have been attenuated. It is hard to imagine that these circumstances wouldn't have contributed to his peculiarly intense self-consciousness. His professed nostalgia notwithstanding, Rousseau couldn't have been all that tightly woven into the community, let alone woven *of* it.

If life in his uncle's house simultaneously safeguarded his religious sensibility and prepared him for philosophy, the same can be said of life with Madame de Warens, except that in the latter case the religious story was less the safeguarding of normative Christian faith than the deepening of a religiosity that some would have regarded as heretical. *"Devout almost in the manner of Fénelon"* is how Rousseau chooses to characterize his religiosity during this period. Francois Fénelon, a Roman Catholic archbishop, insisted that his devoutness remained within the bounds of Christian doctrine. Others disagreed. Does *Rousseau* regard Fénelonian devoutness as Christian? He says that he does. But of course Rousseau's professed understanding of Christianity was always at considerable variance from that of such authorities as the archbishop of Paris.[11] This much we can say: Rousseau indicates that his new piety grew out of a course of studies that he undertook while living with Madame de Warens. These studies were not the continuation of a prior, simpler religious education but rather an exploration of nature. And they led not only to piety but also to philosophy, or perhaps we should say that they led not only to religious piety but also and ultimately to another kind of piety as well. Let's examine again a sentence in which Rousseau speaks of the spiritual effects of these studies: "Secluded meditation, the study of nature, and contemplation of the universe force a solitary person to lift himself up incessantly to the author of things, to search with tender concern for the purpose in everything he sees and the cause of everything he feels" (6). Rousseau specifies three discrete activities in this brief passage. Two of them, meditation and contemplation of the universe, belong as much to philosophy as to religion. And the central activity of the three, the study of nature, is *essentially* philosophic and, in the eyes of some, *anti*religious (antireligious not by discovering truths that contradict religious dogma but because its conception of the world as governed by natural necessity

11. *Letter to Beaumont.*

seems to leave no place for God).[12] Here as in "The Profession of Faith of the Savoyard Vicar" Rousseau almost elides the disjunction between religion and philosophic inquiry. But the disjunction is discernible. And it seems to me that Rousseau begins to elaborate this disjunction in the very next paragraph by suggesting that although philosophy, like religion, is born of awe, gratitude, and piety, it may in turn inspire a *different* awe, gratitude, and piety from those that belong to religious faith. *How* different is a matter of considerable dispute, and the matter isn't made any clearer by philosophers' undeniable dissimulation. But even those who consider the difference between philosophy and faith decisive acknowledge that the same education and beliefs that make possible the ascent to the higher reaches of religiosity may be equally helpful and even necessary to the philosophic life. Whichever peak one aspires to scale, one must have trained extensively for the rigors of climbing. Rousseau will return to his time spent with Madame de Warens in the Tenth Walk, where he recalls with gratitude the role she played in the formation of his soul: "loved by a woman full of desire to please and of gentleness, I did what I wanted to do, I was what I wanted to be; and through the use I made of my leisure, aided by her lessons and example, I was able to give to my still simple and new soul the form which better suited it and which it has always kept" (X, 1). This later reminiscence doesn't contradict what Rousseau says in the Third Walk, but it does differ in two notable respects. In the later passage, Rousseau claims to have given his soul the form it would have thereafter. And he does not say that the lessons and example of Madame de Warens were religious.

One more word about the sentence from the Third Walk on which we've been reflecting. Rousseau attributes his spiritual elevation to the *secluded* meditation, study, and contemplation of a *solitary* person. What can he mean by "secluded" and "solitary" when he was living in the warm embrace of the lady of the house? Clearly Rousseau's use of the word "solitary" does not imply literal isolation. More likely it refers to a certain freedom of mind—a *natural* freedom of mind, since it consists in indifference to what others think of him. This hardly diminishes the significance or the rareness of solitude. Most of us would not be solitary walkers even if we were consigned to complete isolation. Lonely, yes, and the pain of

---

12. Socrates—especially, the young Socrates, it seems—was much occupied with the mutual exclusivity of nature and the popular conception of the gods. For him, however, the crisis arose not from the threat posed by nature to the gods but rather the reverse. This theme is developed extensively by Leibowitz, *Ironic Defense of Socrates*.

loneliness would set us to walking; but not solitary in Rousseau's sense of the word and not walking as Rousseau walks. The meaning Rousseau attaches to solitude is akin to the meaning he attaches to idleness. The decisive thing in both cases is the felt experience of natural freedom.

We turn now to the second subsection of the Third Walk's second section (paragraphs 7 through 16), which, as the central subsection of the Walk's central section, is also in a certain sense the center of the Walk altogether. Does this formal distinction have a substantive correlate? I believe it does.

In this lengthy subsection Rousseau recounts the process of "reform" (8) that he undertook at age forty. The project, he says, had been long planned: "From the time of my youth, I had set this age of forty as the terminal point for my efforts to succeed and as the one for all of my vain ambitions. I was fully resolved once this age was reached that whatever situation I might be in, I would struggle no longer to get out of it and would spend the remainder of my days living from day to day without ever again concerning myself about the future." Rousseau's idea was not to get serious or settle down in any conventional sense but rather to free himself from dubious worries and constraints. And so he did: "I fully gave myself up to carelessness and to the peace of mind which always constituted my most dominant pleasure and most lasting propensity" (7). He "forsook the world and its pomp," "renounced all finery," and quit his job in order to make a simple living copying music. But he did more than this—and more than he had originally planned: "I did not restrict my reform to external things. I felt that this reform was such as to require another of *opinions*, undoubtedly more painful but more necessary; and, resolved not to do it twice, I undertook to submit my inner self to a severe examination which would regulate it for the rest of my life just as I wanted to find it at my death" (8; emphasis added). Rousseau had come to see that settling on a way of life required that he review opinions—not only his own opinions but others too, and not only opinions concerning ways of life but also, and even more so, opinions regarding God and the soul. When he decided to expand his project in this way, he did not foresee *how much* "more painful" his reform would be—not during the inquiry but afterward, and not owing to the views he would adopt but to his publication of those views. Yet even had he been aware of these consequences, it seems doubtful that he would have been deterred from undertaking the review. For the need to examine his opinions had become clear and compelling, owing at least in part to a "great revolution which had just taken place in me; another moral world which was unveiling itself to my observations" (9).

A great revolution. We've already noted the meaning of this term and the momentousness of the change to which it refers. As in the *Second Discourse*, so in the *Reveries* Rousseau speaks of multiple revolutions but only one "*great* revolution." As in the *Second Discourse*, so in the *Reveries* the "great revolution" refers to a fundamental change with respect to personal dependence; and personal dependence, we recall, is the most decisive influence on one's happiness and moral well-being. The "great revolution" of the *Second Discourse* occurred when the invention of metallurgy and agriculture, by making specialization of labor profitable and therefore necessary, brought about ever-increasing and irreversible personal dependence. The "great revolution" of the *Reveries* refers to an equally dramatic step in the opposite direction. Rousseau suggests that with his personal reform he overcame his psychic dependence on others—not entirely, and not as much as he (i.e., the narrator) even now supposes, but very considerably. By recounting it immediately after describing his reform of "external things," he even suggests that his own "great revolution," though an inner or psychic turn, was precipitated by external factors.

By undertaking his personal reform and taking up arms so openly against both the ancien régime and the new regime that was seeking to supplant it—by attacking both the ecclesiastical dogmatism of the church and the atheistic dogmatism of the *philosophes*[13]—Rousseau provoked such enmity in these parties as to ensure that, however much he might have reduced his psychic dependence, his remaining vulnerability would be sorely exploited. The persecution orchestrated by the one camp and the conspiracy spun by the other would lead to the intense anxiety and despondency that we've already encountered (particularly in the Second Walk). It is my contention that Rousseau will overcome personal dependence to a much fuller extent when he takes the decisive step toward being a more perfect philosopher in the Seventh Walk. Even then, as we've noted, he won't have ceased to be vulnerable: amour-propre will persist and will sometimes become inflamed. But even if his amour-propre will remain troublesome, as by its nature perhaps it must, it will no longer exercise tyranny over him.

Revolutions aren't meant to last indefinitely. Rousseau's purpose, he says, had been to "*settle*" his opinions "once and for all" (13).[14] This set-

---

13. That the church was dogmatic needs no explaining. That the modern philosophers were "ardent missionaries of atheism and very imperious dogmatists" is Rousseau's explicit contention (III, 11). That both camps regarded Rousseau with ire is indicated throughout the *Reveries* and is confirmed by the historic record.

14. "Fixons une bonne fois mes opinions, mes principes, et soyons pour le reste de ma vie ce que j'aurai trouvé devoir être après y avoir bien pensé."

tling would require philosophic inquiry, but its purpose was to foreclose the need for a philosophic *life*. And yet a philosophic life ensued—and continues even now. The severe examination recounted in the Third Walk has not ended. Rousseau has continued to live a life of radical inquiry. He has continually *chosen* to do so. Or perhaps the truth is closer to the opposite—perhaps he didn't choose the philosophic life so much as the philosophic life chose him. So much the better. For if Rousseau has led a philosophic life out of necessity, the necessity has been a natural one, a necessity of his own nature, and far more a joyful necessity than a dreadful or tedious one—this notwithstanding his countless claims to the contrary and his continued disassociation of himself from "philosophy." Nowhere in this account does Rousseau claim that his reform is philosophic, let alone the beginning of a philosophic life. As he had in paragraph 5, he again speaks explicitly of philosophers only in order to criticize them. This time the critique focuses not on motive but on effect: "Instead of removing my doubts and ending my irresolution, they had shaken all the certainty I thought I had concerning the things that were most important for me to know. Ardent missionaries of atheism and very imperious dogmatists, there was no way that they would, without anger, put up with anyone daring to think other than they did about any point whatever" (11). Yet Rousseau aims the present critique only at *modern* philosophers, whom he specifically contrasts with their ancient predecessors. The exemption of the ancients from this critique is most instructive for our purposes, for it makes more plausible the idea that Rousseau considers himself a philosopher after all—a *true* philosopher as Socrates and Plato were true philosophers. Again, the suggestion is only implicit. His explicit position is that his inquiry was a matter of painful necessity meant to spare him the need for further such inquiry. But what is implicit is not unclear. Rousseau has a philosophic nature. Since childhood he has longed "to know the nature and destination of [his] being" (5). There can be no denying that in devoting himself to questions of God and the soul, he was devoting himself to the development and expression of this nature and thereby initiating a philosophic life much in the spirit of the classical philosophers.

This notwithstanding Rousseau's *divergences* from his classical predecessors. The classical philosophers emphasized the transpersonal nature of truth and thus the philosopher's need to overcome the partiality that arises from personality. Rousseau, on the other hand, was as palpably present in his own works as Plato was *absent* from his. And yet the distance between Rousseau and the classical philosophers on this matter is more apparent than real. And upon examination the distance is closed from both sides of the divide. Plato, who has Socrates speak of eternal forms and the Good in itself, gives the attentive reader cause to wonder whether the forms and the Good are anything more than problems or presumptions implicit in speech. And to work toward a more adequate opinion about the Good, the philosopher has no recourse but to examine how the universal desire for the Good is variously experienced by particular human beings—which means that the philosopher cannot hope to move toward a more adequate opinion of the Good except by examining private and partial passions. The same logic is at work in the *Reveries*. By examining himself and his own *naturel*, Rousseau uncovers *human* nature. He does not claim to "strip naked [men's] nature" as he claimed to have done in the *Second Discourse* (see *Confessions*, 388–89; 326). But that's just as well, since human nature never *is* naked. It is always embodied and clothed, and there is no end to the multiplicity and diversity of bodies and clothing. This is why philosophy can never complete itself and why Rousseau's example is so valuable. By finding in his private experience a pathway to universals, he shows how other solitary walkers might do the same. And yet if the *what* of Rousseau's inquiries, if the focus of his attention, is inevitably particular and even idiosyncratic, the *how*, by which I mean his way of questioning, is universal. This is nowhere more clearly seen, if we only look, than in his oblique depiction of the beginning of the philosophic life here in the Third Walk. For what he presents is an articulation of the beginning of the philosophic life *as such*. The tasks that mark the beginning of *his* philosophic life are the same tasks that constitute the beginning of *any* philosophic life—and not only the beginning, but the duration. Rousseau's account in paragraphs 7 through 16 is less an account of what he did during his first months as a philosopher than an account of what the philosophic life needs if it is truly to be a philosophic life and not merely an episode. One element in particular, one *task*, stands out from his account. This task, besides being essential to the philosophic life, also ensures that the philosophic life will be a life of *political* philosophy. Namely, one must continually examine and *justify* the philosophic life in the face of all that opposes it. The philosopher as philosopher can never simply take for granted either philosophy's intrinsic goodness or its relation to society. One must perform both a "severe examination" of oneself and a "great review" of the moral needs on whose fulfillment society depends.

If the universal (the philosophic life as such) must be apprehended by way of particulars (one's own philosophic life), some particulars are more illuminating than others. This would explain why *Rousseau has altered or invented particulars*. The story he tells in the Third Walk is at variance with what he had previously reported in the *Confessions* and with what we know from the historic record. Neither the *Confessions* nor any other source (to my knowledge) mentions his supposedly long-held intention to undertake major reform at age forty. And the vivid story told in the *Confessions* (and the *Letters to Malesherbes*), the so-called Illumination at Vincennes, is conspicuously absent from and effectively contradicted by the *Reveries*. This is the story wherein, at age *thirty-seven* (i.e., not forty), Rousseau was struck *spontaneously and by chance* (i.e., not in accord with a long-held intention) by the insight on which all his subsequent thought would be based (*Confessions* 350–51; 294; *Letters to Malesherbes*, 1135–36; 575). Why has Rousseau rewritten his story, particularly when many readers are sure to notice that he has done so? One reason may have less to do with the omission of the Illumination of Vincennes than with what the omission allows him to do—namely, to set the beginning of his personal transformation at age forty. Forty, as it happens, is a number with much resonance in the spiritual history of the West—not in Plato or the classical tradition, however, but in the Bible. And not only forty, but forty *years*. Forty years is the time it took for a band of slaves to become a free people under the leadership of one whom Rousseau regards as a world-historic Legislator (Numbers 14:33; *SC*, 383–84; 156–57). And according to Christian tradition, Moses was forty years old when he fled Egypt for the wilderness (Acts 7:22–33).

There is one more feature of the second subsection that we'd do well to examine before moving on. Rousseau says he had anticipated that a rigorous review of his opinions would lead to painful doubts. This seems believable enough—except that he had previously been no stranger to doubt yet, as far as we can tell, had not suffered for it. Although he had reached age forty "without any principles determined by [his] reason" (6), "carelessness and . . . peace of mind [had] always constituted [his] most dominant pleasure and *most lasting propensity*" (7; emphasis added). Why should doubt and uncertainty begin to bother him now? Perhaps he only now came to see what was at stake; perhaps doubt incurred by philosophy is uniquely troubling. But perhaps Rousseau is also, or alternatively, saying something about a certain *kind* of philosophy.

It is in paragraphs 11 and 12 that Rousseau first reports that he was pained by doubt. He points an accusing finger: "They had not persuaded me, but they had troubled me." The *they* in question are *modern philosophers*, among whom he was then living: "Instead of removing my doubts and ending my irresolution, they had shaken all the certainty I thought I had concerning the things that were most important for me to know" (11). But the modern philosophers couldn't have taken away from Rousseau a certainty he hadn't had to begin with. What, then? My suggestion: they may have inspired in him a felt need for certainty that he hadn't theretofore felt. They may have taught him that he needed to *know* things that, until then, he had been satisfied merely to opine. They may have taught him that, concerning God and the soul, neither faith nor probabilistic reasoning can suffice—and that neither faith nor probabilistic reason *need* suffice since rational certainty has been made possible by Descartes and the new philosophy he had launched. Now Descartes had not inculcated in human beings a need for certainty that hadn't previously been felt. But he had purported to show that certainty about God and the soul, the need for which had surely been deepened and intensified by Christianity, could be achieved by reason. The promise of certainty will in itself make *uncertainty* less tolerable. In this segment of the Third Walk, then, Rousseau presents a sort of symbolic telling, in the guise of a memoir, of the story of modern philosophy and its effects on humanity. Whether his doubts really made him suffer, and why, is finally unknowable. But we do know—at any rate he shows us—that his story took him far from where the modern philosophers would have had it go. Like the ancient philosophers whom he is so careful to distinguish from the moderns, Rousseau is a zetetic skeptic, neither claiming nor suffering for lack of Cartesian certainty.[15]

In the third subsection of the Third Walk's second section (paragraphs 17 through 24), Rousseau articulates the limits of his capacity as a knower and indeed the limits of human reason. He acknowledges that he has never been able to refute "powerful objections" to his beliefs about God and the soul. Strangely, or perhaps not so strangely, with this critique of reason he offers consolation to those who, unlike him, suffer for the lack of certainty regarding God and His justice. For the critique of reason opens space for a rationally oriented *faith*. The same rationality that can't overcome powerful objections to his purported beliefs about God and the soul nevertheless lends support to those beliefs—first, by determining that every other set of beliefs or convictions, including atheism, is also beset by insuperable objections; and, second, by making a theoretical argument in favor of according weight to sentiment in this domain. The faith I'm referring to is that which is articulated in "The Profession of Faith of the Savoyard Vicar," which, he says, is approximately (*à peu près*) his own. The genius of "The Profession of Faith of the Savoyard Vicar" is to make a *reasoned*

15. There is strong reason to suspect that Descartes too was a skeptic, and it is quite plausible that Rousseau would have seen this. On Descartes (without reference to Rousseau), see Kennington, "Essays on Descartes"; and Lampert, *Nietzsche and Modern Times*, 238–49.

argument in favor of appealing to *sentiment*. Rather than trying to meet the need of the suffering skeptic, the Profession attempts to *dissolve* that need, or at least dilute its intensity.

Isn't this an embrace of wishful thinking after all, the determined skeptic might ask? To which Rousseau might answer: no more so than is a starving man's correct intuition that an unknown food will sustain rather than kill him. The determined skeptic might persist in holding that these are inadequate grounds to make a choice, and that one must resolve to remain undecided if an airtight rational argument cannot be made on behalf of any position. But this rational position is rational only for those who are *capable* of remaining undecided. How many of us meet that description? Many who claim to be skeptics are in fact dogmatic nonbelievers. So, at least, Rousseau claims—not implausibly, it seems to me. Thus Rousseau, who says he can no longer recall the reasoning by which he arrived at his beliefs, reports that he has resolved to hold on to them all the same (23). For they give him "self-contentment" and "the hope and consolation" that he needs (24). The critic, again, might hold that Rousseau has all but confessed that he clings to his beliefs only because they are comforting rather than because they are true. To which Rousseau might reply, again, that in certain cases comfort can be a sign of truth. And he might add—this from the standpoint of the most philosophic disposition, in consonance with Plato—that those who find comfort in a certain kind of faith are apt to be more philosophic, not to mention more philanthropic, than those who deny themselves such faith and thereby fall prey to demoralization and resentment.

THIRD SECTION: PARAGRAPH 25

Rousseau continues to elaborate the limits of our capacity to know in paragraph 25, the final paragraph and in itself the final section of the Third Walk. He begins as follows: "Confined thus within the narrow sphere of my former knowledge, I do not share with Solon the happiness of being able to learn each day while growing old and I even ought to keep myself from the dangerous pride of wanting to learn what I am henceforth unable to know well." As he has since the *First Discourse*, Rousseau emphasizes the moral perils that attend learning. Not all learning is equally perilous, however, and not all perils are equally to be avoided. This too Rousseau has maintained since the *First Discourse*. Learning that promises to be *useful*, even if it is not without peril, might be worth the risk. Is there any learning that could be useful to a solitary nearing the end of his life? In fact there is. In paragraph 3 Rousseau had spoken about learning to die. Here in paragraph 25 he answers the question, or at least approaches the answer, differently: "if few acquisitions remain for me to hope for in the way of useful insights, very important ones remain for me to make in the way of the virtues necessary for my condition." The prospect of cultivating virtue so late in life would seem unlikely. Even if we discount the claim that his intellectual vigor has waned, surely the weight of habit, the weight against which it is virtue's task to push, will only have increased with the passing of so many years. But perhaps Rousseau *can* hope to make additional acquisitions in the way of the virtues necessary for his condition, for the virtue that he still needs is not moral virtue à la Aristotle and thus does not require that he overcome long-standing habit. In fact, prior habit is his *ally* in this effort: being a philosopher, his chief habit is thinking. And as it happens, the way to acquire the virtues that he still needs is through *learning*. And so Rousseau, who has just elaborated on his incapacity for knowledge—and who proceeds even here, in the final paragraph of the Third Walk, to condemn the "wretchedness" and "waste" of our vaunted learning—resolves to devote the rest of his life to the "unique and useful study" of the virtues necessary for his condition.

What precisely *is* his condition, and what virtues are necessary for it? To the first question three possible answers are available. The first is the answer that Rousseau has explicitly stressed: he is an old man, nearing death. The second is something he hasn't stated explicitly but that he has communicated extensively throughout the *Reveries* and with particular force in paragraphs 3 and 4 of the Third Walk: he is a philosopher. The third is suggested by the narrative: his condition is like that of one who has just embarked on the philosophic life in that he still needs to perfect his philosophic life. Each of these answers is true, and there is no need to select one above the others, for the answer to the second question, the question of what virtues are necessary for his condition, is the same regardless of which answer we choose to the first question. We have already seen the answer to the second question: "if there is any study still appropriate for an old man"—to which we may add, if there is any study appropriate for the philosopher and especially one setting out on the philosophic life— "it is solely to learn to die" (3). We've already noted the dual meaning of "learning to die." But *how* does one learn to die? In what does this learning consist? This is communicated in paragraph 25, where we left off. Rousseau lists five virtues that he would still do well to acquire: "patience, sweetness, resignation, integrity, and impartial justice." Notice that these are all virtues of character, though not the sort that pertain to particular passions (as courage, for example, pertains to fear and confidence) and thus not the sort that need to be habituated in us by outside tutelary forces. Even resignation is a virtue of character, at least in part. We have seen the difficulty of attaining and sustaining resignation through rational conviction alone. The way to sustained resignation requires that one's rational conviction be joined and supported by certain dispositions of character that rational people can cultivate on their own. "It is to this unique and useful study that I devote the rest of my old age."

Is Rousseau not too old for this unique and useful study? We should hardly assume so. One who could write this book is not old in the decisive respect, whatever his tally of years. And in any case these virtues are needed by everyone, especially the philosopher and perhaps *most* especially the new or aborning philosopher.

That Rousseau is writing for philosophers and perhaps especially for fledgling or aspiring philosophers is indicated by the shape of his narrative. Consider the arc of the Third Walk, whose "severe examination" or "great review" culminates not in the embrace of beliefs about God and the soul (beliefs that are never even explicated) but in "learning to die." But what this means upon reflection is that Rousseau's examination or review never really culminates at all, for learning to die means living the philosophic life. Also consider the arc of the *Reveries* as a whole and the Third Walk's part in it. With its account of Rousseau's severe examination, and by presenting this examination as a decisive moment in his life, the Third Walk highlights the caesura between the philosophic life and whatever kind of nonphilosophic life might have preceded it. This caesura marks not only a new condition or state of being but also a new kind of becoming: although the first-time reader will not yet be in a position to see it, the steps indicated in the Third Walk—the step into the philosophic life and the first steps within it—are the first of an ongoing series of continuous steps across a terrain that, though sometimes quite pleasing and often well lit, can also be more than a little cave-like.

Finally, consider again the virtues listed in paragraph 25: "patience, sweetness, resignation, integrity, and impartial justice." Resignation, which occupies the central place on the list, is a quality that he has long attributed to the wise. By placing it amid these other virtues he suggests its relation to them. On the basis of what we've learned so far from the *Reveries*, resignation can be seen as the *result* of patience and sweetness and, in turn, the *source* of integrity and impartial justice. Of the virtues listed, moreover, resignation is the one with the greatest intellectual component. For Rousseau as for other philosophers as well as for many deeply religious people, resignation properly understood, resignation to necessity, is wisdom: it is practical wisdom born of theoretical insight. That is why philosophers—who after all *love* wisdom more than they *possess* it—will continue to work at securing and perfecting resignation. For Rousseau and perhaps for other philosophers, the continued perfection of the philosophic life depends on the continued perfection of resignation. Resignation to necessity includes—perhaps it begins with—resignation to the compelling character of the apparent good. It is important to remember that resignation to the compelling character of the apparent good does not mean resignation to the power of any *particular* apparent good. That is why resignation or radical acceptance can be seen, as Rousseau saw them, not as the abrogation of freedom but rather its beginning.

Faith and the Philosopher

For Rousseau as for Plato, the philosophic life requires a prior moral foundation, and this moral foundation requires a foundation in belief. For Rousseau as for Plato, teachings about virtue and the divine (*Reveries* III, *Republic* 3) that will later be superseded by a truer teaching (*Reveries* VII, *Republic* 7) prepare the student for that very teaching. Socrates does not address all the virtues in book 3, and still less so does Rousseau in the Third Walk. In each case a single virtue is emphasized—the *same* virtue: "For the first time in my life I had *courage*" (15). As he presents it, "the horrible fate" that would require courage of Rousseau would not be anything intrinsic to philosophy but rather the enmity that his philosophizing—his published and therefore *public* philosophizing—would elicit from others. Rousseau makes no explicit comment about courage being necessary for or even helpful to philosophizing per se. Yet the structure and sequence of the narrative suggest that he did need courage in order to embark on the philosophic life, for he indicates that what *summoned forth* his courage was nothing other than the demands of philosophic inquiry. The first appearance of "courage" in the book—and the first appearance of courage in Rousseau's *life*—occur in response to the acute challenges posed by his inquiry into God and the soul. It is in paragraph 14 that these challenges are articulated, and it is at the beginning of paragraph 15 that courage makes it appearance. It is worth reading the entirety of paragraph 14 and the beginning of paragraph 15:

> I carried out this project slowly and with various fresh starts, but with all the effort and all the attention of which I was capable. I felt intensely that the tranquility of the remainder of my days and my total lot depended on it. At first I found myself in such a labyrinth of encumbrances, difficulties, objections, twistings, and darkness that, twenty times tempted to abandon everything, I was ready to renounce such a futile quest and to abide by the rules of common prudence in my

deliberations without seeking for anything more in principles I had so much trouble unraveling. But this very prudence was so foreign to me, I felt myself so unlikely to acquire it, that to take it for my guide was nothing other than to want to seek—across seas and storms, without a rudder or compass—an almost inaccessible lighthouse which pointed out no harbor for me.

I persisted. For the first time in my life I had courage . . .

As direct as it is, Rousseau's acknowledgment of the significance of courage to philosophy quickly recedes into the background. Rousseau *makes* it recede into the background by the way in which he completes the sentence that I have just truncated. Here are the sentences in their entirety: "I persisted. For the first time in my life I had courage, and to its success I owe having been able to endure the horrible fate which from that time began to envelop me without my having had the least suspicion of it." By turning to his coming "horrible fate" immediately after mentioning his courage—literally, within the same sentence—Rousseau directs the reader's attention away from courage's part in making it possible for him to undertake truly philosophic inquiry. Yet the redirection of attention does not erase the thing from which attention has been directed away. There can be little doubting the importance of courage to his embarking on the philosophic life. And given that the inquiry with which he began his philosophic life would prove unending—not a task to be completed so much as an ever deeper foray into a world he would never leave—there can be little doubting the importance of courage to the philosophic life altogether, not just the beginning but the whole of it, though perhaps the need is most urgent at the start. In indicating the centrality of courage to the philosophic life, Rousseau reminds one of Socrates, who twice in the *Republic* places courage at the center of a list of qualities belonging to the philosophic nature (485a–486d, 489e–490d). And with his enumeration of the "labyrinth of encumbrances, difficulties, objections, twistings, and darkness" that made courage necessary in the first place, he reminds us of Socrates's Image of the Cave. (It is also worth noting how vividly he anticipates Nietzsche. All that's missing is the "Minotaur of conscience" lurking within the labyrinth.)[16]

Rousseau resonates with Plato (and Nietzsche) in yet another way. He not only credits courage for girding him against such challenges as those just cited; he also seems to suggest that courage stoked the fire of his intellectual eros. Only a few lines after speaking of his courage he characterizes

16. Nietzsche, *Beyond Good and Evil*, section 29.

his inquiry into God and the soul as "the most *ardent* and sincere seeking that has perhaps ever been made by any mortal" (15; emphasis added).

Yet even if Rousseau the narrator gives voice here to philosophic eros, he seems not yet to have taken the philosophic turn. At least he seems not to have *completed* the philosophic turn. This is shown in the very sentence from which I just quoted—again, only in part. Here is the whole of the sentence: "After the most ardent and most sincere seeking that has perhaps ever been made by any mortal, I determined for my whole life all the sentiments important for me to have; and though I may have deceived myself in my conclusions, I am at least sure that my error cannot be imputed to me as a crime, for I made every effort to keep myself from it" (15). This hardly seems the voice of a philosopher. A philosopher, one would hope, would not be given to such pathos and self-drama as we hear in Rousseau's superlative claim ("the most ardent and sincere seeking that has perhaps ever been made by *any* mortal"). Nor would a true philosopher have been so eager to find final answers and thus be spared the need to philosophize ever again ("I determined for my whole life"). Finally, and perhaps most revealingly, a true philosopher giving a truthful account of himself would not feel the need to offer anything like Rousseau's preemptive self-defense: "my error cannot be imputed to me as a crime, for I made every effort to keep myself from it." This kind of apologia is a telltale sign of the ordinary moral consciousness and its special queasiness when accused of thought crimes. Rather than a description of the philosophic life as the philosopher experiences it, the passage we've been examining—indeed the Third Walk as a whole—is perhaps best regarded as a description of the philosophic life from the standpoint of the ordinary moral consciousness. As the *Reveries* progresses Rousseau will unfold a more self-respecting account of philosophy if not an altogether frank one.

And yet even here, where the narrator depicts philosophic inquiry as something he undertook more for the sake of living than for the sake of living well, the author points to the truth about philosophy. "Ardent and sincere seeking" bespeaks eros, a *philosophic* eros ignited by wonder and drawn more to questions than to answers. And the narrator's self-dramatization—"the most ardent and sincere seeking that has perhaps *ever* been made by *any* mortal"—can be read as the author signifying the truth about the philosophic life in a particularly Platonic way. This will take a bit of explanation.

Plato links philosophy and immortality in multiple places and in multiple ways. In the *Symposium* he has Socrates recount Diotima's claim that the true lover, by which is meant the philosopher, can partake of the immortal to such an extent that, having followed the right path to its end, "it lies within him to become dear to god and, if it is possible for any human being, to become immortal as well" (212a). But *is* it possible for a human being to become immortal? Or is Diotima's qualification ("*if* it is possible") a reminder that it is *not* possible for a mortal to become immortal? Of course, the reader has already been told that Eros, being a daemon rather than a god, is neither mortal nor immortal but rather in between, both by virtue of shuttling messages back and forth between mortal men and the immortal gods and by periodically dying and then being reborn. But this is more artful than reasonable, for there *is* no position in between mortality and immortality. What then does Plato mean to teach?

Perhaps this:[17] If there is no condition or state of being *between* mortality and immortality, there is something *apart* from them—namely, eternity. Eternity, moreover—that is, the *experience* of eternity—may be the aim or the true object of eros and the core of philosophy and the philosophic life, as we've already briefly discussed. But we can't recognize it as such so long as we can't see beyond the horizon imposed by "our nature in its education and want of education" (*Republic*, 514a), which is maintained by thymos or amour-propre. While we are within this horizon we dimly divine eternity as the object of eros, but we interpret it, or rather misinterpret it, as immortality. Yet this misinterpretation is not for naught, for it would seem that in order to be open to the call of eternity, we must first have come to terms with mortality and our dread thereof. This would explain why Plato has Socrates speak of immortality rather than of eternity. Eternity, though the true name of eros's quarry, is unlikely to appeal to an eros fixated on immortality.

And Rousseau? It seems to me that, in the sentence we've been examining, he does the same thing that Plato does: he too uses "immortality" as a stand-in for "eternity." Sometimes Rousseau does speak of eternity or timelessness by its real name, such as when he describes the experience that belongs to a certain kind of reverie: "time is nothing for [the soul]; ... the present lasts forever without, however, making its duration noticed and without any trace of time's passage" (V, 14). Later I will try to show that what Rousseau signifies in this passage and in the Fifth Walk generally is the centrality of eternity to philosophy, which is a view I also take to be Plato's. In the passage at hand there is no reference to eternity. But if Rousseau does regard eternity as core to philosophy, as Plato does, then we should consider that he might join Plato in employing "immortality"

17. The following brief account is based on an argument I made in chapter 3 of *Eros in Plato*.

as a stand-in for "eternity." So let's do that: let's hypothesize that when he speaks of immortality, Rousseau might be speaking of eternity. Now notice the result: his seemingly overblown and melodramatic formulation is no longer overblown and melodramatic but is simply true. His truth seeking really *was* the most ardent and sincere seeking that has ever been done by a mortal, for to seek more ardently than he did at the moment he is recalling, that is, at the threshold of the philosophic life, would require that the seeker be, so to speak, more than mortal—no, not immortal, but one who has accepted mortality and overcome the ordinary moral consciousness and thus escaped from the fretfulness of those who have not. The seeker I am describing, of course, is the philosopher, both for Plato and, as I have tried to show, for Rousseau as well. Where others seek immortality in one way or another, the philosopher seeks—with some success—to "behold" or "contemplate" and thereby "be together with" the eternal. What initially seemed dramatic exaggeration is in fact an oblique account of real drama: Rousseau's seeking, the most ardent and sincere truth seeking by any mortal, was the seeking of one who was in the process of becoming a philosopher, a daemon, a mortal being engaging eternity and thus, in a sense, in between mortality and immortality after all. Such a being, having experienced eternity—to the extent that this experience stays with him—will have no need for *faith* in eternity.

Faith and Society

We have already examined the ways in which the *Reveries* shows itself to have a keen political consciousness and even a certain political intention. Having been through the Third Walk we may now extend the earlier analysis in two ways. First, by recounting his purported inquiry into God and the soul and by pointing to "The Profession of Faith of the Savoyard Vicar," Rousseau helps his readers toward an ease of mind necessary for virtue, particularly the virtue of courage. In this he performs a service—not only for those who might eventually set out on the philosophic life, but for society as a whole.

Second, by reminding us that it was he who had "recorded" "The Profession of Faith of the Savoyard Vicar" and brought it to the world, Rousseau tacitly acknowledges that he had formerly assumed the part of the Legislator and thus indicates that we might read the *Reveries* as the memoir of a Philosopher-Legislator. In the *Social Contract* he had articulated the Legislator's task and what is required to perform that task. In *Emile* he had articulated what he perhaps regarded as the education best suited to the future Legislator.[18] Here in the *Reveries* he articulates the Philosopher-Legislator's self-understanding. He never explicitly acknowledges any such type as the Philosopher-Legislator, but it's not clear that anyone *but* a philosopher could realize the qualities he attributes to the Legislator as such: "a superior intelligence, who saw all of men's passions yet experienced none of them; whose happiness was independent of us, yet who was nevertheless willing to attend to ours; finally one who, preparing for himself a future glory with the passage of time, could work in one century and enjoy the reward in another" (*SC*, 381–38; 154–57). Many readers will remember the line that immediately follows: "Gods would be needed to give laws to men." Fortunately, gods have been available: "the fathers of nations" have always had "recourse to the intervention of heaven" and have been able to credibly "attribute their own wisdom to the gods." Rousseau, to be sure, never claims to have been vouchsafed divine revelation. But in "The Profession of Faith of the Savoyard Vicar" he purports to show that no such revelation is needed after all. Reason alone will suffice. It will yield a faith like that of the Vicar. Thus Rousseau acts the part of prophet after all, as prior Legislators had. Like them, he propounds a new teaching about God and His relation to us in order to form a new people.

Do Rousseau's insights into the Philosopher-Legislator offer anything useful for us, who have no aspiration to follow his model? But modeling isn't the only purpose of a memoir. By reflecting on his work or even just on himself, a Legislator might instruct us in how to secure or renew what he has made. He offers access to his capacious understanding of politics, particularly if we understand by *politics*—and has it ever been better understood?—"the art whose business it is to care for souls" (Plato, *Laws*, 650b).

By discovering that Rousseau treats the life and soul of the Legislator in the seemingly apolitical *Reveries*, we have taken an additional step in apprehending the book's kinship with the obviously political *Republic*. An even further step becomes possible upon recognizing that if the *Reveries* is not an *essentially* political book, *neither is the Republic*. Both books hold as their highest concern the life of philosophy and the souls of those who might live that life. Yet this *highest* concern should not and indeed cannot be abstracted from *broader* concerns. By addressing the philosophic life,

---

18. The education depicted in *Emile*, however impracticable as a model, instills or rather safeguards the development of independence of mind, a philanthropic disposition, and other qualities belonging to the idealized Legislator of the *Social Contract*.

Rousseau and Plato don't speak only to the few who might aspire to it. They also speak to the greater number of those who, though not aspirants to the philosophic life, might still learn from philosophy and even take their bearings from it. Among their number are many who might play a great part in politics and culture.

✳ CHAPTER 6 ✳

Being a Philosopher
Fourth, Fifth, and Sixth Walks

The first three Walks of the Reveries called for particularly intensive examination because each in some way constitutes a beginning. The First Walk is the beginning of the book and the beginning of a philosophic inquiry. The next two Walks articulate the beginning of the philosophic life—its origin in a certain kind of soul, or its *archē* (Second Walk), and its initial unfolding or its beginning in time (Third Walk). We may permit ourselves to examine the remaining Walks a bit less intensively—still with care, but from an altitude that permits a more spacious view—for the thrust of Rousseau's further development as a philosopher is continuous with the beginnings explored in the first three Walks. The philosopher continues to *become*, yes; but he continues to become a philosopher.

Our focus concerning the remaining Walks will be on that which speaks directly to Rousseau's continued perfection as a philosopher. In the Fourth and Sixth Walks we will see how the philosopher engages the larger world. In the Fifth Walk we will attend to the timelessness of philosophy and philosophizing. In the Seventh and Eighth Walks we will investigate the breakthrough that marks the climax of the *Reveries*, that is, Rousseau's discovery of how better to govern his sight (Seventh Walk) and the self-knowledge that follows from this clearer seeing (Eighth Walk). This makes of the Ninth and Tenth Walks something of a denouement. In the Ninth Walk we will witness Rousseau's reappraisal of solitude and sociability. This reappraisal both reflects and facilitates a better understanding, and therewith a better experience, of both solitude and sociability. For such progress one might be grateful. Accordingly, Rousseau's theme in the Tenth Walk, and therefore ours as well, will be gratitude.

Fourth Walk

The Fourth Walk presents the most sustained recognizably philosophic inquiry in the *Reveries*, and not only because the Fourth Walk is the book's longest chapter. Part of what makes this Walk more recognizably philosophic than the others is that Rousseau *presents* it as a philosophic inquiry. He announces at the outset an inquiry into truthfulness and lying. Although prompted by a random happening—or, rather, by Rousseau's questionable interpretation of a random happening—the inquiry is conducted with evident purpose and care. (The random happening is Rousseau's discovery of a certain remark made by a professed admirer whom he immediately takes to be a malicious detractor.) The Fourth Walk, besides being the most evidently rigorous of the *Reveries'* ten Walks, is also the most obviously duplicitous—which is fitting, for it is here, in his inquiry into truthfulness and lying, that Rousseau makes the case for permissible and perhaps even obligatory falsehoods.

Rousseau's qualified defense of falsehood effectively instructs us to read the *Reveries* with the greatest care, especially when we encounter passages so emotionally compelling that we might be tempted to an overhasty conclusion, and *most* especially where he acknowledges the powerful allure of wishful thinking—as he does, for example, in discussing his purported religious beliefs in Third Walk. (The juxtaposition of his religious profession and his discourse on truthfulness and lying is no accident.)

If we should bring especial care to passages that we find emotionally compelling, we should do the same regarding passages that we find emotionally *repelling*. So Rousseau suggests, albeit very subtly. Late in the Fourth Walk he observes that he had deliberately painted himself in an inaccurately bad light in various parts of the *Confessions*:

> far from having kept silent about anything or concealed anything which went against me, by a twist of mind which I have difficulty explaining to myself and which perhaps comes from my estrangement from all imitation, I felt myself more readily inclined to lie in the contrary sense by accusing myself with too much severity than by excusing myself with too much indulgence; and my conscience assures me that one day I will be judged less severely than I have judged myself. (31)

Readers might wonder about a writer's claim that he had lied to his own disadvantage in a previous book. Why should we believe that it was the former book rather than the present one that is dishonest? But unless we are prepared to convict Rousseau without a hearing, we ought to accept that he might indeed have libeled himself in the *Confessions*. And we ought to remain open to the unstated but equally valid possibility that he libels himself in the *Reveries* too—if not by withholding facts, then by repeatedly depicting himself as touchy, plaintive, self-dramatizing, and even paranoid, and not only in the remembered past but also "now," as he tells his story. Does Rousseau not know how readers are likely to judge an author who claims he had endured "the saddest lot a mortal has ever undergone" (VII, 30)? Remarks in this vein—and they are legion—seem aimed at soliciting sympathy, which they undoubtedly do in many readers. But these same readers, or some of them, are likely to feel impatience and distaste as well. And others are likely to bypass sympathy altogether and go straight to contempt. Did Rousseau not see this? That is the question. Is he unknowingly displaying a grating self-pity and self-importance? Or is he knowingly depicting a character, the narrator, whose discourse reveals for examination the distortions of mind and character familiar to us all as the telltale signs of inflamed amour-propre? Such a question can be adequately addressed only by considering the broad context of the book as a whole. My own answer will come as no surprise. I find in the *Reveries*, especially its final third, sufficient insight and self-awareness to regard the narrator's *lack* of insight and self-awareness in the earlier Walks as the author's literary-philosophic device—or, to put it in terms provided in the Fourth Walk, as a fiction rather than a lie. It is entirely plausible that the author of the *Reveries* would have deployed such a device in order to illustrate the imperfection and the consequent need for further development of one who has taken the philosophic turn. Additional support for this reading is found in the fact that throughout the *Reveries* Rousseau complains far more strenuously even about petty affronts to his amour-propre than about the extensive objective harm he has suffered at the hands of his persecutors.[1] For that matter, even the Fourth Walk's apologetics aren't the apologetics one might expect of a philosopher. Rousseau not only insists that he omitted flattering material from the *Confessions* because it would have cast him in a favorable light; he tells two such anecdotes and claims that he has plucked them from among "a hundred of the same nature" (38). Such apologetics bespeak the kind of needy and insistent self-love that one might have expected the philosopher to have transcended.

By depicting himself in these unflattering ways, Rousseau illustrates for his more careful and perceptive readers the characteristic distortions

---

1. See Gourevitch, "Provisional Reading of Rousseau's *Reveries*," 492.

wrought by inflamed amour-propre even in a philosopher. The example of self-pity and lack of self-awareness that I quoted above ("the saddest lot a mortal has ever undergone") appears late in the Seventh Walk, at which point Rousseau the narrator-protagonist, on my reading, has reached or nearly reached his peak as a philosopher. Thus he shows us that amour-propre and its distortions persist even at this newly achieved elevation. He will also show us that the persistence of this human, all too human vulnerability is not necessarily to be lamented.

The Fourth Walk proceeds not only rigorously but also dialectically. It works its way to a final position by way of positions that are frankly asserted but then superseded. In this the Fourth Walk exemplifies *within itself* a characteristic that we have already noted in the progress from Walk to Walk. Its dialectical character puts the Fourth Walk very much in accord with the ways of classical political philosophy. In many Platonic dialogues Socrates begins an inquiry by affirming an interlocutor's opinion only to move the interlocutor—by examining the opinion and its implications—to a new opinion, and then perhaps to another, and yet another. A likely reason for Socrates proceeding this way is his understanding that one teaches most effectively if one meets the student on the latter's own ground. Another reason, to judge from the progress of so many inquiries, is that common opinion is apt to have some kernel of truth in it. And this kernel in turn is apt to open the way to a further, deeper inquiry. Rousseau's dialectical procedure in the Fourth Walk can be similarly explained. The explicit, animating question of his inquiry is whether he has been as truthful as he has believed himself and has publicly professed to be (1). The inquiry requires him to come to terms with various falsehoods he has told and with his lack of regret for most of them. Like the original opinions of many of Socrates's interlocutors, Rousseau's opinion of himself will be qualified and refined but not simply rejected. And just as Socrates's inquiries into an interlocutor's opinion on a certain matter is apt to open another, more philosophic question, which may in turn open yet another, even more philosophic question, Rousseau's inquiry into his own truthfulness will take him deep into the question of what constitutes truthfulness and lying, which in turn will take him deep into the question of justice.

First, though, the backstory.

"The day before yesterday," on which he happened to have been reading Plutarch's treatise *How to Profit from One's Enemies*, Rousseau came across a pamphlet inscribed by its author, one M. Rosier, with a dedication to him: "Vitam vero impendenti, Rosier," that is, "to the one who consecrates his life to truth" (1). That Rousseau was this "one" couldn't be doubted, since he was known to have adopted as his personal motto the verse from

Juvenal "vitam impendere vero," or "to consecrate one's life to truth."[2] What *could* be doubted, evidently, was the sincerity of Rosier's dedication. Indeed Rousseau immediately "understood" (*compris*) the dedication to have been cruelly ironic. He provides no evidence for this interpretation and gives the reader no reason to believe it. The sole basis of his interpretation is the dedication's "*semblance* of politeness" (emphasis added). His presumption of bad faith on Rosier's part would seem to be yet another indication by the *Reveries*' author that the narrator-protagonist, despite being a philosopher, is still subject to the tendentious distortions of a very touchy moral consciousness. Rousseau responds to Rosier's supposed mockery by determining to follow Plutarch's principle of profiting from one's enemies. In the present case the profit would be self-knowledge, and it would require effort: "I resolved to devote the walk of the following day to examining myself on lying and I came to it quite confirmed in the previously held opinion that the 'know thyself' of the temple of Delphi was not as easy a maxim to follow as I had believed in my *Confessions*" (1).

And now the inquiry itself:

Rousseau begins by recounting "a dreadful lie" that he had told in his "early youth, the memory of which has troubled [him] all his life and even comes in [his] old age to sadden [his] heart again" (2). Those who have read the *Confessions* will recognize that Rousseau is referring to an incident in which he falsely accused a young kitchen maid named Marion of giving him a ribbon that *he*, then a young household servant himself, had stolen (83–87; 70–73). When confronted, he repeated the lie so insistently that both he and Marion were dismissed. He maintains that he had harbored no ill will toward Marion. Indeed, telling the lie went *against* the wishes of his heart:

> considering only how I was disposed while telling it, this lie was simply an effect of mortification; and far from originating from an intention to harm her who was the victim of it, I can swear by Heaven that in the very instant this invincible shame tore it from me, I would joyfully have shed all my blood to turn the consequences on myself alone. This is a delirium I can explain only by saying, and this is what I think and feel, that in that instant my timid natural temperament [*mon naturel timide*] subjugated all the wishes of my heart. (2)

2. Rousseau drew his motto from Juvenal, *Satires*, 4.91. For a brief account of his use of the motto, see Butterworth, trans., *Reveries of the Solitary Walker*, by Rousseau, 59n2. For illuminating reflections on what the motto seems to have meant to him, see Kelly, *Rousseau as Author*, 1–5.

Notice how Rousseau distinguishes here between himself and his shame ("invincible shame tore it from me"), which recalls the story that Socrates tells about a certain Leontius in—yes—book 4 of the *Republic* (439e–440a). Notice too that the conflict in Rousseau is between two expressions of amour-propre: the shame that led him to lie, and the troubling memory that he has lived with ever since. (Here too his story parallels that of Leontius, in which shame battled against the desire to look at what decency forbade looking at.) Rousseau doesn't claim to have overcome his timid natural temperament or his weakness in the face of shame in the years since the Marion episode. But he suggests that his awareness of this weakness has instilled in him, if not greater strength, then something with the same effect: "The memory of this unfortunate act and the inextinguishable regrets it left me have inspired in me a horror for lying that should have preserved my heart from this vice for the rest of my life" (3).

"*Should have* preserved my heart from this vice for the rest of my life." *Has* it? Rousseau is no longer as certain as he once was. "When I adopted my motto," he reports, "I felt deserving of it and I did not doubt I was worthy of it." But upon examining himself he discovered that he has been far freer with untruth than he had supposed: "I was quite surprised at the number of things of my own invention I recalled having passed off as true at the same time that, inwardly proud of my love for truth, I was sacrificing my security, my interests, and myself to it with an impartiality of which I know no other example among human beings" (4). Even more startling than his falsehoods, though, and what will transform this self-scrutiny into a more general philosophic inquiry, is what he noticed next:

> What surprised me the most was that in recalling these fabrications, I felt no true repentance for them. I, in whose heart nothing offsets the horror of a falsehood, I, who would brave punishments if it were necessary to lie to avoid them—by what strange inconsistency did I thus lie with gaiety of heart, unnecessarily, without profit, and by what inconceivable contradiction did I feel not the least regret, I, who for fifty years have not ceased to be afflicted by remorse for a lie? (5)

Rousseau has discovered a glaring discrepancy between his deeds and his principles—or, if one prefers, between how he feels and how he supposes he *should* feel—and he sides with the former. Is this not a rejection of conscience? It is not, for the falsehoods at issue prove on reflection to have been morally permissible or even, in some cases, perhaps morally obligatory. Of course he hadn't reflected so seriously on these falsehoods prior to the current inquiry. But his feelings prove to have been an adequate guide, for they were expressions of natural goodness. Rousseau is keenly aware that natural sentiment can all too easily be overtaken by unnatural passion. He knows that the preservation and recovery of natural goodness in himself is imperfect; and he will readily acknowledge that he has not made up the deficit with virtue (VI, 7). But he deems his goodness robust enough, and his judgment sound enough, to justify taking sentiment as his guide. Is his confidence misplaced? Any evidence we examine in an attempt to answer that question is of course evidence provided by Rousseau himself. But if the evidence has been accurately reported, then there are two bases on which one might deem his confidence justified. First, such wrongs as he has committed as a mature adult have been the result of weakness rather than malice, and temporary weakness at that. His intention has never been malicious. Second, notwithstanding his explicit disavowal of virtue, he lays claim to a quality that we might regard as a virtue after all—and that *he himself* might regard as a virtue. That quality is love of the truth.[3]

Rousseau's trust in his own goodness is apt to strike readers as naive or narcissistic—or both. It is precisely the kind of thing that has earned Rousseau opprobrium from conservatives from Burke to the present day—opprobrium that, in my judgment, has kept these conservatives from seeing how much Rousseau's thought overlaps with and complements theirs. (He never supposes that natural goodness remains remotely as powerful in most others as in himself [*SD*, 202; 74]. Nor does he suppose that natural goodness could be sufficiently revivified in human beings, certainly not by political reform or revolution [*SD*, 187–88; 62]. Rousseau, in short, is not a popular Rousseauan.) His trust in his own goodness also seems to place Rousseau worlds away from the rigorous and unsentimental spirit of classical political philosophy. But appearance in this case is not reality. Rousseau in truth is quite close to the spirit of classical political philosophy. The prerogatives that he exercises on the basis of his presumed goodness are the same ones that the classical philosophers exercised on the basis of their presumed virtue. *His* goodness and *their* virtue yield the same remarkable freedom, which Rousseau calls *natural* freedom.

Aren't goodness and sentiment trustworthy guides only when they haven't been distorted by prejudice and turbulent passion—by, say, the kind of near paranoia that Rousseau evinced in response to Rosier's dedication? Surely so; and *Rousseau clears that bar*—not only Rousseau the author but even Rousseau the narrator-protagonist at this moment, that is,

---

3. Love of truth is informed by strength of soul, which is perhaps the *source* of all virtue. See Rousseau's *Discourse on the Virtue Most Necessary for a Hero*.

when writing the Fourth Walk. The man who speaks from the page is agitated by irrational passion. But this same man demonstrates the presence of mind to stand clear of passion's distortion and see clearly—not in the Fourth Walk's opening paragraph, where he recounts the Rosier episode, but in its forty-one remaining paragraphs. The man—*the philosopher*—who meditates on truth and falsehood with as much penetration and self-awareness as are displayed in those paragraphs is a man who knows how to think and judge clearly when he determines to do so. Indeed, although he is still considerably short of the maturity that he'll ultimately attain, he has made progress toward that end. As yet he hasn't transcended the ordinary moral consciousness in favor of the cognitivist view of morality, certainly not as clearly and securely as he later will; but he is en route to that end. Compare the account of the Marion episode here in the *Reveries* with the version given in the *Confessions*. In the *Reveries* Rousseau acknowledges that he remains "troubled" and "saddened" by what he did to Marion. He exhibits what I would describe as distress born of *regret*. In the *Confessions*, by contrast, he speaks of and from *guilt* and *remorse*. In the *Reveries* Rousseau makes sure to speak of the way in which the episode undergirded *future* improvement. In the *Confessions* we see a man captive to an unchangeable *past*—a man, moreover, who seems to regard the suffering he has experienced in the intervening years as retribution and who claims, though perhaps without fully believing, that between his suffering and his scrupulous behavior he has expiated his sin (*Confessions*, 87; 73).[4] (If the more perfectly philosophic Rousseau feels regret where the less perfectly philosophic Rousseau had felt remorse, what would a *simply* perfect philosopher feel about his own past misdeed? As one who had transcended the ordinary moral consciousness and therewith moral blame, would he even feel personal regret: would he feel any worse about a bad deed of his own than about a bad deed done by another? An important question, and a revealing one. It seems to me that the perfect philosopher would indeed be indifferent to the identity of the doer. But then maybe the "perfect philosopher" would no longer be a philosopher, that is, a lover and pursuer of wisdom, but simply wise—wise like the god of the philosophers, come to think of it. If so, we must conclude—and we must remember—that *true* philosophers are *not perfect* philosophers. They are human beings who were moved to philosophy in the first place because of their finitude and compound nature and who embrace that nature in all its parts, including the moral consciousness.)

4. Regarding the frequently underestimated difference between regret and remorse, see Walter Kaufmann's provocative study *Without Guilt or Justice*, 122–23.

As an inquiry into truthfulness and lying, the Fourth Walk is also, necessarily, an inquiry into justice and injustice. It is only injustice—meaning
a failure to meet an obligation or doing harm—that renders a falsehood a
lie. A falsehood that is not harmful is not a lie but rather, Rousseau determines, a fiction: "everything which, contrary to the truth, hurts justice in
any way whatsoever is a lie. That is the exact limit: but everything which,
though contrary to the truth, in no way concerns justice is only a fiction;
and I confess that anyone who blames himself for a pure fiction as if it
were a lie has a more delicate conscience than I" (20). Thus to determine
what is and isn't a lie Rousseau must determine what justice is. In pursuing this question, the Fourth Walk of the *Reveries* mirrors book 4 of the
Republic, in which justice, the quarry sought by Socrates and his friends,
is finally captured and defined. Indeed, the parallel is more exact than
that, as we can see by considering the structures of the respective texts.
Socrates, having announced at the precise center of book 4 that he and his
fellow hunters had finally cornered justice, proceeds in the first pages of
the second half of book 4 (a) to *define* justice; whereupon, after (b) investigating the question of whether the *city* and the human soul are similarly
structured (they are), he (c) leads his hearty band through an investigation
of justice in the *individual* human being.[5] Rousseau's procedure parallels
Socrates's. Just after the midpoint of the Fourth Walk he examines "the
man [he] calls *truthful*" (23; emphasis in the original), and on this basis
he (a) *defines* justice as truthfulness. Unlike Socrates, Rousseau has not
constructed a city in speech and thus doesn't need to declare what justice
is *except* in the individual. And yet he does comment on another view of
truthfulness, the view held by society's leading lights and which we might
therefore effectively consider (b) *society's* view of justice. But he references
this view only to show that it is wanting and thereby to aid his investigation
into (c) the justice and truthfulness of the just and truthful *man* (23–34).
Chief among this man's characteristics—the thing that animates him and
explains his scrupulous honesty where matters of consequence are concerned and his laxness where justice is not at issue; the thing even deeper
and more determinative than his "ardent love for truth"—is his *love of
justice*, of which his love of truth "is only an emanation" (24). To be sure,
Rousseau never gives as explicit and formulaic a definition of justice as

5. Book 4 of the *Republic* runs from Stephanus page 419a to 445e, or twenty-six pages,
making 432 the midpoint. It is at 432d that Socrates, having just identified wisdom, courage, and moderation, claims to have "caught sight of" justice and then proceeds to define it,
establish its importance to the city, establish that the city and soul are similarly structured,
and explicate what justice means in the soul and how it expresses itself in the just man.

the one Socrates gives in book 4. Yet what Socrates captures and defines isn't really what his companions had been asking for, and it falls far short of his own final position in the dialogue.

But what about the divergence between Rousseau and Socrates concerning the identity and character of the just man? Socrates nominates the philosopher, though this isn't made clear until book 6. Rousseau, by contrast, puts forward . . . himself. That he identifies himself as the just (because truthful) man is clearly indicated at the start of paragraph 25, where, having devoted the entirety of the previous two paragraphs to characterizing the truthful man, he says, "Such were *my* rules of conscience about lying and truth" (emphasis added). I have been arguing, of course, that Rousseau is and understands himself to be a true philosopher. That closes the distance between him and Socrates considerably. Now I would like to close the distance from the other side. Not only is Rousseau a true philosopher; the philosophers described by Socrates are *false* philosophers. By professing knowledge of what is not humanly knowable, they are sophists, either in the literal sense of that word (meaning wise men) or in the colloquial sense (meaning false pretenders to wisdom). Why Plato would have Socrates depict as philosophers those who differ so much from himself is a long question but one whose answer seems to me to begin and end with the thymoeidetic character of the *Republic*. The dialogue's dubious characterization of philosophy and the philosopher is apparent in philosophy's first mention in book 2, where Socrates says that the city's guardians must be philosophic in the same way that *dogs* are philosophic (376a). No less thymoeidetic, and thus no less questionable, is that the dialogue investigates philosophers only in response to the city's purported need for philosopher-*kings*. The *Republic*'s *truly* just man is the true philosopher, who acknowledges his ignorance and is animated by eros for the truth. That man is Socrates.

The *Reveries*' truly just man is also the true philosopher. That man is Rousseau himself. Rousseau holds himself to the standard of the perfectly truthful or perfectly just man, and although he sometimes falls short, his lapses are minimal. He still lies on occasion, but this is "due to embarrassment and mortification" rather than envy, spite, or interest (28). Moreover, the standard by which he judges himself and others hasn't been given to him; he determines it himself—which, as strange as it might sound, is itself a mark of the truthful or just man. (When a sufficiently meticulous and demanding standard is not on offer, the truthful or just man develops it for himself.) To develop such a standard and examine oneself in its light are demanding tasks, tasks befitting a philosopher as understood both by Rousseau and by Socrates. And if Rousseau credibly qualifies as a philosopher à la Socrates's conception, so too does he do justice in the way and in the spirit of Socrates's just man. Socrates's just man conducts himself honestly toward others—not, however, because he disregards his own good but because he understands where his good truly lies (442d–443b). From the standpoint of the ordinary moral consciousness, such justice must seem suspect and unsatisfying, at best only a kind of incidental justice. So too is Rousseau's just man, that is to say, Rousseau himself, peculiarly just. He too conducts himself beneficently toward others because it follows from his resolve to do justice to himself, which is an expression of his natural goodness.

Finally, consider how well Socrates's just man meets Rousseau's criteria of justice and how well Rousseau meets Socrates's criteria of justice, notwithstanding the considerable differences that seem to separate the two conceptions of justice. For both thinkers the just man is truthful, indeed, an ardent lover of truth whose soul is well ordered *by* this love. If Socrates and Rousseau meet one another's criteria so well, that's because their respective conceptions of justice are closer to one another, not to mention less odd, than they appear. Socrates's strange formulation, according to which justice entails everyone doing his or her own job, isn't so strange after all, especially when applied to the soul's various parts or forms. And Rousseau's narrow formulation isn't so narrow after all. Truthfulness, when applied in all respects, means nothing short of a way of life. It is the natural expression of a well-ordered soul—which is to say that Rousseau's formula is the natural expression of Socrates's formula. But truthfulness isn't only the *expression* of a well-ordered soul. If the well-ordered soul is understood to mean the philosopher's soul, truthfulness is also a way, perhaps *the* way, to achieve that good order in the first place. Love of truth is what drives a nonphilosopher to become a philosopher and what drives the one who is already a philosopher, like our protagonist at this stage of his story, to become a more perfect philosopher.

If justice *allows* fictions, does it sometimes *demand* them? Rousseau never says as much, though if he thought so he likely wouldn't have said so. One who had ever passed off fictions as the truth because he considered it his duty to do so wouldn't publicly condone the practice, not if he wanted his fictions to be believed. What we've seen of Rousseau as Legislator in light of his explication of the Legislator's task in the *Social Contract* suggests that he believed this duty to have befallen him long ago. We've seen him fictionalize his own character and experience in the *Reveries*. He may also fictionalize others—or so I would suggest, based on his slight but curious misspelling of certain names. He calls by the names of Rosier and Madame Vacassin a man and woman whose names were Rozier and Vacassin. Might these be indications that he has made fictional use of real persons for philosophic purposes? And then there is Marion. Some scholars have suggested that the story about Marion was made up, that it was one of many fables invented by Rousseau for pedagogical purposes.[6] I am not convinced one way or the other, but if it *is* a fable, either in whole or in part, then we might wonder whether giving the name of "Marion" to the victim of his injustice was yet another instance of deliberately misspelling a name—in this case, the misspelling of the name of the eponymous heroine of *La vie de Marianne*, a prominent eighteenth-century "antiromance," antiromances being novels in which characters blame fortune, rather than themselves, for their travails.[7]

A final word on justice. Recall that Socrates, although he purports to uncover justice in book 4 of the *Republic*, has already effectively articulated a principle of justice in book 1, and that this principle, which is to help one's friends who are good and to harm no one, seems to govern his dealings with others. I take this same principle to be *Rousseau's* principle in *his* dealings with others, even if he occasionally stumbles. And for these reasons I take this principle to express Socrates's and Rousseau's shared understanding of the justice of the just man as such, remembering that for both thinkers the good and just *man* is not synonymous with the good and just *citizen*.

Fifth Walk

In the Fifth Walk of the *Reveries* Rousseau recounts his blessed if brief exile on St. Peter's Island. The exile, a verifiable historic fact, also serves to reveal the ahistorical, indeed atemporal, dimension of the philosophic life.

Rousseau's time on St. Peter's Island was a kind of island in time, or rather an island *outside* of or unmoved by the currents of time. Rousseau admits that his happiness on the island was troubled by the knowledge that his stay there could be cut short, as indeed it would be after only two months. To this extent time did intrude on him. But the intrusion wasn't

6. Mercier, *De J. J. Rousseau*, 262; cited in Kelly, *Rousseau's Exemplary Life*, 18. Ann Hartle argues that the conspiracy Rousseau recounts in the *Confessions* (which is the same conspiracy that he speaks of in the *Reveries*) was his own knowing invention. See Hartle, *Modern Self in Rousseau's Confessions*, 212.

7. Regarding *La vie de Marianne* as an antiromance, see Pagani, "Living Well Is the Best Revenge," 415. Pagani does not mention Rousseau's Marion in this connection.

decisive. He reports that his time on the island was "the happiest time of [his] life" (5), which may signify that happiness requires an easing of time's grip on us. His days on the island were devoted almost entirely to idle and mostly solitary pursuits, the most exquisite of which were the rapturous reveries that we've already noted. These reveries were accompanied by, or perhaps brought about by, or perhaps productive of, but in any case connected to what I would call the *forgetting* of time if it weren't for the fact that Rousseau did *not* forget time; rather, he would cease to *experience* his *existence* as temporal. When he would turn his attention inward, when he would remove himself from the world and experience nothing but the sentiment of his own existence and be fully satisfied in doing so—at these times he would live altogether timelessly. "Time is nothing" for the soul at such moments, he reports (14). Notice the use of the present tense in a story otherwise told in the past tense.

As Rousseau's sojourn on St. Peter's Island was a kind of island in time, the Fifth Walk is a kind of island in the *Reveries*. To be sure, Rousseau speaks of past experience in the Fifth Walk just as he does in other walks. But as we'll see, he recounts his past experience of timelessness in a sort of timeless way. That he does so is more than a nice literary touch. It carries an important philosophic teaching in that it communicates to readers that what he experienced once upon a time on St. Peter's Island continues to be available to him in the present, away from the island. The island in time has proved to be portable. Rousseau can return to it when and as he sees fit.

Of course the ability to transport oneself to another place is only as meaningful as the experience on offer there. Are Rousseau's depictions of rapturous and ecstatic reveries believable? There is reason for skepticism. Yet even if there is something fictional about the Fifth Walk, the fiction, both its substance and the fact that it *is* fiction, communicates something factual about philosophy and the philosophic life. Irrespective of whether the reveries that Rousseau relates in the Fifth Walk were as joyous and fulfilling as he says, the timelessness that he highlights in these experiences belongs to philosophy and the philosophic life. He suggests as much, as I've already noted, by placing his account of his time on St. Peter's Island at the center of his book on the philosophic life.

The happiness that Rousseau enjoyed on St. Peter's Island, at least as he recalls it, was so rapturous as to be *erotic*. Indeed eros and its relation to our well-being is the overarching theme of the Fifth Walk. In this the Fifth Walk corresponds to book 5 of the *Republic*. Book 5 of the *Republic* is almost entirely devoted to Socrates's articulation of three radical institutions or practices, the "three waves of paradox," that place the *kallipolis* at its furthest and most shocking remove from any known society. What makes the three waves so shocking is their progressively more radical engagement with and transformation of eros. The first wave, the equal nurture and employment of male and female guardians, would entail a commingling of the sexes, including physical exercise in the nude, that would be possible only if eros were strenuously disciplined. The second wave, which consists in the elimination of private attachments among the guardians in favor of a "community of women and children" (449d, 461e) along with a eugenics program aimed at producing only noble progeny, entails a more obvious and more comprehensive management of eros—indeed, what most would consider the *denaturing* of eros. And yet the third wave, rule by kings who are true philosophers, would arguably require an even more ambitious governance of eros—not only disciplining or redirecting but sublimating it.

That Rousseau's happiness as depicted in the Fifth Walk is indeed erotic is suggested in several ways. There are "raptures" (*ravissements*) and "ecstasies" (*extases*) (7, 15, 17). There is an exultant sense of complete fulfillment: "a sufficient, perfect, and full happiness which leaves in the soul no emptiness it might feel a need to fill" (14). There is no felt awareness of, no suffering, the passing of time: "time is nothing for [the soul]; . . . the present lasts forever without, however, making its duration noticed and without any trace of time's passage" (14). This is not eros in any ordinary sense, to be sure. Rousseau makes no reference to being erotically attracted to another human being during this period. But it is eros all the same, *philosophic* eros. Rousseau's philosophic eros, his eros for *Sophia*, drives his two most notable activities on St. Peter's Island. The first of these is what he himself describes as a "passionate" engagement with botany, which centers on the ambition to describe, to observe, to *know* all there is to know about the island's flora. This, we might say, is an expression of intellectual eros proper: intellectual in that it consists in discursive inquiry, eros in that it is the source of "raptures and ecstasies" (7). Rousseau recounts that he set out to describe "all the plants of the island, without omitting a single one. . . . It is said that a German did a book about a lemon peel; I would have done one about each stalk of hay of the meadows, each moss of the woods, each lichen that carpets the rocks; in short, I did not want to leave a blade of grass or a plant particle which was not amply described." What is this but a labor of love—a labor of intellectual eros? The other erotic activity recounted in the Fifth Walk, if one can call something an activity that is as inward and still as this one, consists not in investigation or analysis (though it may require prior investigation and analysis) but in beholding or being with. Here I am referring to the reveries in which

Rousseau claims to have found perfect fulfillment by gathering his soul into itself, whereupon he would feel nothing but the sentiment of his own existence, and feel it so fully that he would want nothing more. This is the experience that he describes as timeless and as perfectly happy. If his botanizing was animated by intellectual eros proper, these reveries were animated by philosophic eros of a different shade, which we might call *contemplative* eros. We can accept that these reveries were erotic so long as we are prepared to recognize two things: first, that the immediate object or focus of philosophic eros needn't always be discursive knowledge—which is something one might learn, and that Rousseau himself perhaps learned, from Plato;[8] second, that the *aim* of philosophic eros and indeed all eros, even if it is rarely recognized as such, might be eternity (timelessness), which too is something Rousseau perhaps learned from Plato.

The correspondence between Rousseau's Fifth Walk and Plato's book 5 extends to their respective structures and subthemes. Each is subdivided into three discrete parts with corresponding discrete foci. The first section of the Fifth Walk (paragraphs 1–5) and the first wave of *Republic* 5 introduce nature as a source and touchstone of happiness and thus as a standard by which to judge our deeds and pursuits. Socrates's appeal to nature is simplistic to the point of ridiculousness—the natural differences between men and women are casually presumed to be no more significant than those between long-haired and bald men (454c–455a)—so much so that it serves only to raise nature as a *question*. We learn at one and the same time that the question of nature is an enormously long and difficult one but one that we often presume to have answered all the same. Comparably, it is in the first part of the Fifth Walk that Rousseau gives us the *Reveries'* single portrait of nature, as it were. Elsewhere in the book Rousseau speaks of *his own* nature and of the *study* of nature. Only in the Fifth Walk does he describe nature in its beauty and diversity. And it is in the Fifth Walk that he explicitly ties nature to happiness. The section begins and ends with statements about his own happiness. Here is the first line of the section (and thus of course the first line of the Walk): "Of all the places I have lived (and I have lived in some charming ones), none has made me so truly happy nor left me such tender regrets as St. Peter's Island

8. That the object of philosophic eros needn't be discursive knowledge is suggested both by what Socrates *says* about philosophers and by what he *does* in his own life. The most striking instance of the latter was his habit of standing stock-still in meditation for extended periods (*Symposium*, 175a–b and 220c–d).

in the middle of Lake Bienne" (1). And here is the last line of the section: "I consider these two months the happiest time of my life, so happy that it would have contented me for my whole existence without the desire for another state arising for a single instant in my soul" (5). It is also only in Fifth Walk—though in the second section, not the first—that Rousseau recounts his *direct experience* of nature.

The second section of the Fifth Walk (paragraphs 6–11) and the second wave of *Republic* 5 both deal with the inner workings or character of eros, which arguably means with the innermost workings or character of *nature*. In the first wave, that is, the equal treatment of men and women and their complete intermingling, eros was most notable for being overlooked or discounted. It was taken for granted that sexual attraction and jealousy could easily be overcome. In the second wave, that is, the abolition of private personal attachments and the institution of a wholesale eugenics scheme, eros is not overlooked or discounted but rather enlisted into service to the city. It is enlisted, however, in a dubious way that also arises from an oversight. The second wave doesn't overlook eros's existence or power, but it does overlook eros's resistance to rational governance. The assumption that eros can be rationally governed—that it can easily be directed toward objects deemed fitting by civil authorities—is the second wave's most dubious feature. Perhaps a totalitarian state could curtail the expression of erotic passion. Perhaps it could even have some success at redirecting erotic passion toward objects it prefers. But it's hard to imagine that eros could be so easily controlled, or indeed that efforts at control wouldn't provoke resistance and rebellion. And even if eros could be successfully directed by civil authorities, it is doubtful that it would be directed wisely, for that would require the civil authorities to have a greater mastery of eros and sexuality than anyone has yet demonstrated. And Rousseau? He too ostensibly affirms the amenability of eros to rational mastery. He even indicates that he has attained this mastery himself—though with a qualification. The mastery that Rousseau highlights and demonstrates is the mastery of reproductive structures and processes *in plants*. Human eros, which is to say eros simply, does come into play here. Rousseau speaks of his "botanical fervor . . . which soon became a passion," and of the "raptures and ecstasies [he] felt with each observation [he] made on plant structure and organization, as well as on the role of the sexual parts in sporulation" (7). But the contrast between Rousseau's eros and the "eros" of the plants he studied only serves to underscore that eros is *not* amenable to rational mastery, and why. Rational mastery requires predictability. Rousseau's own case points to two sources of eros's *un*predictability. By recounting his passion for botany, he highlights the prevalence of idiosyncrasy in erotic affairs. And by recounting his rapture and ecstasy, he highlights the wildness and boundlessness to which eros is given. The heart of eros—and its greatness—lie in their not lending themselves to calculations of utility. Rousseau is as alive to eros's power and importance, and thus to the need for good governance, as anyone. Knowing something of the sources of eros's power and importance, however, he knows something about how eros can and cannot be governed. He knows, to begin with, that reason demands respect for the reality of unreason. In all of this, Rousseau is of one mind with Plato.

Botany certainly involves direct engagement with nature. But it was Rousseau's other main activity on St. Peter's Island, the rapturous reveries in which he felt nothing but the sentiment of his own existence unmediated by discursive thought, to which I was referring when I suggested that in the Fifth Walk Rousseau relates his *direct experience* of nature.

Is such an experience possible? To conceive of the pure sentiment of existence as the most direct or purest experience of nature sounds plausible in principle. But does it comport with the facts of our experience and capacities? Or is it rational only in the way that Socrates's use of nature in connection with the first two waves is rational, which is to say simplistic or rational*istic*? *Can* one withdraw one's attention from the world so completely as to be filled with nothing but the sentiment of one's own existence? I am inclined to answer both yes and no. Yes, perhaps one can—perhaps *Rousseau* can—fix his attention fully on himself and his experience. And in that, he may well be experiencing nothing but the sentiment of his own existence. But he experiences this sentiment in connection with, or as it is solicited by, things other than itself—that is to say, through the use of faculties that engage the world or the contents of one's mind. To sense nothing but the sentiment of existence *in itself*—that would seem doubtful, except perhaps in brief peak moments. It would be to abstract from the body to an impossible degree—just as Socrates does in the *Republic*, and nowhere more so than in connection with book 5's second wave.

If botany and reverie were Rousseau's major activities on St. Peter's Island, another is worth mentioning, which too bears on eros and is recounted in the second section (7). I am referring to his rabbit-breeding project, which is surely his counterpart to the eugenics scheme and the abolition of private erotic attachments of the *Republic*'s second wave. What better way to show the implausibility of the kallipolis than this? Here too Rousseau is affirming Plato, who also knows that his kallipolis, and the second wave more than any of the rest of it, pushes hopelessly against nature.[9]

Rousseau's response in the third section of the Fifth Walk (paragraphs 12–17) to Socrates's third wave, rule by philosopher-kings, is more extensive than his response to either of the first two waves. With respect to the third wave alone Rousseau responds affirmatively not only to the wave itself but also to its psychic analogue. (Recall that the city in speech was created in the first place as a larger and therefore easier-to-read reflection of the soul.) The psychic analogue of the third wave is surely the rule of the soul by reason. Rousseau exemplifies and thereby effectively advocates this very principle, notwithstanding his embrace of sentiment and his celebration of rapture. He does so throughout the *Reveries*, but most particularly in the Fifth Walk, where he first and most extensively *depicts* himself in a way that implies reason's governance of his soul, however tenuous and vulnerable to disruption this governance might still be. As for philosopher-kingship itself, he embraces the idea in the same sense that Plato did—namely, that philosophers might "legislate" for peoples by propounding new, compelling teachings regarding the most important and determinative matters.

9. A final observation from the second section of the Fifth Walk: a minor detail—a minor *error*—of a sort we've already seen: Recalling his time on St. Peter's Island, Rousseau says that the memory still "arouse[s] intense, tender, and lasting regrets in my heart at the end of *fifteen* years" (V, 11; emphasis added). Butterworth points out that Rousseau's arithmetic is in error: "The interval is really only twelve years, for the Fifth Walk was probably written in 1777," and Rousseau spent his months on the island in 1765 (Butterworth, "Interpretive Essay," 173n11). We've seen the erroneous use of this number before (II, 1), whereupon I suggested that Rousseau meant to liken his work during the period in question to the fifteen years spent by Socrates's guardians tending to political and military affairs in the cave following their education in dialectic. It seems to me that we may read the current line from the Fifth Walk in the same way. Rousseau devoted the years between his expulsion from St. Peter's Island and the *Reveries* to the defense of himself and his thought. What could be more political—and military—than that?

Once Socrates's philosophers have completed their fifteen years of service, we recall, they return from the cave and are compelled to behold the Good. Rousseau too might be seen as being compelled to discover the good, in that the new insight and happiness he has managed to find at the end of "fifteen years" in his own cave were prompted by the intense suffering imposed on him by his enemies. Finally, Socrates's philosophers, even after they've beheld the Good, are compelled from time to time to "drudge in politics" at the highest level—this is their service as philosopher-kings properly speaking (539e–540b). And Rousseau? Might such "drudgery" be exactly what he is doing "now," in writing the *Reveries*?

There is an element of philosopher-kingship that we have not yet seen, however. In the final paragraph of the Fifth Walk Rousseau gives us what I take to be his most emphatic avowal that he regards himself as a true philosopher—not because he calls himself one (he doesn't) but because he applies to himself, or hopes to be able to apply to himself, the term with which he frequently designated true philosophers. Imagining what his life might have been had he never been expelled from St. Peter's Island, he writes the following: "Delivered from all the earthly passions the tumult of social life engenders, my soul would frequently soar up above this atmosphere and commune in advance with the celestial intelligences whose number it hopes to augment in a short while (17)." *Celestial intelligences*: In the current context, the term seems to apply to angelic beings. In prior writings, as we've noted, Rousseau uses it to describe the greatest of philosophers, those who live the theoretical life because they love the truth and who have the practical wisdom and beneficence to shield society from the potentially subversive effects of their theoretical inquiries. Appearing as it does in the final paragraph of the Fifth Walk, Rousseau's self-assessment corresponds in placement to the introduction of the third wave at the end of book 5 of the *Republic*, which launches Socrates's extensive elaboration of the philosopher as a human type.

That Rousseau had once aspired to be a kind of philosopher-king is most incontrovertibly shown in his claim on behalf of the "revolutionary" potential of "The Profession of Faith of the Savoyard Vicar" (III, 17), which we've already noted. But the same aspiration is evident in the Fifth Walk with its compelling depiction—its advertisement—of the happiness of a certain kind of contemplative life. In this the *Reveries* is continuous with the works Rousseau published in his lifetime, from the *First Discourse* through *Emile* and the *Social Contract*. Each of those works taught, with great poetic power and intellectual force, unconventional ways of conceiving of human nature and the human good, ways that must inevitably *change* those who are persuaded by them. Offering a compelling worldview or an advertisement for a way of being is perhaps the chief means whereby a philosopher might hope to legislate for a civilization. It is not the only means, however. Although he does not mention it in the Fifth Walk, we know that Rousseau devoted considerable time during his stay on St. Peter's Island to drafting, per invitation, a constitution for Corsica.[10] And if *we* know this, so did a number of those who would have been among the first to read the *Reveries* upon its circulation.

---

10. See Meier, *On the Happiness*, 105–6; also 173–76. It is also worth noting something that Rousseau does divulge in the Fifth Walk—namely, that he did much more reading and

Let us return briefly to how the Fifth Walk functions in the *Reveries*. I've suggested that the Fifth Walk's graphic centrality to the *Reveries* reflects its *substantive* centrality to philosophy and the philosophic life—that is to say, the centrality of timelessness or eternity to philosophy. Centrality, however, does not imply visibility or accessibility; the opposite is more nearly the case. Nor does it imply an ongoing consciousness of eternity, let alone ongoing absorption of the kind depicted in the Fifth Walk. As if to highlight the rareness and elusiveness of the pure engagement with eternity—though admittedly, as highlighting goes, this is rather low wattage—Rousseau opens both the preceding and the succeeding Walks by accentuating their placement in time.[11]

The Fifth Walk not only signifies, but it also enacts, as it were, the centrality of eternity to philosophy as Rousseau understands it. Rousseau doesn't emphasize philosophy's *inquiry* into the eternal so much as the philosopher's *experience* of eternity. (If it seems unlikely that Rousseau, one of the great discoverers of the historicity of human nature, would put eternity at the center of philosophy, it shouldn't. For inquiring into the eternal does not mean inquiring into eternal entities or even presupposing that such entities exist; it means inquiring into principles or forms that, regardless of when or whether they have been perceived, exist apart from time.) As Rousseau depicts it—that is, with reference to his own case—the philosopher attains to the experience of eternity not by forgetting or repressing past and future but by being fully present. The Fifth Walk is the only place where Rousseau explicitly treats this experience of eternity (14). He does not use precisely that word, however, which is itself worth thinking about. Rather than speaking of "eternity" or "the eternal," he chooses to speak about "timelessness." His choice is prudent, for the word "eternity" was commonly misinterpreted in Rousseau's time, as it is in ours. When people hear the word "eternity," they commonly take it—they commonly *mis*take it—to mean sempiternity, everlastingness, or immortality. But the latter words signify indefinite persistence *in time*, whereas "eternity" means being apart from time. If he had spoken of "eternity," Rousseau would have risked summoning and appealing to the longing for immortality. (Indeed, in the single instance in the *Reveries* in which he does use the word "eternity"—this is in the fifth paragraph of

---

writing than he says he did. Although he claims not to have unpacked his books or writing tools, his subsequent description of his botanizing includes a project, a *Flora petrinisularis*, that was to have become a book.

11. Meier, 98.

the Fifth Walk—he uses it to refer to immortality.) Rousseau follows the Socratic practice of meeting people where they are in order that he might lead them, or at least some of them, someplace else. With his moving depictions of reveries in which the experience of timelessness is equated with happiness and sufficiency, he moves the reader who might be open to it toward the philosophic standpoint and experience.[12]

If eternity is central to the philosophic life, that is because to experience eternity is to experience *existence* in the purest way possible. As it happens the Fifth Walk contains the majority of the *Reveries'* mentions of

---

12. Rousseau's awareness of the decisive difference between eternity and immortality might explain a strange error in the Fifth Walk, namely, his substituting Habakkuk for Baruch in a story he tells about La Fontaine in order to describe something about himself. The obviousness of the mistake suggests that it may have been intentional. It appears in paragraph 7:

> Nothing is more singular than the raptures and ecstasies I felt with each observation I made on plant structure and organization, as well as on the role of the sexual parts in sporulation, which was then a completely new system for me. I was enchanted to discover generic features of which I previously had not the slightest idea and to verify them on common species, while waiting for rarer ones to offer themselves to me. The forking of the two long stamens of the self-heal [etc., etc.] filled me with joy and I went around asking whether one had seen the horns of the self-heal plant like La Fontaine asking whether one had read Habakkuk.

Why Habakkuk rather than Baruch, if indeed we may presume that Rousseau knew whereof he spoke? The brief book of Habakkuk, as it happens, recounts the words of a prophet for whom God's splendor lies in His (still awaited) punishment of the wicked. Meier persuasively suggests that Rousseau means to contrast the life-giving horns of the self-heal to the horns on God's hands with which He will justly destroy the wicked (Habakkuk 3:4); see Meier, *On the Happiness*, 106–7. To this I would add that Habakkuk is notable among Hebrew prophets for singing of God's and the human soul's *immortality*: "Art Thou not everlasting, my God, my Holy One? we shall not die" (1:12). Thus does Habakkuk offer Rousseau a particularly incisive contrast with the philosopher's cognitivist view of morality. In Habakkuk's vision of divine justice Rousseau would have recognized a lofty expression, perhaps the loftiest possible expression, of the ordinary moral consciousness. And in Habakkuk's invocation of immortality Rousseau would have recognized the *ground* of the ordinary moral consciousness. Scholars suggest that, in the original Hebrew, the immortality invoked in the final part of Habakkuk 1:12 is not ours but rather God's— not "we shall not die" but rather, per Robert Alter, "you shall not die"; see Alter, *Hebrew Bible*. Rousseau, however, being no reader of Hebrew, would in all likelihood not have known this. The Vulgate, like the King James from which I quoted above, imputes deathlessness to ourselves: "Numquid non tu a principio Domine Deus meus, sancte meus, et non *moriemur*?" (emphasis added).

"existence," and the *Reveries'* central discussion of existence appears in the central paragraph of the Fifth (which of course is the central) Walk.[13]

As we've noted, there is reason to wonder whether Rousseau hasn't idealized his experience on St. Peter's Island. Can one really be aware of nothing but the sentiment of one's existence *in itself*, that is, without corresponding awareness of anything else? And if not—if we necessarily experience ourselves in relation to and in contact with the world—then mustn't his account of the experience of eternity also be exaggerated? Perhaps so. Yet this needn't count against the goodness and choiceworthiness of the philosophic life any more than does Plato's idealization of the ascent from the cave. If Plato exaggerated or idealized the philosopher's wisdom, he still embraced the *love* of wisdom as the most humane and fulfilling stance toward being. If Rousseau exaggerates or idealizes the kind of reverie that he recounts in the Fifth Walk, he still embraces *openness* to eternity as the most humane and fulfilling stance toward being.

There is one more sense—a more literal and more promising sense—in which Rousseau has idealized his experience of St. Peter's Island. The experience has become an ideal to which he will have access always and everywhere, even in the Bastille, were he to find himself there (16). The same is perhaps true for us, whether or not we've ever set foot on that heavenly island in Lake Goodness (*lac de Bienne*).[14]

Sixth Walk

The Sixth Walk is a meditation on freedom. It begins with Rousseau's observation that benefactions he has performed spontaneously, out of the goodness of his heart, become tedious and unpleasant to him when his beneficiaries have come to expect them. What had been a joyous act of freedom has become a burdensome obligation (4). The exploration of freedom versus obligation continues through the entirety of the Walk.

13. The word "existence" appears thirteen times in the *Reveries*, in eleven paragraphs. Of the thirteen appearances of the word, seven—the central seven—occur in the Fifth Walk. Of the eleven paragraphs in which "existence" is discussed, five—the central five—occur in the Fifth Walk. And the central paragraph of the eleven, or the *Reveries'* central discussion of existence (also the Fifth Walk's central discussion of existence), appears in the Fifth Walk's ninth or central paragraph.

14. Rousseau not only idealizes his experience on St. Peter's Island; he idealizes the island itself and the surrounding lake. By comparison with his account of the island in book 12 of the *Confessions*, his account in the Fifth Walk of the *Reveries* makes lac de Bienne more circular and thus, in a sense, more perfect. See Davis, *Autobiography of Philosophy*, 170 and 187n2; and Meier, *On the Happiness*, 101.

More than freedom as such, however, or freedom in its various senses, the theme is *natural* freedom. Natural freedom is a rarefied condition. In a well-known passage from the *Social Contract*, Rousseau distinguishes between natural, civic, and moral freedom (364–65; 141) But from the standpoint of nature, only natural freedom is real freedom. Civic and moral freedom are conditions of self-rule, but the part of the self that rules the other parts has been formed and thus is ruled by a will whose origin is beyond the self. Entailing as it does independence of mind, natural freedom can plausibly be claimed by few human beings, and *perfect* natural freedom by none. Among those who can make a plausible claim to natural freedom are true philosophers. They may be the only ones, depending on whether independence comparable to theirs could be achieved by one who has considerable strength of soul but lacks the philosophers' ardent intellectual eros—by someone like Emile, for example. But of course no one like Emile is likely to be found in the world, even if, as Rousseau insists, such a person is possible in principle. Practically speaking, the philosopher is *the* exemplar of natural freedom.[15]

The philosopher, however, lives in society, which exists only and precisely at the *expense* of natural freedom. This puts the philosopher in a most extraordinary situation. On the one hand the philosopher might occupy any one of a number of positions in society, from high governmental official to dissident, from moralist or defender of the faith to hedonist and scandalous nonbeliever, not to mention scientist, essayist, perhaps novelist or playwright, and even university professor.[16] But philosophers *as philosophers* hold no place in the social order. They move among their fellows seeing but unseen, vulnerable yet barely inciting notice, at least if they so wish, living as it were in a kind of bubble. (Passing through society as if in a bubble also means that the philosopher's translucence may occasionally give way to flashes of iridescence visible to those positioned just so.) Inevitably, then, the theme of natural freedom resolves into the theme of the philosopher's relationship with society, or the politics of philosophy—which is also the major theme of book 6 of the *Republic*.

Book 6 of the *Republic* divides into three major sections. The first section explicates the nature of those with the potential to develop into phi-

15. For an alternative understanding of natural freedom as understood by Rousseau, some of whose elements are consistent with my own understanding, see Miller, "Forced into Freedom," 129–38.

16. Rousseau himself took on the tasks of dissident (a republican critic of monarchy), moralist, defender of the faith (rather, defender of *a* faith), amateur scientist, novelist, and humble, or perhaps not so humble, music copyist.

losophers (484a–487a). The second section explains why philosophy has such a poor reputation (487b–497a): philosophers are seen by the general public as useless at best and more often as wicked, and not without reason. True philosophers, Socrates explains, *are* useless, but only because they have been made so by the city itself, which does not recognize their wisdom. And many who call themselves wise or philosophic are in truth vicious and incapable—capable perhaps of gaining rule, but not capable of ruling well. These lessons are neatly conveyed by the famous Image of the Ship, in which the true pilot is dismissed as a stargazer while those who violently battle for the helm call themselves pilots though they have no piloting skill. Finally, book 6's third section (497b–511e) takes up the question of what kind of regime—what practices and, in particular, what studies—favor the proper development of the philosopher. The discussion culminates in Socrates's revelation and nonrevelation of the greatest study of all, the Good. The revelation is multipartite: Socrates discloses that the Good is indeed the greatest study, in that knowledge of the Good is what makes possible, or would make possible, our profiting from other studies; that each of us somehow divines that this is so, even as none of us knows what the Good is; and that the Good is beyond and indeed the source of being and knowing. The nonrevelation is Socrates's demurring to explicate his opinion of the Good, on the grounds that he could not make his opinion understood in the present context ("it looks to me as though it's out of the range of our present thrust to attain the opinions I now hold about it" [506e]). Instead he agrees to present "what looks like a child of the good and most similar to it" through two images, the Sun and the Divided Line.

Rousseau's Sixth Walk addresses these same three themes—the first and second in so obvious a way that, despite their being treated together, they make the Sixth Walk the chapter of the *Reveries* whose connection with the *Republic* is clearest.

Where Socrates explicates the nature of potential philosophers in the first section of book 6, in the first section of the Sixth Walk (paragraphs 1–9) Rousseau explicates two important features of his own nature, features that seem to me to constitute what he regards as the philosophic nature in its outward or political expression.[17] The first feature is his love of freedom and dislike of obligation. The second is his goodness, as manifest in his

17. Unlike Socrates, Rousseau doesn't provide a systematic account of the factors that favor or inhibit the long-term development of the philosopher (though the *Reveries* as a whole can be seen as addressing this matter extensively). However he does speak in these paragraphs about factors that "elevate and strengthen the soul" or "strike it down and kill

love of benefiting others. Rousseau's articulation of his love of freedom culminates in the admission that he altogether lacks virtue, understanding by "virtue" the performance of duty over and against inclination: "virtue consists in overcoming them [inclinations] when duty commands in order to do what duty prescribes, and that is what I have been less able to do than any man in the world" (7). But of course the meaning of Rousseau's goodness is that his inclinations are thoroughly benevolent (3). One might suppose that a lack of virtue would be no problem so long as the person in question is truly good. And one would be right—but only if the person in question was not a social being. Society requires of human beings things that are not natural. Even the best of inclinations won't suffice to make good *citizens*.

In the Sixth Walk's second section (paragraphs 10–16) Rousseau restates the argument of *Republic* 6's second section. His lack of virtue, no matter how great his goodness, renders him a deficient citizen. But he is, or at least he could be, something greater than a citizen—greater even from the standpoint of society itself—if only society would let him. Rousseau, a true philosopher who wishes to do good, is useless to society because, like Socrates's true pilot, he has been made useless. "I know and feel that to do good is the truest happiness the human heart can savor; but it is a long time now since this happiness has been put out of my reach, and it is not in such a wretched lot as mine that one can hope to perform wisely and fruitfully a single really good action" (3). Rousseau has already told us that whatever good his books might have done for society has been undone by the poisoning of the public mind against him. He has even lost hope that he might reach future generations (I, 10). Meanwhile, as he sees it, the well-known *philosophes* of his time were a pernicious social force. *His* uselessness and *their* wickedness: this was Socrates's explication of the uselessness of the true philosophers and the wickedness of the pretenders.

Rousseau also treats, or rather points to, another of his qualities, in addition to or rather behind his goodness and love of freedom and thus behind his untapped ability and desire to do good for humankind. That quality is love—more particularly, a certain kind of love of himself; more particularly yet, the desire to extend his being. In paragraph 14 he insists that his self-love or desire to extend his existence are what have kept him from hating men for their falseness and dissembling. He has felt repugnance, yes; but not aversion or hatred. "I love myself too much to be able to hate anyone whatever. That would be to constrict or repress my ex-

---

it" (12), and he gives us to understand that various factors have favored or inhibited the expression of his natural qualities.

istence, and I would rather extend it over the whole universe." Indeed, Rousseau is so far from hatred that the malevolence of his enemies moves him to "real pity." But the self-love that saves him from hatred is ambiguous: "Perhaps pride is still mingled with these judgments: I feel I am too much above them to hate them." His pride is serving a good end, an end that secures amour de soi and furthers its interests. Yet the perfection of the philosopher as philosopher, or the perfection of the natural man as natural man, will require the further taming of pride and the amour-propre of which it is an expression. Alignment of amour-propre's interests with those of amour de soi is far better than the alternative. Best of all, though, would be to enlist amour-propre into the *service* of amour de soi.[18] It is worth noting that Rousseau's mention of the desire to extend his being, one of only three such mentions in the *Reveries* and the broadest of the three,[19] corresponds in placement to the *Republic*'s most extensive discussion of eros as part of the philosopher's nature.[20]

18. Perhaps it is pride's role in the story that accounts for the specific placement of this passage. Rousseau discusses the sentiment of existence at a number of places in the *Reveries*, but he references the desire to *extend* his existence only three times. The first reference appears in paragraph 14 of the First Walk. The second, which is the one we have been examining, appears in paragraph 14 of the Sixth Walk. The third appears in paragraph 17 of the Seventh Walk. Although such a thing is unprovable, those acquainted with certain conventions might find it reasonable that the first two references, being informed by or arising in part from amour-propre (pride) and to that extent unnatural, might deliberately have been associated by Rousseau with a multiple of the number seven. The third reference, on the contrary, which appears at the moment when Rousseau has freed himself from the tyrannical hold of amour-propre, merits association with the number seventeen. (It may also be worth noting that Rousseau's famous celebration of the perfect happiness and sufficiency he enjoyed when abstracting himself from every sentiment except the sentiment of his own existence begins in paragraph 14 of the Fifth Walk. Might he thereby be signaling that we should think again before taking the Fifth Walk's testimony at face value? Might his purported ecstasies have been a fiction?)

19. Here, at VI, 14, Rousseau says that to hate others "would be to constrict or repress my existence, and I would rather extend it over the whole universe." Later, at VII, 17, he will observe that even when he wishes it not to, his "expansive soul seeks to extend its feelings and existence over other beings." The later reference, though less broad than the earlier one (Rousseau desires to extend himself over "other beings" rather than "the whole universe"), is more active and passionate, more *erotic*: Rousseau speaks of *seeking* to extend himself, whereas the earlier reference merely expresses a preference ("I would rather").

20. If Rousseau means to note the shadow cast by pride over the desire to extend his existence in VI, 14, does Plato mean to do something comparable? Those who recognize a difference between the philosopher that Socrates *is* and the philosophers that he *depicts* should be open to this reading. Indeed, the difference between the truly Socratic philosopher and the philosophers of the kallipolis may be nothing more or less than the difference between eros and thymos.

Even as he recounts his incapacity to do good for others, Rousseau quietly indicates that he has discovered or attained greater agency with regard to himself. Significantly, this surge of felt agency came about once he had been thoroughly disabused of his trust in men. With trust goes passivity: "Ever since then I have been disgusted with men, and my will, concurring with theirs in this respect, keeps me even more removed from them than all their machinations do" (13). That Rousseau would discover his agency only after his trust has been disappointed is a rough lesson, a Machiavellian lesson, but hardly less useful for that. He has taken a further step toward the fuller freedom that still lies ahead.

Rousseau's agreement with Socrates on the uselessness of true philosophers and the wickedness of false ones is clear enough to require no more elaboration here. But what about the third section of *Republic* 6? Does Rousseau really offer anything corresponding to "the greatest study," that is, the Good in itself? He doesn't appear to, and the reason seems obvious enough: he nowhere embraces any kind of metaphysical doctrine. And yet it seems to me that Rousseau offers something responsive after all in the third and final section of the Sixth Walk (paragraphs 17–21). Where Socrates had discoursed allusively about the Good, Rousseau hypothesizes about what he would do were he given the ring of Gyges—a thought experiment whose purpose is to reveal what one considers the greatest good that one might hope to possess or engage. The *Republic* includes its own notable mention of the ring of Gyges, of course, in book 2. Yet it is not incongruent, indeed it is fitting, for Rousseau to invoke the ring only here in the Sixth Walk. For the ring is introduced by Glaucon in connection with the challenge he puts to Socrates, and Socrates begins to answer the challenge only in book 6, in connection with the philosopher. Let's look at how Rousseau develops the hypothetical: "Master of contenting my desires, able to do anything without anybody being able to fool me, what could I have reasonably desired? One thing alone: that would have been to see every heart content. Only the sight of public felicity could have affected my heart with a permanent feeling, and the ardent desire to contribute to it would have been my most constant passion" (18). What Rousseau seems to be saying is that for him the greatest good is not metaphysical or contemplative but rather moral or political—in which case he might have been pursuing the greatest good by writing and publishing his oeuvre and perhaps even by writing this book.

Now if Rousseau is indicating that the greatest good is moral or political, this would seem to *separate* him from the *Republic* and from classical political philosophy more generally, for which the greatest good is transmoral and transpolitical and accessed by contemplation. Yet there is reason to resist concluding that Rousseau's greatest good truly is moral or political. By posing the hypothetical as he does, Rousseau indicates only what he would want to do if given powers he doesn't already have, that is, what *additional* good he would seek. It may well be—in fact, he indicated in the Fifth Walk—that the greatest good is already in his power: this would be the happiness of the philosophic life that he already enjoys. Or to formulate it more Platonically, the good that "every soul pursues and for the sake of which it does everything" (*Republic* 505d) is, in Rousseau's view, the sentiment of existence, for, as we noted in chapter 1, the sentiment of existence is what constitutes the goodness of other goods and thus the goodness of life itself. The best life is the most fully felt life. But Rousseau *doesn't* speak Platonically. He doesn't say of the sentiment of existence or anything else that it is "beyond being, exceeding it in dignity and power" (509a–b). Then again, perhaps Plato doesn't speak as "Platonically" as he seems to. By saying that the good gives rise to being and truth he might simply be saying that it gives rise to being and truth *for us*. Our world comes into being and is intelligible only insofar as it is structured by our concerns. Without such structuring, there can be no world; there can be no being or truth for us. If this is what Plato has in mind—to the extent that this is what he has in mind—he and Rousseau are in close company.[21]

None of this is to deny that Rousseau finds happiness in beneficence. There is no reason to deny that he regards beneficence as *a* good, perhaps even the *crowning* good, even if it isn't the greatest good or the good as such. Beneficence perhaps derives from or is subsumed by a greater good that is transmoral and transpolitical. Nor did the classical philosophers dismiss the goodness of beneficence for the beneficent one or its relation to the philosophic life. Though they held the greatest good to be transpolitical, they too allowed that political activity can be a good, even a great good, for the philosopher.[22] Thus in the Sixth Walk Rousseau follows Plato

---

21. At *Emile*, 280; 189–90, Rousseau hypothesizes about a mind fully formed with respect to structures and capacities but altogether bereft of experience. A person with such a mind would have no world, only a sensorium.

22. Both Plato and Aristotle allow for the goodness of a kind of political activity—meaning legislative or architectonic activity—for the philosopher. In Plato's case, as we've seen, this possibility is implicit in the Image of the Cave: might not the philosopher supplant the poet and the prophet as maker of the artifacts whose shadows are projected onto the wall? And might that not be at least part of what Plato himself is doing with his dialogues? Aristotle, for his part, seems to me to vindicate the same possibility in a line from the *Nicomachean Ethics* that has drawn remarkably little notice—hiding, as it were, in plain sight. Aristotle begins a discussion of pleasure late in book 7 by noting that the one who studies politics philosophically is "*the master craftsman of the end to which we look when we speak of each thing as bad or good simply*" (1152b2–4; emphasis added). Perhaps

in book 6 of the *Republic*, where the good and philosophy are treated from a political perspective.

It may be that this practical dimension of the philosophic life meant more to Rousseau than to his classical predecessors. Certainly Rousseau *depicts* himself as given more to moral passion than the classical philosophers did. He says in the Sixth Walk that "the sight of injustice and wickedness still makes my blood boil" (16), and he gives no indication in the remaining Walks that he has overcome this disposition. Consider by contrast Socrates's sangfroid, which holds up even when what he most cherishes is subjected to abuse: having spoken, seemingly with heat, about those who "splatter" philosophy "with mud," Socrates pauses and observes that he had spoken "*as though* [his] spiritedness were aroused," as if to indicate that his apparent indignation was feigned (536c; emphasis added). Nor does Socrates—or Plato or Aristotle—ever express anything like Rousseau's professed "ardent desire" or "constant passion" "to see every heart content." In his moral passion Rousseau appears closer to the biblical tradition than the classical. Or, if we want to stay within the classical tradition, he seems closer in this regard to the Legislator than to the philosopher[23]—though we should not forget that Plato too was wont to "play the lawgiver."[24] Nor should we discount the possibility that there is an element of play in Rousseau's expression of moral passion. The passion might well be real, but a philosopher *as* philosopher, holding the cognitivist approach to morality, would not be thoroughly overtaken by it. Yet he might choose to give it vent and stoke it even as he directs it, or tries to direct it, this way or that. Such directing might be compared to diking and damming flood waters à la Machiavelli, though an even better comparison would be to making use of a fierce but loyal dog, or even lion (*Republic*, 375d–376a, 440c–d, 588e–589b). The question is whether Rousseau really is seething with resentment, or whether, to the contrary, he is *playing the role* of indignant moralist, a role that had once been more than a role for him and thus perhaps a role that is natural for him to play even now.

This last point steers us back to the core issue of the Sixth Walk and poses a challenge in the process. Rousseau presents himself as one who

---

readers tend to miss the import of this line because they focus instead on Aristotle's presentation of the contemplative life, which he declares the best of lives, in book 10. Yet the latter account is strangely thin and seems to describe a different kind of contemplative life from the one Aristotle himself exemplifies.

23. Indeed, as we've already noted, it's not implausible to read Rousseau's description of the Legislator in the *Social Contract* as a description of a philosopher, i.e., as something of a self-description.

24. Montaigne, *Complete Essays of Montaigne*, 879.

enjoys natural freedom. But is role-playing consistent with natural freedom? Perhaps in his case it is, since he has assumed the role voluntarily
and since, although he is subordinating moral passion to something else,
that something else is his own, his reason. But this response only shifts the
focus of the question from Rousseau to natural freedom itself. How free
is natural freedom? Doesn't Rousseau himself admit that natural freedom
is dubious? When he declares in the *Second Discourse* that human beings
are by nature free, he immediately acknowledges that this claim is faced
with many difficulties (148–49; 26); and later he refers to the faculty of
self-perfection as "*the* specific characteristic of the human species" (217;
83; emphasis added). Yet even as he seems to concede that human freedom
is only a conceit, he signals that freedom can be *attained*. His ostensible
case for man's natural freedom is that where the beasts are compelled by
instinct, man experiences impulses that he is free to resist. The attentive
reader might wonder whether this isn't a distinction without a difference.
The savage denizen of the pure state of nature, in connection with whom
the argument for natural freedom is made, would have had no reason to
resist impulse and no thought of doing so, unless by "resist" we mean that
one impulse is overpowered by another one. And yet the overpowering
of one impulse by another does merit being called freedom—not in the
instance of the primordial savage but in the case of a reasoning and self-
aware being. In a reasoning and self-aware being, after all, the relative force
of the impulses will be informed by reason and self-awareness. Natural
freedom lies not in the exercise of will over inclination—the freest will is
still compelled by the apparent good—but rather in the exercise of *intellect*, whereby we can reflect on what is good, and why, and come to a more
perfect understanding thereof. Even when we are not investigating what
is good but simply hold uncritically to what we have been taught, we still
need to rationally determine what is demanded in this or that situation.
This too is freedom, though of a lesser order.

From the standpoint of the ordinary moral consciousness the cognitivist
view of morality seems to deny human freedom. And indeed the cognitivist view holds that the freedom that the ordinary moral consciousness claims and on which it stakes human dignity, or what Rousseau had
called moral freedom (*liberté morale*) in the *Social Contract* (364–65; 141),
is not the reality that its believers claim. But the cognitivist view recognizes the possibility of considerable freedom of *mind*, which it regards as
true human freedom and the ground of human dignity. What's more, the
cognitivist view claims for itself, or rather for its subscribers, a unique
degree of this freedom precisely by virtue of recognizing the compelling

power of the apparent good. Freedom of mind is the core if not the whole of natural freedom. This may explain why Rousseau would characterize human freedom in the final paragraph of the Sixth Walk in strictly negative terms: "I have never believed that man's freedom consisted in doing what he wants, but rather in never doing what he does not want to do; and that is the freedom I have always laid claim to, often preserved, and most scandalized my contemporaries about" (21). Doing what one wants is freedom only to the extent that what one wants (one's conception of the good) has been freely determined, by which I mean two things: first, that it has been arrived at by free thinking; second, to recall the opening paragraphs of the Sixth Walk, that it has not become an obligation. These two strictures suggest, respectively, the limits and the tenability of natural freedom. A cautionary note, to be sure. But also a hopeful one. For while natural freedom's tenability is fixed, its limits are not. We can extend the limits by attaining greater self-awareness and freedom of mind. And in doing so we will be enhancing our well-being. For even if Rousseau elides some of the difficulties surrounding the nature and extent of human freedom (SD, 148–49; 26), there is no reason to doubt the sincerity of his equating it with happiness.

CHAPTER 7

Becoming a More Perfect Philosopher

Seventh, Eighth, and Ninth Walks

In the next Walks we encounter a Rousseau who has begun to see nature differently. This change isn't trumpeted; nor are its effects. Yet both the change and the effects, though subtle, are profound. In the Seventh Walk we learn something about what characterizes this new way of seeing, especially regarding the meaning and apprehension of *wholes*. Rousseau introduces and develops this theme in connection with botany, but there is reason to understand botany as a proxy for nature as such. One reason for taking this view is indicated by his crediting botany—which is to say, his new way of botanizing—with "not letting any germ of revenge or hatred spring up in [his] heart" and with purifying his natural temperament of "all irascible passions" (VII, 3). That Rousseau makes this claim without fanfare, almost as if in passing, does not keep it from being the *Reveries'* most decisive and credible claim with respect to his further philosophic perfection and the resulting enhancement of his happiness, for these irascible passions—irascible yet masterfully dissembling—are what have chiefly been keeping him from making good on his long-standing claim to the wisdom of acceptance. His new way of regarding nature, we might say, has removed what had diluted or covered over his natural goodness. How? The answer is given in the Eighth Walk, where we see his newly clear sight trained not on plants or external nature but on himself. In the Eighth Walk Rousseau gives readers something like a travelogue from which they might take some guidance in their own self-examination, especially concerning the machinations of amour-propre, for he is hardly alone in having been deluded by this complicated and complicating force. Where he *is* outstanding is in his insight. Perhaps only a few readers will make good use of the travelogue. But without it, these few would be fewer still. The Eighth Walk has perhaps the narrowest compass of all ten Walks. It also has perhaps the deepest focus, however, and it may therefore be the most practically instructive of all ten Walks—and not only for those drawn to the philosophic life but for anyone who recognizes the unhealthfulness of revenge, hate, and the other irascible passions, at least insofar as one is held in their thrall. To diminish this thralldom would be to make progress toward freedom and therewith wisdom and happiness as well.

If Rousseau means to provide instruction toward freedom, it makes sense that he would also teach, à la Plato, the insuperable limits of said freedom even in the best case. In the Eighth Walk Rousseau indicates the limits of his own liberation from tyrannical amour-propre. In the Ninth Walk he addresses the limits of his freedom with respect to *society*. He has freed himself from the most painful and stifling of his former limits. He now lives under sunnier skies, which brighten sight and mood alike. His skies are still far from cloudless, however, and one dark cloud in particular, the work of his enemies, is never altogether out of sight.

Seventh Walk

Unlike its predecessors, the Seventh Walk finds Rousseau pointedly directing his attention away from himself. His primary focus in the Seventh Walk is *botany*. The shift from the Sixth Walk to the Seventh is a shift from philosopher-kingship, as it were, to the vegetable kingdom.

Somehow, Rousseau's turn to botany—more precisely, his *return* to botany, though in a new key—is the setting of his most important step forward with respect to self-knowledge and the perfection of his philosophic life. His renewed embrace of botany is sanctioned and even commanded by *wisdom*: "wisdom itself wills" (*la sagesse même veut*) that he follow his inclinations, of which the inclination to botanize is the strongest (VII, 1). It is because the Seventh Walk recounts this step forward that I regard it as the thematic and narrative peak of the *Reveries*. But the Seventh Walk isn't only an ascent. It divides into three major sections, the last of which seems to be a kind of *de*scent or concession, though it turns out that the apparent concession testifies to something good. In this tripartition the Seventh Walk parallels book 7 of the *Republic*. The first section of the Seventh Walk (paragraphs 1–17) recounts an ascent and an abiding on high: it gives us Rousseau, as botanist, living according to wisdom. Similarly, the first section of *Republic* 7 gives us the Image of the Cave, the very paradigm of intellectual ascent, which tells of the arduous rise from ignorance and slavery to wisdom and freedom (514a–521b). In the second section of the Seventh Walk (paragraphs 18–24) Rousseau compares botany, that is to say *his* botanizing (which is different from most), with other natural studies, to the decided disadvantage of the latter. He does not engage in any of these other studies during the time recounted here, but he does comment on them in order to compare them unfavorably to botany. Thus the second section of the Seventh Walk concerns the study of nature as such. It shows how one might *look* at nature, and with what result. In so doing it sketches an education to philosophy, or, as Socrates might have put it—as Socrates *does* put it in the second section of *Republic* 7—"in what way such men [philosophers] will come into being and how one will lead them up to the light" (521c). Socrates proceeds to take up the question of "what studies have such a power" (521d). He outlines a curriculum that begins with a "prelude" comprising five studies (number and arithmetic, plane geometry, solid geometry, astronomy, and harmonic movement) and culminates with "the song itself," meaning dialectic (521c–535a).

The Seventh Walk's third section (paragraphs 25–30) consists mainly of three anecdotes, the first of which is notable because it shows that Rousseau remains susceptible to overblown amour-propre. In this the Seventh Walk speaks to the *limits* of Rousseau's greater perfection as a philosopher that makes it in a certain sense a kind of descent. Yet the way that Rousseau responds to his amour-propre—his gently comic perspective on his limitations—amounts in the end to a deeply affirmative testimony. Indeed, the final two paragraphs of the Seventh Walk affirm botany (explicitly) and philosophy (implicitly) for their rich and humanizing effects on their practitioners. Similarly, the third and final section of *Republic* 7 (535a–541b) seems lower and darker than *its* preceding sections. It opens with Socrates asking, "To whom shall we give these studies and how shall we do it?" But the focus of the ensuing discussion is not the qualities of those who should be selected for philosophic education but rather what happens when one brings unqualified students to philosophy. Thus the third part of *Republic* 7, too, is a kind of descent. Yet as in the third section of Rousseau's Seventh Walk, the descent is no crash but rather a climbing-down from exaggeration and idealization to something still high—and *real*. And like Rousseau, Socrates experiences a flare-up of amour-propre (*thymos*)—or at least pretends to—and then responds in the same spirit in which Rousseau responds to the unveiling and puncturing of his own amour-propre. Upon exclaiming that bringing unqualified men to philosophy would undermine the city "and also pour even more ridicule over philosophy," Socrates interrupts himself with a gentle statement of comic self-reproach. "I seem to have been somewhat ridiculously affected just now," he observes. "I forgot that we were playing and spoke rather intensely. For, as I was talking I looked at Philosophy and, seeing her undeservingly spattered with mud, I seem to have been vexed and said what I had to say too seriously as though my spiritedness were aroused against those who are responsible" (536b–c).

Socrates's statement is charming. It also signifies something quite serious, however, for where he pretends to have suffered aroused spiritedness and playfully reproaches himself for it, others would have been overtaken by the real thing and, far from reproaching themselves for it, would have embraced it all the more. And among these others are some who purport to be philosophers. Thus, it seems to me, Socrates calls attention to yet another danger arising from philosophy, a danger that he does not address explicitly but which he sets before us all the same. I am referring to the danger that arises from idealizing philosophy and the philosopher. Idealization serves constructive purposes in the dialogue, but it can also lead to an illiberal perversion of both philosophy and politics. Both of these perversions, I would hold, are on display in the kallipolis. Socrates's cautionary notes regarding philosophy in the final pages of book 7 can help us see the kallipolis as a warning against prideful self-certainty. And Rousseau? As we'll see, he provides a comparable warning in the final section of the Seventh Walk.

FIRST SECTION: PARAGRAPHS 1–17

The Seventh Walk has a dual character. It is about botany, and it is about wisdom. In its first lines, Rousseau announces his newly all-absorbing pastime. By the middle of the first paragraph, he claims the mantel of wisdom. What wisdom permits—what "wisdom itself *wills*"—is that he do "whatever gratifies" him. Why? Two reasons suggest themselves. First, Rousseau is powerless to do anything about his lot. Second, he has "only innocent inclinations." The first reason means that there's nothing else in particular that he should be doing; the second means that there's no reason not to do what he wants to do. That the claim to be living wisely is made without fanfare amid a colorful, larger introduction to his botanizing does not cut against its enormous import. Neither does its correspondence in placement to the *Republic*'s Image of the Cave, whose anonymous hero must struggle tenaciously to get to the sunlit flora where Rousseau already is. If this isn't enough, Rousseau soon makes a second, perhaps even more astonishing claim. To the mantel of wisdom—now said to be *great* wisdom—he adds that of great *virtue*: "I do not seek to justify the course I take in following this fancy [i.e., botany]. I find it very reasonable, persuaded that in my present position it is great wisdom and even great virtue to give myself up to the pastimes that gratify me" (3). This claim marks a decided shift. Heretofore, not only in the *Reveries* but in Rousseau's corpus more generally, "virtue" had signified the overcoming of inclination by duty. That is the virtue that Rousseau, by his own admission, lacks (VI, 7). Here in the Seventh Walk, however—in connection with the philosophic life—"virtue" means living *according to* inclination. It seems to have been redefined into its opposite.

If the two conceptions of virtue oppose one another with respect to inclination, however, they agree with respect to reason. Reason is what determines when inclination ought to be resisted (in the case of virtue as Rousseau has normally conceived of it), and reason specifically sanctions his giving way to inclination now (in the case of virtue as he has just redefined it): "without a doubt, reason permits me, even commands me, to give myself up to every propensity which attracts me and which nothing prevents me from following" (4). Why does reason permit Rousseau what it denies others? The answer is that whereas sociable men and women need virtue of the conventional sort, he, a solitary man of nature, can trust in his goodness. And yet trusting goodness—determining that it can be trusted—is a judgment made by reason with reference to principles and results. Or to say it more simply, Rousseau trusts his inclinations and judges that he may indulge them because they comport with the principles of natural right as reestablished by reason (*SD*, 15; 126). This is how goodness becomes virtue. In Rousseau, goodness has become moral. Like all moral beings, Rousseau is accountable to his conscience. Like very few moral beings, his conscience takes its bearings from nature. A conscience oriented to nature is strict, but only rarely does it impose on Rousseau. For, as it happens, all his inclinations are innocent (1).[1] Indeed, in his case yielding to inclination is not only morally permissible; it is the means to moral *improvement*. Let's look again at paragraph 3:

> I do not seek to justify the course I take in following this fancy. I find it very reasonable, persuaded that in my present position it is great wisdom and even great virtue to give myself up to pastimes which gratify me. *It is the means of not letting any germ of revenge or hatred spring up in my heart*; and, given my destiny, to still find delight in any amusement, it is surely necessary to have a natural temperament quite *purified of all irascible passions*. I thus avenge myself of my persecutors in my way: I

1. Although he claims that in botanizing he is following reason's command, Rousseau admits that reason does not tell him *why* he is or should be attracted to it. Friedlander reads this admission as an indication that Rousseau's botanizes without intention and without the possibility of justification. See Friedlander, *J. J. Rousseau*, 78–84. What Friedlander takes to be an eschewal of intention and justification I take to be an eschewal only of instrumental intention and instrumental justification. The difference between our readings may seem trivial. But from small things large ones can arise. To see Rousseau as lacking intention and justification is to see him as lacking freedom, even natural freedom.

would not know how to punish them more cruelly than to be happy in spite of them. (emphasis added)

In Rousseau nature has become morality without ceasing to be nature. Goodness has become virtue without ceasing to be goodness. Natural freedom and moral freedom have become one and the same.

Rousseau's virtue is not *simply* moral virtue. Indeed, strictly speaking, it isn't moral virtue at all, but rather, as he calls it in this very passage, great *wisdom*. For Rousseau as for Socrates, true virtue is wisdom, of which moral virtue is but a phantom. The virtues as Socrates had defined them in book 4 of the *Republic* turn out to be only vulgar imitations of the real things: they are characterized by certain salutary *opinions* whereas true virtue is *knowledge*. Although he disavowed for himself the knowledge he attributes to the kallipolis's philosopher-kings, Socrates did lay claim to what he called *human* wisdom, which is still far more substantial, far wiser, than received opinion. The same is true of Rousseau's wisdom.

It may seem strange that Rousseau's decisive step toward wisdom and virtue should be presented in connection with botany rather than, say, intense introspection. But that's just the point. Wisdom and self-knowledge come when Rousseau, rather than contemplating himself, observes himself contemplating nature—when he observes himself contemplating nature in a certain *way*. Unlike other botanists, he sees nature for itself and thus *in* itself rather than in relation to his own needs, much less medicinal needs. Does one need to look away from oneself in order to see oneself? It would seem so, at least sometimes, and it seems to me that Rousseau means to teach this to readers. More particularly, one must look away from oneself to *nature*, that is, to external nature. What is natural in ourselves is so overlaid by and intermingled with artifice that in order to see it we would do well to start by directing our attention outside ourselves. We stand a greater chance of resisting the necessarily distorting allure of egocentrism when studying green nature rather than human affairs or even, perhaps especially, ourselves. Not that it's easy to resist the temptation of egocentrism anywhere. And even the most disinterested contemplator isn't *entirely* disinterested. One cannot hope to contemplate nature except as it presents itself to human beings with human needs and desires. But the chances of avoiding egocentric and anthropocentric prejudice are better when looking at plants rather than at ourselves and our fellows. Learning to see green nature clearly, learning to see it as it presents itself to us rather than as we might want to see it, is training for seeing ourselves clearly. Plants are not human beings, of course, and not even the most crystalline apprehension of plants would reveal anything about *human* nature, not unless there is some deep continuity between all natural beings—*which, in fact, there is.*

No, Rousseau does not deny human distinctiveness or indicate that he wishes he could.[2] Nor does he suggest that the study of nonhuman nature is sufficient for self-knowledge. Botany is not philosophy, and Rousseau never suggests that it is. But to botanize and to observe and study oneself botanizing, to study nature and to observe and reflect on oneself as student and part of nature—together these may be a gateway to philosophy. There are other natural sciences besides botany, of course, but botany seems to be the best one for Rousseau's purposes. In the second section he will discuss the particular virtues of botany vis-à-vis the other natural sciences. But we need hardly wait until then to see something of what makes botany the uniquely protophilosophic science that it is for Rousseau. The point is driven home from the start of the Walk. Either plants provide special entrée into nature altogether, or Rousseau uses them as a synecdoche for nature as such, or both. The first section culminates in a summary account of botany in which Rousseau describes an almost magical elaboration: "I feel ecstasies and inexpressible raptures in blending, so to speak, into the system of beings and in making myself one with the whole of nature" (16). Not the system of *plants*, but "the system of *beings*." Not one with *verdant* nature, but "one with *the whole* of nature."

Readers have not failed to take note of the ecstasies and the experience of oneness that Rousseau attributes to botanizing. What has garnered much less notice, however—indeed, hardly any notice, even though *it may be the most important revelation in the Seventh Walk and perhaps of the* Reveries *altogether*—are the *effects* he attributes to his new way of studying nature, that is, that it has afforded him "the means of not letting any germ of revenge or hatred spring up in [his] heart" and has "purified [him] of all irascible passions" (3). For with this claim, which was attended by none of the stylistic embroidery that attends the report of ecstasy and oneness, Rousseau indicates nothing less than that he has finally if still imperfectly embraced the cognitivist view of morality. He doesn't make this claim

2. To take Rousseau as lamenting human distinctiveness is an understandable error. What is more distinctively human than thinking, which Rousseau purports to find tiresome? Or than amour-propre, whose baleful consequences Rousseau has so tirelessly exposed? And yet as we've seen, a close reading of the *Reveries* reveals the goodness of thinking and the utility of amour-propre in the philosophic life (and not only in the philosophic life—think of Emile), if not in most of our lives.

explicitly, but he doesn't need to, for nothing else (apart from a religious faith he doesn't have) could have released him from the logic of retribution that ignites and sustains the irascible passions.

As we know all too well, this is not the first time in the *Reveries* that Rousseau has professed to be free of vengeance or hatred. It is, however, the first *credible* profession, in part because he finally if only tacitly concedes that prior to his return to botany he *had* been subject to vengefulness and hatred. I don't want to claim too much on Rousseau's behalf. We know that he will continue to be subject to inflamed amour-propre, and this may mean (though it is unclear) that he will continue to be subject to the recurrence of vengeful feelings. If so, Rousseau's purification is complete only when he is engaged in or perhaps mindful of his study of nature. Or perhaps his resistance to being *overcome* by amour-propre is sufficient to keep him from vengefulness. A clue that points to the latter alternative, though not conclusively, appears in the immediate sequel to the passage just quoted: "I thus *avenge* myself of my persecutors in my way: I would not know how to *punish* them more cruelly than to be happy in spite of them" (3; emphasis added). To some readers this line indicates that Rousseau has not been freed from vengefulness and hatred.[3] On the view of these readers, bad feeling has only been compounded by bad faith. But I see no indication that Rousseau believes that his so-called vengeance causes his enemies to *suffer* or that he wishes them to suffer. Absent such a wish, "vengeance" is at best a figure of speech. Not that figures of speech are meaningless. Rousseau has chosen to speak the language of vengeance and punishment for a reason. What reason? The likeliest candidate, in my view, is that by claiming to have avenged himself and to have punished his enemies he means to appease his calm but still inflammable amour-propre. That he knows to appease his amour-propre, and knows *how* to do so, is testimony to his skill at what I have previously referred to as statesmanship within and over the soul. Rousseau has learned how to govern his amour-propre. Or, if one likes, *in* Rousseau *reason* has learned how to govern amour-propre. Reason has even learned to enlist amour-propre in its own service, as we'll soon see.

This statesmanship, like all good statesmanship, seeks the good of the whole—not just the overcoming of certain difficulties but happiness and overall well-being. Rousseau is now credible when he claims to be happy. His tone is believable. So is his explanation of the *mechanism* whereby a new way of studying nature has led to greater happiness. This mechanism

3. See Pagani, "Living Well Is the Best Revenge."

is the calming of his imagination, or, perhaps better stated, the adoption of new principles by which to govern his imagination. That the calming of imagination might enhance one's happiness is not hard to understand (*Emile*, 303–7; 210–14). Thus we needn't doubt that Rousseau has related a real step into greater clarity and happiness, even if, as we'll soon see, we *can* doubt the character and intensity of his purported happiness. This step is the culmination of the *Reveries'* main drama. And like all living culminations, it is also a new beginning.

That the Seventh Walk marks a new beginning is signified from the start. The *Reveries* began, we recall, with the words *Me voici donc* (I, 1), a phrase that appears nowhere else in the book. But in the first paragraph of the Seventh Walk Rousseau uses a phrase that echoes that one as nearly as possible without repeating it. This phrase too appears only once in the entire book: *Me voilà donc*.

Voici versus *voilà*: the subtlest of differences, but not an unimportant one. The *voici* of the First Walk bespeaks melodramatic self-centeredness; the *voila* of the Seventh Walk, a more capacious, decentered perspective on the self. This reading is borne out in the immediate sequels. In both cases Rousseau proceeds to give an overall account of his condition in terms of what he has and what he lacks. Objectively speaking, the two accounts are very similar. Subjectively, however, or with respect to what Rousseau emphasizes in the respective passages, there is a great difference. In the passage from the First Walk, he emphasizes what he lacks: "Here I am, then [*Me voici donc*], alone on the earth, no longer having any brother, neighbor, friend, or society other than myself. The most sociable and the most loving of humans has been proscribed from society by a unanimous agreement" (I, 1). In the passage from the Seventh Walk, by contrast, he emphasizes what he *has*: "Here I am, then [*Me voilà donc*], with grass as my only nourishment and botany as my only preoccupation" (VII, 1). The respective emphases are maintained. The First Walk continues to be plaintive and even self-pitying. The Seventh Walk continues to be affirmative and even cheerful. The good cheer of the Seventh Walk may explain why Rousseau doesn't elaborate there on his deliverance from irascible passions. He prefers instead to dilate on the *positive* benefits of his new way of seeing nature. The alleviation of moral ills is certainly a benefit of his new way of seeing nature—it may be the greatest benefit—but to explain it in detail would require discussing previous unpleasantness and thus diminish the Seventh Walk's sunniness and lightness of tone. This descent is left for the Eighth Walk, though it is broached in the concluding paragraphs of the Seventh.

More instructive than the difference between the Seventh Walk and the

Eighth, however, is that between the Seventh and the Fifth. The Fifth Walk too reports rapturous reveries. But Rousseau gives no indication that *those* rapturous experiences had any effects that outlasted the experiences themselves. Evidently all ecstasies are not alike. But what is it that makes those of the Seventh Walk so much more beneficial? The answer, as Rousseau sees it, has to do with where and how one's attention is directed. Botanizing directs one's attention outside oneself, whereas the reveries recounted in the Fifth Walk are altogether inner-directed. To be sure, attention to what is outside oneself can be a way of avoiding self-awareness. But for one who does not seek self-escape but rather self-knowledge, directing attention outside oneself is favorable to the quieting of imagination and thus to clearer sight of the world. It makes one less susceptible to the prejudices and delusions of amour-propre and, when joined with adequate learning and openness, enables one to apprehend nature as a system and to reflect on one's relation to it.

Let us examine the events recounted in the Seventh Walk's first section more closely. The story begins with Rousseau suffering great apprehension: "In my reveries I even had to fear lest my imagination, frightened by my misfortunes, might finally turn its activity to this side and lest the continual sentiment of my troubles, gradually constricting my heart, crush me at last with its weight" (7). Silencing one's imagination under the pressure of such conditions might be regarded as an emergency measure, except that the word "measure" would imply forethought and deliberation whereas Rousseau depicts it as spontaneous: "In this condition an *instinct* which is natural to me, making me flee every depressing idea, imposed silence upon my imagination" (emphasis added). But that is not the whole of the sentence as written. Rousseau proceeds to introduce what I take to be the signal breakthrough that marks the peak of the *Reveries*. Here is the sentence in its entirety: "In this condition an instinct which is natural to me, making me flee every depressing idea, imposed silence upon my imagination and, fixing my attention upon the objects which surrounded me, made me consider in detail for the first time the spectacle of nature which until then I had hardly contemplated except in a mass and all together [*en masse et dans son ensemble*]" (7).[4] What an amazing report, all the more so for the casualness with which it is made. What is presented

4. Here I have departed from Butterworth (in *CW*), who renders the phrase "en masse et dans son ensemble" into English as "in a mass and in its *wholeness*." Wholeness, however, is precisely what one does *not* see when regarding things *en masse*.

as instinct transforms thought. Flight turns out to be a great step forward. Self-protection has become self-perfection.

What *was* this instinct that imposed silence on Rousseau's imagination? Was it simply an instinct for self-protection—was it an instinct at all—or did it partake of something larger and more varied? There is good reason to think that the latter is the case, since for Rousseau the concern for self-preservation is an expression of our naturally expansive self-love. Unlike Plato in his treatments of eros, Rousseau never suggests that our expansive self-love is directed toward a pregiven telos or even in any particular direction. Did the quieting of his imagination cause his attention to be directed to the natural world only by default, then, because there was no place else for his attention to go? Or did he somehow intuit that the desire to extend his being would find gratification in *knowing*? And if the latter was the case, does that imply the working of a natural intellectual eros? Rousseau doesn't answer these questions. He doesn't even pose them so much as tacitly allow them. Yet in light of his determination not to further stimulate the appetite for popular enlightenment, merely leaving open the possibility that his great step forward was propelled by intellectual eros is notable. And in fact he soon suggests that his botanizing was indeed animated by something like intellectual eros. In paragraph 8 he speaks of green nature as the earth's enlivening *"nuptial dress."* And later he observes that "plants seem to have been sown profusely on the earth . . . to invite man to the study of nature by the attraction of *pleasure and curiosity*" (23; emphasis added). A few lines later he remarks that the pleasure of botany, or at least one pleasure of botany, is painless, which might seem to indicate that eros is *not* at work here. Erotic pleasure, after all, presupposes the pain of prior longing. But perhaps that's not always the case; and the full line suggests that what is at work here is eros after all: the botanist "walks about, wanders freely from one object to another, examines each flower with interest and curiosity, and as soon as he begins to grasp the laws of their structure, he enjoys, in observing them, a painless pleasure *as intense as if it had cost him much pain*" (23; emphasis added). Such intensity of pleasure suggests eros, pain or no pain. Indeed, the painlessness may suggest that such experience as this, far from being unerotic, was *more perfectly* erotic than ordinary erotic experience, not unlike the philosopher's eros as described by Socrates.

With the quieting of his imagination Rousseau has adopted a new way of seeing, an integrative and noetic way of seeing. And with this new way of seeing has come a new way of experiencing life and even a new way of being that themselves might be called integrated and noetic. These terms are mine, not Rousseau's. I proffer them not for the sake of labeling what Rousseau has chosen not to label but to underscore that however peculiar or idiosyncratic his experience might have been, he understands it to have been grounded in nature and human nature as such. Indeed, in the immediate sequel he shifts without explanation from recounting his *own* experience in the first-person voice to speaking, scientifically, of *man* and of a certain *kind* of man in the third-person voice. He is done recounting how "an instinct which is natural to *me*, making *me* flee every depressing idea, imposed silence on *my* imagination and . . . made *me* consider" the spectacle of nature in a new way. Instead, he speaks of the harmonious spectacle that the earth "offers *man*," meaning all of us (8; emphasis added). People vary with respect to how much they are moved by this spectacle, but this variation can be expressed scientifically, in terms something like those of a mathematical function: "The more sensitive a soul a contemplator has, the more he gives himself up to the ecstasies this harmony arouses in him" (9).

An inconsistency now confronts us, however. No sooner has Rousseau noted the different experiences of differently sensitive contemplators than he proceeds to speak of only a single experience: "A sweet and deep reverie takes possession of his senses then, and through a delicious intoxication he loses himself in the immensity of this beautiful system with which he feels himself one. Then, all particular objects elude him; he sees and feels nothing except in the whole [*dans le tout*]" (9). The variation of experience from contemplator to contemplator is forgotten. Rousseau speaks as if every contemplative experience is exalted. He has *idealized* contemplation—just as Plato has in book 7 of the *Republic*.

We've already noted *Republic* 7's idealization of philosophy and philosophers. Philosophers as Socrates *describes* them are far more knowledgeable than the philosopher that Socrates *is* or ever claims to be. And yet Socrates's imperfection by comparison to the idealized philosophers is not clearly a defect. Few readers with a philosophic disposition, it seems to me, would prefer the ideal that Socrates articulates to the reality that he embodies. Unlike Socrates himself, the idealized philosophers show no sign of eros. Nor would they *know* anything about eros. Certainly they wouldn't have learned anything about it from their education, which, though it culminated in dialectic, completely neglected human affairs. There is no study of soul or politics, only number and arithmetic, geometry, astronomy, and harmonic movement. A true education to philosophy would be an education in the *whole* of physis. It would have to engage what Socrates engages: *human* virtue, *human* passions, and the like.

Rousseau's idealization of the contemplative life at this point in the text mirrors Plato's. As the *Republic*'s idealizing is evident in the discrepancy between philosophy as Socrates describes it and philosophy as he practices and lives it, the *Reveries'* idealizing is evident in the discrepancy between contemplation as Rousseau describes it and contemplation as we see him practicing and living it. In his *descriptions* of contemplation, Rousseau celebrates dreamy expansiveness and purports to find reflection tiresome (5). Yet we see him engaging in rigorous reflection—*choosing* to engage in rigorous reflection—throughout the *Reveries*. That he has been idealizing contemplation is indicated by Rousseau at the end of paragraph 9, right after the point at which we left off. Immediately following the mention of the contemplator's felt oneness with the system of nature and the disappearance from awareness of all particular objects such that "he sees and feels nothing except in the whole," Rousseau proceeds to answer a question that he has not asked and which, by answering as he does, he obscures: "Some particular circumstance must focus his ideas and close off his imagination for him to be able to observe the parts of this universe he was straining to embrace" (9). The question that is both answered and obscured is why someone who has dissolved into oneness with the whole of being would be "straining to embrace" particular parts of the whole. Who would want to descend from ecstatic oneness? Answer: Rousseau would. *A philosopher* would. Rousseau's botanical recollections show that he delights not only in the whole but in the parts as well. It belongs to contemplation to oscillate between a view of the whole and a focus on particular parts. But this oscillation doesn't happen automatically. It requires that "some particular circumstance . . . focus his ideas and close off his imagination."

Close off his imagination? Hadn't Rousseau's imagination *already* been silenced? Evidently not, or else being silenced does not mean *staying* silent. If imagination has to be closed off in order for the contemplator to direct his attention from the whole to the parts, it must have been at work while the contemplator was apprehending the whole as whole—which suggests that imagination was *needed* to apprehend the whole as whole. But if it requires imagination to see the whole, that doesn't make the whole a figment. Just the reverse is true: imagination allows one to hold many particulars in mind and thereby see the whole as whole. And if particular objects continue to elude the contemplator, that doesn't mean that imagination is again obstructing sight of what is: what eludes the contemplator are particular objects *in themselves,* that is, seen apart from the whole that they constitute. What eludes the contemplator is the sense, in fact the *delusion,* that the objects he sees are independent and freestanding, that they are not parts of a whole but rather self-subsisting wholes in themselves. A world consisting of independent and self-subsisting objects is the world as seen by amour-propre. To amour-propre, the world appears as an arena in which separate objects contend with one another; and the *social* world appears as an arena in which separate *selves* strive and contend with one another.[5] A mind freed from amour-propre's tyrannical grip, by contrast, can attend by turns to both parts and whole; its attention can oscillate from parts to whole and back again without denying the reality of what it has oscillated *from*. There is no contradiction between attention to details and contemplation of the whole. Nor, we might add, is there a contradiction between the contemplator's self-awareness and his loss of self in the "system with which he feels himself one." In an important sense, as we noted in chapter 1, the self does *not* lose itself. One still remains aware of one's experience as one's own. This is evident from Rousseau's detailed and patently self-aware accounts. What one loses—what one transcends—is the self that is structured or constituted by amour-propre.

If the foregoing is correct—if there is no contradiction between attention to particulars and awareness of the whole and no contradiction between self-awareness and losing oneself in the system of nature—that is because there is no contradiction between the different cognitive processes at work in the philosopher. Specifically, there is no contradiction between, on the one hand, reasoned, scientific analysis that reveals the details of nature and the details of one's own soul (and hence the *system* of nature and the overall *character* of one's own soul), and, on the other hand, the process through which one sees the whole as whole and experiences oneself as one with the whole. There is a radical difference between these faculties, yes, of course; but not a contradiction—no more so than there is a contradiction in Plato between the rigorous discursive analysis for which Socrates is so famous and the presumably *non*discursive and strangely *un*famous contemplation wherein Socrates abstracts himself from his environs for extended periods (*Symposium*, 174d–e, 220c); or between the modes of cognition represented by the upper and lower segments of the *Republic*'s Divided Line (509d–511d). Both Plato and Rousseau idealize contemplation. But idealization can have a basis in truth: it can be a fic-

---

5. "It is very natural that a person who loves himself should seek to extend his being and his enjoyments and to appropriate for himself through attachment what he feels should be a good thing for him. This is a pure matter of feeling in which reflection plays no part. But as soon as this absolute love degenerates in amour-propre and comparative love, it produces negative sensitivity, because as soon as one adopts the habit of measuring oneself against others and moving outside oneself in order to assign oneself the first and best place, it is impossible not to develop an aversion for everything that surpasses us, everything that lowers our standing, everything that diminishes us, everything that by being something prevents us from being everything" (*Dialogues*, 805–6; 112).

tion rather than a lie. And so we must remain open to the idea that the nondiscursive activities as well as the experience of oneness with nature that are recounted in the Seventh Walk are consistent with reason and even a part of it, just as the fruit is part of the tree. This openness requires a more capacious conception of reason than that which has prevailed in modernity, a conception more like Plato's. But let us leave that aside as a broader suggestion for a broader discussion. For present purposes the important thing is that we remain open to the possibility that the nondiscursive experiences recounted in the Seventh Walk may indeed belong to the philosophic life understood as the life of reason.

Let us not conclude this discussion of imagination without posing a discomfiting question. Even if calming his imagination made Rousseau a better philosopher, and even if it spared him undue anxiety, did it not also cost him something precious—namely, "those dear ecstasies which for fifty years had taken the place of fortune and glory and, without any other expense than that of time, had made me, in idleness, the happiest of mortals" (VII, 6)?

Perhaps not. I suggested earlier that his claim in the Third Walk to have undertaken "the most ardent and most sincere seeking that has perhaps ever been made by *any mortal*" allows and even suggests that his subsequent seeking *as a philosopher* was even *more* ardent and sincere since it was the seeking of one who, by virtue of learning to die or training his sights on eternity rather than immortality, is, in a sense, no longer mortal (III, 15; emphasis added). A similar interpretation is available in the current situation: Rousseau's claim that the reveries of the first fifty years of his life made him the happiest of *mortals* allows for and even suggests that his subsequent happiness *as a philosopher* was greater still. This reading further aligns Rousseau with the classical philosophers. Plato gives us a Socrates who calls eros, including philosophic eros, *divine* madness. And Aristotle flatly asserts that the contemplative life partakes of divinity and that we should not settle for merely human or mortal activity.[6] As for Rousseau, whenever he explicitly refers to himself as a mortal in the *Reveries*, it is in connection with limitations and almost always in connection with misfortune. The most revealing instance of this usage is his claim that he has endured "the saddest lot a mortal has ever undergone"—this at the very end of the Seventh Walk (30), just after he has elaborated his *happiness* as a *philosopher*.

6. Aristotle, *Nicomachean Ethics*, 1177b–1178a.

Why botany? Is the study of plants uniquely conducive to the study of nature as such? Or is it perhaps a uniquely apt synecdoche for philosophy? Or is botany simply Rousseau's favorite study, or even just the natural science he knows best? The answer perhaps embraces all these meanings. As the Seventh Walk tells the story, it was in and through botany that Rousseau learned how to study nature as it is, which is to say disinterestedly, though perhaps it would be more accurate to say that he learned how to study nature for the *love* of it, since one seeking pleasure is not really disinterested. Or maybe we should say Rousseau learned how to study nature for the love of *them*, both nature and the study of nature, though the latter is ultimately an expression of the former. Both of these loves, moreover, promise lovers even greater love than that with which they began. Nature becomes more loveable as one studies it, and the study of nature— philosophy—becomes more loveable as one deepens one's awareness and understanding of what one is doing and why. That this description applies to Rousseau is confirmed by the *Reveries* in its entirety, both in what is recounted and in the recounting itself. That he studies nature in order that he may come to love it all the more he states outright: "Attracted by the cheerful objects which surround me, I consider them, contemplate them, compare them, and eventually learn to classify them; and now I am all of a sudden as much a botanist as is necessary for someone who wants to study nature only to find continuous new reasons to love it" (21). But we've drifted from the question before us: why botany? After all, people pursue other natural studies for the love of it. There is no reason to regard the amateur astronomer or chemist as a botanist manqué. All nature and all the natural sciences have their passionate enthusiasts. Nevertheless Rousseau finds some kinds of natural beings and domains more loveable than others. They are more loveable for just the reason one would expect upon recalling that the love in play is eros. Eros, as everyone knows, is inspired by and drawn to the beautiful as seen by the erotic one. And for the erotic Rousseau it is plants and verdant nature as a whole that shine with the greatest beauty. It is for this reason that botany seems to him especially loveable and edifying. He goes so far as to perform a comparative analysis of several natural sciences, measuring botany against geology, anatomy, and astronomy. The contest is not close. Geology is the first contender to be dispatched. "In itself," Rousseau asserts, "the mineral realm has nothing lovely or attractive" (18). Moreover, the student is confronted by serious "difficulties," "encumbrances," "distasteful elements," and "labors" (20). And if geology comes off as brutalizing and unhealthful, anatomy is even worse, for it requires either the caging of animals, which is physically demanding and disheartening besides, or sifting through carcasses, which is repugnant for its intimacy with "stinking corpses, slavering and livid flesh, blood, disgusting intestines, dreadful skeletons, pestilential fumes!" (20). And like geology, anatomy imposes formidable logistic difficulties. Botany, by contrast, is inviting and immediately rewarding and elevating. The "brilliant flowers, diverse colors of the meadows, fresh shady spots, brooks, thickets, greenery," and the like not only please Rousseau but also purify his imagination.

Yet there is a strange inconsistency here. Prior to this point, Rousseau had been much more respectful of the other sciences. Consider the following passage from paragraph 8 in which not only botany but the other sciences are given respect as well:

> Trees, shrubs, and plants are the attire and clothing of the earth. Nothing is so sad as the sight of a plain and bare countryside which displays only stones, clay, and sand to the eyes. But enlivened by nature and arrayed in its nuptial dress amidst brooks and the song of birds, the earth, in the harmony of the three realms, offers man a spectacle filled with life, interest, and charm—the only spectacle in the world of which his eyes and his heart never weary. (8)

In the light of this treatment, Rousseau's critique of geology and anatomy in paragraphs 18–20 can't but strike us as partial and unjust. Is eros intrinsically unjust? Unjust or not, it serves a purpose whose justice and beneficence more than outweigh the slights done to these sciences. I would suggest that Rousseau denigrates the other sciences for the sake of more effectively celebrating botany—and that he *wants* to celebrate botany more effectively because there is something about plants that renders the study of them, at least his way of studying them, particularly conducive to philosophy.

Compared to the objects of the other natural sciences, plants are uniquely *purposive*. And their beauty and fascination can help us set aside our own almost inevitably distorting purposes. In this botany is indeed unique. Unlike objects in the mineral realm, plants have purposes of their own and thus cannot quite as easily be regarded merely as raw materials to be shaped by our own purposes. Unlike domesticated animals, plants can't so easily be made to appear to adopt the purposes of those who raise them. Yes, plants can be cultivated and doctored quite effectively; but they can't be made to act upon our spoken command as can domesticated animals. And unlike *wild* animals, plants, at least when studied in their natural settings, neither impose purposes on us nor solicit purposes from us. (A natural science that Rousseau does *not* include in his comparative analysis is the study of human beings, perhaps because human beings as they present themselves are too far removed from nature to belong in this discussion. Or perhaps Rousseau *has* considered the study of human beings after all—under the rubric of studying wild animals.)[7] Is it not a worrisome thing from the standpoint of philosophy that botany's advantages seem to depend so much on the beauty of its subject matter? In the passage quoted from paragraph 8, Rousseau likens plants to attire; but attire covers up the wearer. Is the study of nature to be pursued only in surfaces? *Can* it be? Not that surfaces are without philosophic interest, if only because there is no getting to depths except through or even *in* them.[8] And not that plants don't also have an exquisite interior beauty, though of course even this beauty, though not belonging to outward surfaces, is surface beauty all the same. (The interior becomes surface to the one who has penetrated the outer surface.) But we needn't worry too much about this surface orientation, for as we have seen, another kind of beauty presents itself to the student of nature. Some kind of sublimation seems to take place, likely by the faculty of imagination governed by reason. And if some will be so enchanted by the beauty of surfaces that they don't care to go any further? Well, this would hardly be the worst course for those who will have shown themselves not to be philosophers at heart.

But Rousseau's comparative analysis of natural sciences isn't quite done. It still remains to consider astronomy, the only one of the sciences he has reviewed that is included in *Republic* 7's prephilosophic curriculum. Rousseau does not denigrate astronomy. In fact he likens it to botany with respect to the broader study of nature: "Plants seem to have been sown profusely on the earth, *like the stars in the sky*, to invite man to the study of nature by the attraction of pleasure and curiosity" (23; emphasis added). Like botany and *un*like geology and anatomy, astronomy is acknowledged to be a promising entryway to philosophy. But even astronomy does not seem to him quite *as* promising an entryway. In the very next lines, Rousseau suggests that astronomy is less effective than botany as an invitation to the study of nature as a whole because the heavenly bodies are so re-

---

7. "For injustice is harshest when it is furnished with arms; and man is born naturally possessing arms for [the use of] prudence and virtue which are nevertheless very susceptible to being used for their opposites. This is why, without virtue, he is the most unholy and the most savage of the animals, and the worst with regard to sex and food." Aristotle, *Politics*, 1253a35–40.

8. See Nietzsche, *Gay Science*, section 4 of the preface.

mote while plants beckon from close by. Rousseau's correction of Plato is grounded in a certain Platonic logic: surely the prospect of sunlit, green nature is a more effective inducement to ascend from the cave than the cold, distant, starry heavens. Or might the sunlit uplands be *too* attractive? Might they lure people only to green nature, that is, only to botany and the like and not to philosophy? They well might. In fact Rousseau presumably trusts that they often *will*. As Socrates would have those who lack a philosophic disposition live lives of moral and civic virtue, Rousseau, writing in an age he believes has sacrificed its right to speak of citizens and fatherlands, would have them live lives of nature and *goodness*.

THIRD SECTION: PARAGRAPHS 25–30

The Seventh Walk's concluding section is structured around three anecdotes. The first and by far the longest concerns Rousseau himself and is told at his own expense (25–27). He sets it up thematically in paragraph 24, where he dilates on botany's power both to deliver him from men and to supply the deficit that this deliverance necessarily creates: "The more profound the solitude in which I then live, the more necessary it is that some object fill the void; and those my imagination denies me or my memory pushes away are replaced by the spontaneous products that the earth, not violated by men, offers my eyes on all sides." We have no reason to doubt that natural objects would enter the void that imagination and memory have left unfilled. But we might doubt whether the products of the earth have completely filled the void, leaving no emptiness into which untrammeled imagination might rush. For that is what turns out to be the case. The story that Rousseau proceeds to tell finds him alone, on a botanizing expedition, in a particularly wild and remote place. The story is told well and in detail: "I went deep into the winding crevices of the mountain; and passing from wood to wood and boulder to boulder, I arrived at a retreat so hidden that I have never seen a more desolate sight in my life" (25). Further description follows, now including not only foliage but also the difficult and indeed frightening terrain. Rousseau speaks of "horrible precipices, which I dared to look over only by lying down on my stomach." He recalls birds—first the cries of predatory birds, then small birds that "tempered the dreadfulness of this solitude." This dizzying Alpine experience was not so overpowering as to make him to forget about botany: he reports the names of the plant species he encountered in this place. But the experience seems to have *altered* his botanizing: he refers to the plants he encountered by their Latin names. Why Latin? Perhaps to signify that his botanical discoveries on this occasion in fact had little purchase on him. Rousseau *had* forgotten botany. He tells us so: "imperceptibly dominated by the strong impression of the surrounding objects, I forgot botany and plants." Instead,

> I sat down . . . and began to dream more at ease thinking that I was in a refuge unknown to the whole universe where persecutors would not unearth me. A flash of pride soon inserted itself into this reverie. I compared myself to those great travelers who discover an uninhabited island, and I said to myself with self-satisfaction: "Without a doubt, I am the first mortal to have penetrated thus far." I saw myself almost as another Columbus. (25)

Imagination has stepped in where the reality before him has lost its interest. And yet it is not imagination per se that Rousseau depicts as the primary psychic actor in this story but rather *pride*. Imagination is the operative faculty, but it is pride, a species of amour-propre, that drives and feeds imagination even as it is fed by imagination in return. As always, the driver behind events is passion.

We already know that amour-propre persists in Rousseau's soul even now, in his fullest maturity. Does it also remain ungoverned? Yes and no. Yes, in that amour-propre can temporarily direct his thoughts and feelings, as it did in this episode, either unconsciously or with his complicity. But no, in that, once he realizes what has happened—not just that his amour-propre has flared, but that it has led him into ridiculous self-conceit—he can recover himself, as he did in this very episode when, in this most remote and wild place, he stumbled upon . . . a stocking mill! Evidently our Columbus had unknowingly doubled back to the Old World. With this, reason and amour de soi were restored to rule. More precisely, the reason of amour de soi was restored to rule. Amour-propre's coup had failed. What's more, the restoration was gentle. No purges, no martial law, no settling of scores; just a brief series of steps, not without some displeasure, but pleasant in the end. Step one: upon discovering the stocking mill, Rousseau's "first impulse was a feeling of joy to find [him]self back among humans when [he] had believed [him]self totally alone." But, alas, step two was quick to arrive. His joy "soon gave way to a painful and more lasting feeling of being unable, even in the deepest recesses of the Alps, to escape from the cruel hands of men eager to torment" him (26). For Rousseau was "quite sure" that the mill workers had been enlisted into a plot against him orchestrated by a certain Pastor Montmollin. But this feeling too would soon be eclipsed, and what would follow would be something we have not yet seen from Rousseau. This was step three: "I hastened to *drive away* this depressing idea and ended up *laughing* to myself about both my puerile vanity and the comic manner in which I had been punished for it" (26; emphasis added). What a profound if undersold change this reaction bespeaks. Our hero freed himself and laughed at himself; he laughed at his vanity and at the puncturing of his vanity. Justice ("punishment") *was* exacted, but it was a gentle and truly corrective justice, justice that improved the offender, much gentler than the formerly moralistic Rousseau would have supposed justice could be. An easy spirit would soon prevail, a gently comic spirit—*the spirit of philosophy*.[9]

The same comic spirt pervades the two remaining anecdotes, each of which, like the first, centers on a faintly ridiculous but harmless idiosyncrasy that nevertheless illuminates something deep-seated and consequential. This time, however, the character revealed to us is not Rousseau's but rather that of a *people*—*two* peoples: first the Swiss, then the French Savoyards (27–28). With these little tales Rousseau teaches us something about the posture from which to observe and think about peoples as such. The story about the Swiss concerns a man whose house is the only one on a certain mountain but who makes a good living all the same—as a bookseller. In him is revealed the "mixture of wild nature and human industry" that one finds only in the Swiss. "It seems to me that a single fact of this kind makes Switzerland better understood than all the descriptions of travelers" (27). The story Rousseau tells about the French Savoyards, "a quite different people" from the Swiss, is similarly revealing. One Squire Bovier, who had made it his mission to act as Rousseau's bodyguard and accompany him on a botanical expedition, did not say a word when he saw Rousseau eating berries that he, Bovier, like the rest of his countrymen, believed to be poisonous. What kind of a bodyguard is that? One who protects the *standing* of his charge even more than his life. One of Bovier's friends, seeing Rousseau partaking of the berries, rushed over to stop him, whereupon Rousseau "looked at Squire Bovier and said to him: 'Why, then, didn't you warn me?' 'Ah, sir,' he replied to me in a respectful tone, 'I didn't dare take the liberty'" (28). What a funny and rich comment on nature and humanity. Nature proves not to have been as harsh as thought: the berries, as it happens, did not sicken Rousseau. And so the humanity of the Savoyard was aligned with nature—but only accidentally, or, rather,

9. For further observations about the shift of perspective signified by Rousseau's laughter in the Seventh Walk, see Scott, "Rousseau's Quixotic Quest." Scott does not link Rousseau's laughter to philosophy or the philosophic spirit per se, but he comes as close as possible: the laughter of the Seventh Walk signifies the narrator's recognition of the tragicomic character of his pursuit of solitary satisfaction and self-knowledge.

erroneously. His humanity, surely grounded in natural goodness, had been commandeered on behalf of falsehood.

All three anecdotes are circumstantially connected to botany. The same is true of the Seventh Walk's final two paragraphs (29–30). Here, though, Rousseau brings our attention back to himself and what he owes to botany. Given what botany has done both for his perfection as a philosopher and for his happiness—or, if one prefers, given what *he* has done with botany—it seems only appropriate for him to return to himself in the Seventh Walk's denouement.

Or *are* the final paragraphs a denouement? Certainly paragraph 30 seems to be. It and thus the Seventh Walk as a whole end on a complicated note, bathed at once in splendor and sadness. Having noted in paragraph 29 that he is no longer able in his old age to scale the splendid peaks that botany had offered him, Rousseau indicates in paragraph 30 that he is able to *relive* them after all. Key to this happy possibility is, of all things, *imagination*: "Botany gathers together and recalls to my imagination all the ideas which gratify it more. The meadows, the waters, the woods, the solitude, above all, the peace and rest to be found in the midst of all that are incessantly retraced in my memory by my imagination" (30). Imagination performs two critical functions here: it receives, and it conveys. But notice an interesting discrepancy. What imagination receives are *ideas*. What it then conveys, what it retraces in memory, are *images* or remembered perceptions (the meadows, the woods, etc.). Thus we may infer that imagination also performs a third, intermediary task that might be described either as converting ideas into images or as distilling images from ideas. Perhaps the best name for this task would be—*imagining*. We see again that imagination, the faculty that had obstructed Rousseau's philosophizing and undermined his happiness, *contributes* to them once it is has been brought under rational governance:

> Botany makes me forget men's persecutions, their hatred, scorn, insults, and all the evils with which they have repaid my tender and sincere attachment for them. It transports me to peaceful habitats among simple and good people, such as those with whom I formerly lived. It recalls to me both my youth and my innocent pleasures; it makes me enjoy them anew and, quite often, still makes me happy in the midst of the saddest lot a mortal has ever undergone. (30)

Botany made Rousseau a more perfect philosopher and a happier man only after his imagination was first checked and then wisely deployed. And judging from the lines just quoted, the concluding lines of the Seventh Walk, botany *continues* to serve him in these ways.

But how can botany still serve Rousseau when advanced age keeps him from making the needed expeditions? Here too, even more wonderfully, imagination is key. This point is made very subtly but emphatically in paragraph 29, through a slight linguistic variation. The paragraph begins with an emphasis on place: "All of my botanical jaunts, the diverse impressions of *the place* in which the objects which struck me were located, the ideas that it [the place] brought forth in me, the incidents which were mingled with it, all of that has left me with impressions which are renewed by seeing the plants that I had looked for in *those very places*" (29; emphasis added). Rousseau then proceeds to enumerate "those very places" by type. They include "beautiful landscapes, forests, lakes, groves, masses of rock," and "mountains whose sight has always touched my heart." From here he proceeds to observe that although he can no longer visit these places, he can recall them, indeed he can be "transport[ed] there." But let us return to the first sentence, for within its brief compass is a significant linguistic shift that one is bound to overlook in English translation. The sentence ends with reference to places in the plural; the word is *lieux*. And since Rousseau proceeds to enumerate these places, the plural is apt to stay in the front of our minds, perhaps leading us to forget, if indeed we even noticed, that the sentence's first reference to place was in the singular, and made use of a different word to boot: *du local*. It was this single and indeed singular place whose "diverse impressions" struck Rousseau and brought forth ideas in him. We could read the singular *local* to refer to each particular place in which Rousseau examined plants, that is, to each of the plural *lieux* that he goes on to enumerate. But a more persuasive reading sees *local* as referring to a fundamentally different kind of place from the places referred to as *lieux*. *Lieux* refers here to physical or geographical places—landscapes, forests, lakes, and the like. And *local*—what might *it* refer to? An answer comes to light if we restate the question. What kind of "place" could have left Rousseau with "diverse impressions" and "brought forth" in him (literally, "gave birth in him to") ideas? Such a place could only be a mental space: a cognitive field, a mind, a soul. This possibility becomes a strong probability in the second sentence of the paragraph, a sentence from which I selectively quoted above. Here is the entirety of the sentence: "I will never again see those beautiful landscapes, forests, lakes, groves, masses of rocks, or mountains whose sight has always touched my heart; but now that I can no longer roam about those happy regions, I have only to open my herbarium, and it soon transports me there." Transports me *there*. The French allows for the referent of "there" to be either singular or plural. No matter, though. What does matter is that Rousseau need only open his herbarium in order to be transported there. This transportation could only be the work of imagination—particularly since, as he had related in paragraph 2, *he no longer has a herbarium*. He sold it years ago, thinking that his days of botanizing were over. (He did add in paragraph 2 that he had resolved to make another herbarium. But the sequel makes clear that he has not yet made good on this resolution.) The herbarium that transports Rousseau in these latter days can only be the herbarium of imagination. This new herbarium is more expansive by orders of magnitude than the one he sold. It includes "all the plants of the sea and the Alps and all the trees of the Indies in it." The only eye that could begin to take in such a wide expanse of nature is the eye of imagination. The only eye that could glimpse the whole of nature is the eye of imagination in the service of philosophy.

Eighth Walk

Like book 8 of the *Republic*, the Eighth Walk of the *Reveries* sets out to survey life under a sweeping array of different conditions. Book 8 begins with Socrates, after briefly restating the chief features of the kallipolis, preparing to discuss the remaining forms of regime that "it is worthwhile to have an account of" and "the men who are like these regimes" (544a). Similarly, the Eighth Walk begins with Rousseau preparing to discuss how *he* has fared across a variety of life circumstances. He opens the Eighth Walk by observing that his well-being has not tended to track with his prosperity. "In meditating upon the dispositions of my soul during all the situations of my life, I am quite struck to see so little proportion between the different phases of my fate and the habitual feelings of well-being or uneasiness by which they affected me" (1). In paragraph 2, however, what has just been described as "so little proportion" turns out to be a strong correlation—a strong *negative* correlation that bespeaks causation. "When all was in order" around him, Rousseau explains, his "expansive soul extended itself" so profligately that it effectively vacated itself: "I somehow forgot even myself. I was entirely devoted to what was alien to me; and in the continual agitation of my heart, I experienced all the vicissitudes of human things" (2). The story that he tells about himself is also the story of humankind, familiar to us especially from the *Second Discourse*. As with humankind as a whole, so with Rousseau in particular the cascading effects of this expansion-cum-self-forgetting culminated in a perplexing unhappiness—perplexing because it defied the expectations that had prompted his soul to extend itself in the first place. He had reached out. He had gained what he'd sought. "What was I lacking, then, to be happy? I don't know, but I do know that I was not happy" (2). The author of the *Reveries* pretty clearly does know what Rousseau the narrator may not. The author stands toward the narrator just as he had stood toward the Genevans when he dedicated the *Second Discourse* to them: "your happiness is all established," he had told his (former) countrymen; "it is only necessary to enjoy it; and to become perfectly happy you have no other need than to know how to be satisfied being so" (*SD*, 115–16; 7). The full import of this line is apt to go unnoticed until one proceeds through the *Discourse* proper, where it becomes all too clear that this seemingly small lack is no small thing at all. Neither the Genevans nor any other people "know[s] how to be content."

Both *Republic* 8 and the *Reveries*' Eighth Walk describe a *decline*. Socrates narrates the decline of the kallipolis into a series of four progressively worse regimes: timocracy/timarchy, oligarchy, democracy, and tyranny. Rousseau too presents a four-stage narrative, but the decline that he articulates is not in the narrative per se. In fact the second and third stages of his narrative trace an *ascent*. Stage 1 is the intense agitation and fury into which he plunged upon learning of the conspiracy against him. Stage 2 is his long struggle to come to terms with this condition, a struggle that culminated in his embrace of the wisdom of acceptance. But this embrace, which ought to have restored him to equilibrium, didn't. Considerable time would pass before he would finally come to understand the reason—that is, that what he had believed to be a passion for justice in his heart was really only petty pride passing itself off as a passion for justice. It was only with this discovery that stage 3, the attainment of equilibrium, finally began. Rousseau does not identify these three stages as such, but they are recognizable all the same. The fourth stage, however, is not so clearly demarcated, for Rousseau presents the third stage as if it were the end of the story. But although Rousseau had presented his discovery of amour-propre's insidious machinations as something close to a total victory, with amour-propre degraded to the point at which it could no longer seriously undermine his well-being, we soon see that his victory hadn't been as clean as he had suggested. The sway of his amour-propre has diminished, but not to the degree that Rousseau had indicated. It mounts a serious insurgency. Accordingly, Rousseau must launch and maintain a counterinsurgency. This is stage 4.

If the final stage of Rousseau's narrative can be seen as a decline, the narrative as a whole cannot—which would seem to mark a breakdown of the parallelism between the *Reveries* and the *Republic*. Yet the break is not as severe as it seems. Indeed, at a deeper level there is no break at all. The apparent distance between the two texts is narrowed from both sides. Rousseau, whose *story* (as I have just argued) recounts an ascent rather than a decline, nevertheless reports a kind of net decline in the Eighth Walk after all: "My soul—clouded and obstructed by my organs—sinks down day by day and, [beneath the] weight of these heavy masses, no longer has enough vigor to thrust itself out of its old wrapping as it used to do" (3). And Socrates's tale in *Republic* 8 is only superficially a story of decline. The first indication of this is his announcement at the outset that he is going to tell his story of decline in "high tragic talk," that is, that in what follows he will be speaking playfully (545d–e). Second, and more important, Socrates investigates the progressively corrupt regimes for the sake of making possible an ever *greater* wisdom. If his companions listen well, they will be progressively disabused of extravagant political idealism. They will learn that even the best regime must inevitably decline. They may even learn that the defects of the defective regimes have their origins in the kallipolis itself. The more thoughtful among them may thereby come to see that the so-called kallipolis, "beautiful city," is no such thing. And the *most* thoughtful of them, having been disabused of extravagant political ambition, may become open to the less flattering but more rewarding life of philosophy. The narrative of political decline is a pedagogical or philosophic *ascent*.[10]

But wait. If Socrates's story is really one of ascent, doesn't Rousseau's

10. This is not the place to lay out the argument, but the kallipolis itself can be seen—in my view, *should* be seen—as a tyranny. And not only with respect to overall governance, but even with respect to philosophy. Its ostensible philosopher-kingship notwithstanding, the kallipolis *constrains* philosophy. By pretending that its rulers are wise, it subverts awareness of ignorance and eros for the truth. Once we see this, we are prepared to consider whether the seeming four-stage descent from the kallipolis isn't an *ascent*—if not with respect to civic virtue, then with respect to favorability to philosophy. The case turns on whether the final regime, the one described as tyranny, could be thought to be somehow favorable to philosophy. In fact it can be. What makes the kallipolis tyrannical and anti-philosophic is that its so-called philosopher-kings are not true philosophers. The regime most favorable to philosophy, and perhaps to civic well-being too, would be one ruled by *true* philosophers, i.e., Socratic philosophers. This would be *true* philosopher-kingship, in which philosophers would "rule" by persuading people to salutary beliefs—the kind of rule that Socrates exercises over the dialogical community at Cephalus's house and, on a much greater scale, the kind of rule attempted by subsequent philosophers beginning with Plato and including Rousseau. True philosopher-kingship can exist only surreptitiously—which would make it, in the strict sense of the word, a tyranny (*tyrannia*), i.e., the ruling without legal right.

decline in vigor, which I introduced as *mitigating* the break in the *Reveries-Republic* parallelism, now prove to be a break in itself? It would—if it truly were what it appears to be. In fact, though, just as Socrates's apparent story of decline proves to be something else, so does Rousseau's, and for the same reasons. Rousseau too, it seems to me, elaborates his supposed decline in vigor in "high tragic talk." To be sure, it is perfectly plausible that a man of his years would have become less vigorous than he once had been. Let's stipulate that he has. But there are different kinds of vigor. And even as a man declines in one way, he might hold his own or even become stronger in another way. The *Reveries* tells just such a story. It recounts—and *demonstrates*—Rousseau's further perfection as a thinker. That, it seems to me, is what the story told in the *Reveries* is most of all about. And the culmination of the story, Rousseau's insight into amour-propre as told in the Eighth Walk, *is the same insight that is taught in Republic 8*, irrespective of whether Socrates's interlocutors learn it.

Like Glaucon (at least briefly),[11] Rousseau too is progressively disabused of a false and deeply debilitating conception of justice. The conception was false for being grounded in the ordinary moral consciousness, which is to say, for denying the compelling power of the apparent good. It was debilitating because it added agitation and resentment to the pain inflicted on him by his enemies. The agitation and resentment gave way, or at least ceased to hold Rousseau in thrall, with his discovery that what he had taken to be a noble passion for justice was in fact "petty self-pride." This discovery has allowed him to divest himself from the expectation that, because he *should* be treated justly, he *would* be—and from the underlying, implicit belief that if he is not treated justly, then life itself must be radically defective and can't be come to terms with. Rousseau has overcome the ordinary moral consciousness. He has finally made good on his many-times pronounced but only now credible claim to have achieved acceptance and equanimity through the wisdom of resignation. The claim began to be credible in the Seventh Walk, as we've seen, with his account of how he quieted his imagination and developed a new way of seeing and experiencing the world. The claim has become more credible still in the Eighth Walk.

---

11. I take Glaucon to have been persuaded by Socrates regarding the limits of politics and the political life. Whether he would remain persuaded is another question. Jacob Howland argues that Socrates's spell over Glaucon would later wear off and that much of the *Republic*'s dramaturgy, as it were, means to indicate just that. See Howland, *Glaucon's Fate*.

The story told in the *Reveries* is paradoxical, and its value lies chiefly in the resolution of the paradox. Rousseau had ostensibly embraced the cognitivist view of morality for many years. He had subtly indicated as much in the *Second Discourse* and had articulated its core principle, that is, the compelling power of the apparent good, in *Emile*[12]—if not in the terms I am using, decidedly all the same. Yet the resignation and peace that should have followed continued to elude him. How can this have been? How could Rousseau have believed something yet not attained that which ought to have followed from the belief? The only logical answer—also the most intuitively persuasive answer—is that, in truth, he had *not* believed in the compelling character of the apparent good and thus had not embraced the cognitivist view of morality—not completely, not in his bones, not all the way down. His account of finally seeing through amour-propre's disguise is the dramatic peak of the Eighth Walk. Few readers will altogether miss the import of this discovery. Something that readers *are* apt to miss, if only because Rousseau never calls attention to it, is why amour-propre's disguise should have been so effective in the first place—not why it should have succeeded in passing itself (in this instance, petty pride) off as a noble passion for justice, but why it should have caused him to lose sight of the compelling character of the good and thus remain captive to the ordinary moral consciousness that he has repeatedly professed to have overcome. Rousseau does not pose this question, let alone offer an explicit answer. Yet it is a question very much worth thinking about. Upon raising it, a subterranean world opens up to us. The disguise adopted by Rousseau's petty self-pride was far more than a disguise. It was a multipartite lie. Not only did it deceive Rousseau (a) about itself and thus (b) about *himself*. It also implicitly (c) denied the compelling character of the apparent good while (d) allowing Rousseau to believe that he accepted the compelling character of the apparent good. Amour-propre doesn't only mislead us about ourselves; it also weakens the strength of those of our convictions that dispute its understanding of the world, or, more precisely, the strength with which we hold those convictions. It thus diminishes our strength of soul by dividing us against ourselves. This is hardly a complete explication of amour-propre's insidiousness and its effectiveness at keep-

12. "A savage has a healthier judgment of us than a philosopher does. The latter senses his own vices, is indignant at ours, and says to himself, 'We are all wicked.' The former looks at us without emotion and says, 'You are mad.' He is right. No one does the bad for the sake of the bad. My pupil is that savage, with the difference that Emile, having reflected more, compared ideas more, seen our errors from closer up, is more on guard against himself and judges only what he knows" (*Emile*, 535; 399).

ing one from acceptance, but it is a necessary beginning, and perhaps more than a beginning.

Another question passed over in silence is what it was that finally enabled Rousseau to see what amour-propre had been up to. The answer to *this* question, as I have suggested, is nothing other than the story told in the Seventh Walk: that is, Rousseau's silencing his imagination and thereby coming to see what *is*, including what *he* is, more clearly and comprehensively. What he depicts as an impressive but narrow accomplishment belonging to his work as an amateur botanist was in fact a wholesale transformation of his way of looking at the world. And what he depicts as a welcome but less than monumental emotional cleansing, that is, his purification of revenge and hatred, was nothing less than his overcoming the ordinary moral consciousness. The former seems to have been the cause of the latter. By attributing his freedom from revenge and hatred to botany, Rousseau suggests that change of heart follows change of mind. He suggests that the overcoming of the ordinary moral consciousness follows from learning how to see the world more clearly. Plato suggests the same thing in the *Republic*. Socrates's account of philosophic liberation in book 7 makes it possible for his interlocutors to see the shortcomings of politics and thereby open themselves to a deeper wisdom in book 8. Rousseau's new way of seeing as recounted in the Seventh Walk has enabled him to see the shortcoming of his own psychic politics (amour-propre's illegitimate influence) and has thereby cleared the way to a deeper wisdom in the Eighth Walk.

The foregoing discussion has sketched what I take to be the main tenets of Rousseau's teaching in the Eighth Walk. But "teaching" has two meanings. It refers not only to what is taught but also to how it is taught. And with a writer of Rousseau's stature we can't do justice to the one without attending to the other. Let us therefore examine a bit more closely how the Eighth Walk's four-stage narrative works.

In the first stage (paragraphs 1–5) Rousseau establishes the constant against which the changes depicted in the narrative take place. He observes that his inner well-being or happiness has always tended to correlate negatively with his prosperity or external well-being. Men have inflicted great misfortune on him, Rousseau says. "And yet in this deplorable condition I still would not change being or destiny with the most fortunate among them, and I still prefer to be by myself in all my misery than to be any of those people in all their prosperity" (3). This pronouncement

echoes, in form and perhaps in more than form, Socrates's pronouncement at his trial that he preferred his own ignorance to the false wisdom
of others (*Apology*, 22d–e).

The second stage of the narrative (paragraphs 6–13) begins with Rousseau posing a question, "How have I come to that?" (6), whose answer
consists of a step-by-step account. Most of the steps are already familiar
to us. First came distress—the "indignation, fury, delirium" that took possession of him—upon discovering the conspiracy (6). In paragraph 7 he
reports that he found his way to peace and calm despite the conspiracy's
ongoing success. Paragraph 8 poses another question—"How was this
transmission made?"—and proceeds to an answer: he finally learned not
to struggle against the injustice inflicted on him and not to hope that
others would recognize the injustice of his condition (8). It was only by
giving up hope that he "again found serenity, tranquility, peace, even happiness" (9). With paragraph 10 come yet another question and answer:
"What gives rise to this difference? A single thing: I have learned to bear
the yoke of necessity without murmur" (10). This would seem to be the
end of the story. It *is* the end of the story as we have known it thus far.
But what sets the Eighth Walk apart from its predecessors is the inclusion of an additional step. Rousseau has come to see that learning to bear
necessity means more than just learning that one *should* bear necessity. It
requires looking at one's persecutors in a new way: "I understood that in
relation to me my contemporaries were nothing more than automatons
who acted only on impulse and whose action I could calculate only from
the laws of motion" (12).

Yet even this proves not to be the end of the story. Regarding one's
contemporaries as automata does not in itself produce the desired resignation and tranquility. Why not? Rousseau doesn't answer this question
explicitly. Indeed, he doesn't even explicitly acknowledge the insufficiency
of the automata strategy. But an answer comes into view upon examining
the automata strategy in light of the cognitivist view of morality. From the
standpoint of the cognitivist view Rousseau's formula both overshoots and
undershoots the truth. It overshoots by denying that human beings are
moral or spiritual beings. It goes beyond conceding that human beings are
compelled by the apparent good into denying the power and meaningful
existence of *any* kind of good. Rousseau's formula *under*shoots the truth
with respect to scope. It speaks to how he should regard those with whom
he already has dealings but says nothing about how to regard anyone else,
let alone human beings in general. These defects are theoretical, not practical. But theoretical defects become practical defects when they obtrude

into one's awareness, especially if one is a philosopher. This likely explains why Rousseau almost immediately begins to refine his strategy.

The undershooting ends in paragraph 13, where he speaks about human beings in general. "In all the evils which befall us," he begins, meaning by "us" *all* of us, "we look more to the intention than to the effect. . . . Material suffering is what we feel least in the blows of fortune; and when the unfortunate do not know whom to blame for their misfortunes, they blame fate which they personify and to which they ascribe eyes and an intelligence to torment them intentionally." Rousseau's exemplar of this cast of mind is the gambler who, "vexed by his losses, becomes furious at he knows not whom. He imagines a fate which relentlessly and intentionally torments him and, finding fuel for his anger[,] . . . becomes irritated and inflamed against the enemy he has created for himself." And yet if this propensity is the rule, there are exceptions; at least there can be exceptions. Against the gambler Rousseau juxtaposes *the wise man*. "The wise man, who sees only the blows of blind necessity in all the misfortunes which befall him, does not have this insane agitation. He cries out in his suffering, but without being carried away, without anger. He feels only the material blow of the evil to which he is prey, and the beatings he receives injure his body in vain—not one reaches his heart." The wise man distinguishes himself not only from the gambler but also from the practitioner of the automata strategy. He neither personalizes fate (like the gambler) nor depersonalizes human beings (like Rousseau in paragraph 12). Whether one might plausibly hope to *be* this wise remains to be seen.

The path to this wisdom, or *toward* it, is mapped out in the third stage of the narrative (paragraphs 14 through 16). The path begins with Rousseau's realization that everything he had theretofore understood, true and important though it might be, would not suffice for freedom and peace. To understand is not enough: Rousseau had "understood that the causes, the instruments, and the means of all that [befell him], unknown and inexplicable to [him], ought not to matter to him"—but what ought not to have mattered continued to matter. He had "understood that [he] ought to regard all the details of [his] fate as so many acts of pure fatality to which [he] ought not ascribe direction, intention, or moral cause"—but he had continued to ascribe direction, intention, and moral cause. He had "understood that [he] had to submit to [his fate] without reasoning and without struggling, because that would be useless"—but he had continued to reason and struggle (14). To which we might respond by asking, *Had* Rousseau really understood these things, then? Can one be said to have understood something if one's actions contravene one's supposed understanding? Certainly one cannot be said to have understood them firmly or all the way down: "It is a lot to have reached this point, but it is not all. If we stop here, we have indeed cut out the evil, but we have left the root" (14).

For a long time Rousseau had done just this: he had left the root. It was only when he finally asked why he "still felt this heart of [his] grumble" that he would find the root that he had not seen or perhaps even suspected: "What gave rise to this grumbling? I sought for it and found it: it came from amour-propre which, after having become indignant about men, also rebelled against reason." Reason had failed to deliver the peace and freedom of radical acceptance because amour-propre had been staging a successful rebellion. So successful had the rebellion been that reason hadn't even known of it, let alone quelled it.

Amour-propre's insidiousness had kept Rousseau from this discovery. Once the discovery had been made, however, things improved quickly and easily, as a matter of course:

> This discovery was not as easy to make as one might believe, for an innocent persecuted man considers his petty self-pride as pure love of justice for a long time. Still, once the true source is known, it can easily be dried up or at least diverted. Self-esteem is the greatest motive force of proud souls. Amour-propre, fertile in illusions, disguises itself and passes itself off as this esteem. But when the fraud is finally discovered and amour-propre can no longer hide itself, from then on it is no more to be feared; and even though we stifle it with difficulty, we at least easily overcome it. (15)

With this assessment of reason's limits and capacities Rousseau adumbrates a paradoxical new rationalism. Reason had long proved incapable of mastering passion, and it had compounded its insufficiency by supposing itself to be more powerful than it was or could have been. (Reason, it would seem, has its own amour-propre.) Yet this same reason, by finally discovering and acknowledging its own insufficiency, has become a more reasonable reason and indeed a more powerful reason that opens the way to real practical wisdom. Reason has been humbled, but it has been empowered by this very humbling. Its domain has not been enlarged, but within its domain it has become a more effective governor. Amour-propre, though it can't easily be stifled, *can* easily be overcome. What gives reason the power to overcome amour-propre, it would seem, is amour-propre itself. Reason has turned the tables and enlisted amour-propre into *its* service. "Self-esteem is the greatest motive force of proud souls," Rousseau has told us. As such, it is too strong to be conquered. But it is not too strong or too clever to be recruited into an alliance.

Overcoming amour-propre means ceasing to be ruled by it. It does not mean ceasing to suffer from it. Passions will continue to arise from irrational principles and judgments. Even if reason should identify and refute these principles or judgments, that is no guarantee that the passions will dissolve or be transformed. Passion always has its reasons, but it is also grounded and experienced in the body. There can be no passion where either of these elements is missing, any more than there can be a physical object that lacks either matter or form. Indeed, the somatic element is something like the matter of a passion; and the reasoning element, the principle and judgment, determines what we might regard as the passion's form. It is the bodily element that places the passions beyond the command of even the most empowered reason, both before they are triggered and, especially, in the aftermath of the triggering. *Before they are triggered* because our investment in suspect principles and judgments, though cognitive, is not *only* cognitive: with firm belief comes a tenacity that is somehow bodily. *In the aftermath of the triggering* because where passion is felt, physiological processes are at work that must run their course once they have begun. All of which is to say that irrational passions will continue to arise and must run their course. Knowing this, Rousseau has come to see that any effort to resist passions by repudiating them must be futile or indeed worse than futile. Resistance compounds suffering by keeping one engaged in battles that can never be won. He also knows that this is hardly cause for despair from the standpoint of well-being or even from the standpoint of reason. What he has told us about amour-propre is true of any passion. Once its true source is known, "it can easily be dried up or at least diverted." In short, discovering the limits of reason's power is the beginning of its capacity for effective *governance*.

We might wonder if Rousseau hasn't overstated the ease with which amour-propre can be governed. And perhaps he has. But there is also reason to think that he has understated what such governance can mean. In the line just quoted he speaks as if diverting amour-propre is a lesser good than drying it up. And so it is—*from the standpoint of one whose aim is to diminish the discomfort of being human.* But a different view is possible and indeed suggested. In the *Second Discourse* Rousseau had identified amour-propre (the "universal desire for reputation, honors, and preferment") as the source not only of the worst but also of the best things we possess. "Our philosophers" are among the six things he lists, and the one whose status is least clear: is it among the worst or the best or both?

(*SD*, 189; 63). But whatever might be said of "our philosophers" in toto, *true* philosophers surely land on the good list, at least when viewed from the standpoint of nature or human flourishing. (When viewed from the standpoint of civic health, true philosophy has a more complicated status.) In the *Reveries* we see amour-propre at work in impelling Rousseau toward the philosophic life in the first place and then toward his further perfection as a philosopher, not to mention the part it plays in any number of other worthwhile activities and experiences.

That Rousseau underestimates the capacity for good self-governance is suggested most vividly in a description of how he handles his own indignation:

> at each blow, I let my blood boil. I let anger and indignation take possession of my senses. I yield this first explosion, that all my strength could neither stop nor delay, to nature. I try only to stop its consequences before it produces any effect. . . . But after having let our natural temperament have its first explosion, we can become our own master again as we regain our senses bit by bit. . . . I wait for the moment when I can conquer by letting my reason act; for it speaks to me only when it can make itself heard. (23)

These lines capture both the meaning and the limits of rational self-governance. But it is only in the next lines that Rousseau's critique of reason's practical potency reaches its full extent: "Alas! What am I saying, my reason! I would be very wrong to honor it with this triumph, for it hardly plays a role in any of this. Everything comes out the same when a changeable temperament is irritated by an impetuous wind, but becomes calm again the instant the wind stops blowing." But what seems to be a depreciation of reason is no such thing. How *does* Rousseau handle his negative passions so much better than he once did? Has there been climate change? If so, it's a change brought about by nothing other than reason. It is reason—statesmanlike, practical reason—that directs him to places where the winds are calmer or where he can find a way to escape the more powerful gusts. He has become like the philosopher described by Socrates who "keeps quiet and minds his own business—as a man in a storm, when dust and rain are blown about by the wind, stands aside under a little wall. Seeing others filled full of lawlessness, he is content if somehow he himself can live his life here pure of injustice and unholy deeds, and take his leave from it graciously and cheerfully with fair hope" (496d–e).

Why does Rousseau veil the potential efficacy of reason? The likeliest answer, by my reckoning, is that here, as in so many other places, he veils something good for fear that he might stimulate something bad. To openly vindicate and articulate reason's power for good would also be to vindicate and articulate reason's power for what *seems* to be good but isn't. In particular, Rousseau would have wanted to avoid encouraging the more technical and thus less statesmanlike conception of self-governance implicit in modern rationalism.

Rousseau's recognition of the somatic grounding of passion has great practical implications. If we regard the passions only as they would have us regard them—which is to say, as strictly moral forces, independent of the body and its needs—then, when we wish to calm a passion, we'll try to reason with it: either we'll challenge the judgment or principle that informs it, or we'll try to explain that, questions of merit aside, there is practical advantage in regaining calm. In either case, our effort is likely to fail. The physical component of passion is deaf to reason, and the moral component is apt to be suspicious of if not hostile to reason because it will already be invested in its own reasons. By contrast, when we are cognizant that the passions are grounded in the body, we can more easily accept that they are beyond our immediate and complete control—that sensations, being physical phenomena, must run their course, and that even the rational or moral component of a passion is not *simply* rational or moral, since it will have been informed and even spurred by subrational and submoral phenomena. Above all, awareness of the physical basis of the passions will make it easier to regard them with some detachment. We generally tend to regard the body as something we *have*, and the mind or soul as what we *are*.[13] Consequently, to the extent that we are cognizant of the passions' grounding in the body we needn't regard them as revelations of our essential or deepest self. We needn't feel quite so invested in them, or so accused on account of them when they're less than noble. Such detachment doesn't imply indifference any more than enlightened political statesmanship implies indifference toward those one has been charged to lead.

13. Aristotle is instructive here. Although he says repeatedly that human beings have a composite nature, he also says of *intellect* that "each person would even seem to *be* this part, if it is the governing and better part" of oneself (*Nicomachean Ethics*, 1178a). "*If it is the governing and better part*"—does this leave in question whether intellect truly *is* each person? It doesn't matter, and that's just the point: mind seems to us to be our true self. A vivid example of the tendency to regard one's mind as one's self and the body (and its desires) as something other than one's self is seen in Leontius, who chastises his eyes in the second-person voice for desiring to look upon an unwholesome sight. "Look, you damned wretches, take your fill of this fair sight (*Republic*, 440a). The eyes are *you*. The *I* who despises them is someone else.

Statesmanship over or within the self is a classical idea that finds its preeminent expression in the *Republic*. But for all that Socrates likens the soul to a city, the model he invokes to describe reason's governance of the soul is a wax image in which the soul's different desires are represented by different *animals* (588b–589b). Spiritedness is represented by a large and powerful lion, and the appetites are represented by an even larger multiheaded beast, some of whose heads are tame while others are savage. Alongside these great beasts, however, is a human being, who, though small and with little power of the blunt sort, can govern the large and powerful beasts all the same—not by overpowering them, but in the way that human beings might govern such beasts out in the world: "the human being within will most be in control of the human being and take charge of the many-headed beast—like a farmer, nourishing and cultivating the tame heads, while hindering the growth of the savage ones—making the lion's nature an ally and, caring for all in common, making them friends with each other and himself, and so rear them" (588b–589b). Likening self-governance to animal husbandry doesn't express a degraded view of humanity. It is reason, after all, that rules in Socrates's scenario—as it does in Rousseau's conception of self-rule in its fullness. In Rousseau's view as in Plato's, this fullness is only rarely approached. But in Rousseau's view as in Plato's, all human beings seem to have the faculties with which they might acquire virtue and achieve a measure of rational self-rule (435e; *Emile*, 651–52 and 813–26; 495 and 630–40).

The subrational parts of the soul are not likely to look favorably on the prospect of being ruled by reason. The appetites are likely to regard the idea as hidebound or cruel. The passions are apt to regard reason as a trimmer. To gain their acquiescence, reason will have to persuade them that their interests would be served by its rule. It will have to propose a social contract with attractive and credible terms. To the appetites it must guarantee an adequate degree of gratification. To the passions it must guarantee something that could plausibly be called freedom. The particulars of the contract would surely vary from person to person, as would the ways and means and even the aims of reason's statesmanship, though certain principles would presumably be common to all cases, beginning with those we have encountered in the Eighth Walk. The passions would be allowed to express themselves but only in such ways that would not directly or indirectly cause injury; and interaction with others, or the self's foreign policy, would guard against the gratuitous inflammation of amour-propre. The implementation of these principles would vary from person to person, but, again, not indefinitely. In most cases, it seems to me, any wise course as seen by Rousseau is one that would steer clear of unnecessary social and, especially, psychic entanglements.

Rousseau's story thus far has been sober but hopeful. It will end soberly and hopefully. But between now and then—which is to say, over the course of the fourth and final stage of the narrative (paragraphs 17–23)—it will take a turn. Amour-propre turns out to pose a more formidable challenge going forward than it had seemed to only a short time ago. This is a remarkable change from the account given only a few paragraphs earlier. *There*, although Rousseau had made no secret of how difficult it had been for him to see through amour-propre's disguise, he claimed that with the seeing had come profound relief: "when the fraud is finally discovered and amour-propre can no longer hide itself, from then on it is no more to be feared" (15). *Here* he gives a very different account—if not a different story, then the same story told from a very different perspective. He acknowledges that during the three-quarters of the time that he is not made to be in unwanted company, he lives "the happy and sweet life for which [he] was born"—a life, he stresses, in which amour-propre has no part: "In all this, love of myself [*l'amour de moi-même*] does all the work; amour-propre has nothing to do with it" (19). The remaining quarter of the time, however, turns out to be much more difficult than the account of just a few paragraphs earlier would have led us to expect—so much so that these shorter periods of distress seem to outweigh the longer periods of happiness in Rousseau's mind. Consider how he describes the inflammation of his amour-propre in paragraph 19:

> No matter what I might try to do, amour-propre then comes into play. The hatred and animosity I discern through the coarse wrapping of their hearts tear my own heart apart with sorrow; and the idea of being taken for a dupe in this foolish way adds a very childish spite to this sorrow—the result of a foolish amour-propre whose complete folly I sense, but which I cannot overcome. (19)

What had been treated in paragraph 15 as a manageable problem—manageable because its chief cause lay within himself—is now made to seem overwhelming and the deliberate doing of outside enemies. Instead of annoyance we hear of heartrending sorrow, and a very childish spite to boot. (So much for having been purified of irascible passions.) Instead of depicting himself as an effective agent, Rousseau casts himself as "a *plaything* of [men's] treacherous flattery, bombastic and derisive compliments, and honeyed malignity" (19; emphasis added). Worst of all is how he now *understands* his distress. He regards the continued inflammability of his amour-propre not just as a misfortune but as a degrading failure or defeat. And so devastating does this defeat seem to him that it effectively negates all the gains he has made both as a philosopher and with respect to happiness:

> The efforts I have made to become inured to these rude and mocking looks are unbelievable. A hundred times I have passed along the public walks and through the most frequented spots with the sole intention of inuring myself to those cruel taunts. Not only have I not been able to succeed, I have not made any progress; and all my painful, but vain, efforts have left me as easy to disturb, to grieve, and to render indignant as before. (19)

What has caused Rousseau to take such a dim view of what he had seen so differently just a short time ago? And what should we make of this darkening? The answer is perhaps what we should have expected. What has happened—what *is happening*—is amour-propre. Rousseau is not only writing *about* amour-propre; he is writing *from* it: our narrator is writing while in the grip of inflamed amour-propre. To feel defeated and humiliated, to discount progress because it has not been complete—even to go to such great lengths in the effort to inure himself to inflamed amour-propre—all of this is the work of amour-propre. We even catch a whiff of amour-propre in Rousseau's description, at the start of this very paragraph, of the happiness he enjoys during the three-fourths of the time that he is supposedly free of it:

> Everything brings me back to the happy and sweet life for which I was born. I pass three-fourths of my life occupied with instructive and even agreeable objects in which I indulge my mind and my senses with delight, or with the children of my fancy whom I have created according to my heart and whose company sustains its sentiments, or with myself alone, satisfied with myself and already full of the happiness I feel to be due me. In all this, love of myself does all the work; amour-propre has nothing to do with it. (19)

"The happiness I feel to be *due* me"—this too is amour-propre speaking.

How shall we weigh the contradictory accounts of paragraphs 15 and 19? Which, if either, is the truer account? And what lesson, if any, can we draw from the inclusion of both accounts?

The view conveyed in paragraph 19, being deeply shaped by amour-propre, might seem to warrant suspicion. And so it does, though the palpable influence of amour-propre on a judgment doesn't make that judgment false. And for that matter, we don't know that the view taken in paragraph 15 wasn't also influenced by amour-propre, albeit it the opposite direction. Just as amour-propre will tend to further darken our dark moods, it can also further brighten our brighter ones. However that may be, it is paragraph 19 that yields the chief practical lesson of this section of the Eighth Walk and the second maxim of wise statesmanship of the self. The first maxim of wise statesmanship of the self is to avoid situations in which one's amour-propre is apt to be gratuitously wounded insofar as this avoidance is consistent with other needs and goods, including the legitimate needs of amour-propre itself. The second maxim, the one taught by paragraph 19, is that, when amour-propre *has* been wounded, we should *disengage* from the situation—again, insofar as this is consistent with other needs and goods, including amour-propre's own legitimate needs. The second maxim is undoubtedly more demanding than the first, partly because it will be more difficult to determine where the legitimate needs of amour-propre end (the legitimate needs of wounded amour-propre will be more extensive than the legitimate needs of unwounded amour-propre) but mostly because one will be sorely tempted to go beyond meeting those needs. But disengagement is perhaps a misleading term—and, on reflection, not the thing most needful. Disengagement from situations in which one's amour-propre has been wounded will often be the course of wisdom. But the deeper and dispositive principle is dis*identification*: one must cease identifying with wounded amour-propre as one's essential self. Disidentification demands great strength of soul, for until one has disidentified with wounded amour-propre, it will purport to speak as one's true self and will regard disidentification as outrageous and even humiliating. The strength of soul required by disidentification is great indeed—if not greater than most of us have, greater than we are usually willing to devote to such a task as this. Our strength of soul is commanded, like everything else about us, by the apparent good. What's most needed, then—and more promising than trying to build ever greater strength—is to deploy well the strength that we have so that we might attain the perspective from which what *seems* good to us actually *is* good.

Skillful statesmanship of the self will limit one's vulnerability to the gratuitous wounding or inflammation of one's amour-propre. But it's when amour-propre *has* been wounded or inflamed, it seems to me, that the *most* skillful statesmanship is called for—the most skillful because it is bound to appear to one gripped by amour-propre the least promising route to gratification. Though itself a master of appearances, amour-propre is nevertheless easily fooled by appearances. The most promising route to acceptance and freedom is statesmanship that casts a cold eye on the hot demands of wounded amour-propre. Such statesmanship is already in itself acceptance and freedom.

Rousseau's politic teaching on self-governance demands that we consider an impolitic question: Is statesmanship of the self entirely truthful? *Can* it be? Or does it require, just as *political* statesmanship requires, occasional or even more than occasional dissimulation?[14] And if so, of what sort and degree?

The case of Rousseau himself is instructive if not dispositive. We find Rousseau telling himself a falsehood as late as the twelfth paragraph of the Eighth Walk, namely, that his contemporaries were "nothing more than automatons who acted only on impulse and whose action I could calculate only from the laws of motion" (12). By the standard articulated in the Fourth Walk this falsehood is a fiction rather than a lie, for it helps him come to terms with the injustices inflicted on him. How *much* it helps him is still open to question, but at a minimum it is a step toward the more truthful and beneficial view that he will adopt later in the Eighth Walk.

How truthful is *that* view"? Does Rousseau ever cease to rely on fictions? Could he plausibly hope to do so?

In paragraph 17 Rousseau seems to say that he has finally graduated from reliance on fictions. At the end of this long paragraph he declares that he worries about nothing and is indifferent to everything. Thus he no longer needs to contrive fictions. In particular, he no longer needs to regard his persecutors as automata. But consider what he has said earlier in the paragraph about how this ease of mind has come about:

When amour-propre is quiet and reason speaks, reason eventually consoles us for all the bad things we have not been able to avoid. Reason annihilates them insofar as they do not immediately affect us; for by ceasing to be preoccupied by them, we are sure of avoiding their most poignant blows. They are nothing for the person who does not think about them. Offenses, acts of revenge, slights, insults, injustices are

14. If political *founders* make use of fictions—and they do, in Rousseau's view—then succeeding generations of statesmen must maintain those founding myths.

nothing for the person who, in the bad things he endures, sees only the bad itself and not any intention. (17)

Reason *annihilates* bad things. These bad things are nothing for one who *doesn't think* about them. This person *does not see* intention. Rousseau has come a long way from converting his persecutors into automata. Yet he still does not look open-eyed at all that is. He may not actively distort reality, but he looks at it selectively. Rather than see something that isn't real, he avoids seeing something that is real. This may well be the most wholesome and rational policy that he could have adopted, and the one most favorable to the greatest degree of truthfulness that is within his reach. All the same, the intentions that Rousseau doesn't see do exist. And so we find him, at last call, so to speak, still employing a cognitive practice that falls short of complete truthfulness. Note too that the same characterization applies to "the wise man" of paragraph 13, who "sees only the blows of blind necessity in all the misfortunes which befall him."[15]

Finally, let us look at the concluding lines of the Eighth Walk. "The evil that men have done me in no way bothers me. Only the fear of the evil they can still do to me is capable of disturbing me. But certain that they have no other new hold by which they can affect me with a permanent feeling, I laugh at all their intrigues and enjoy myself in spite of them." Is Rousseau believable here? It does seem plausible that he could accept without distress what his enemies have done to him. It even seems plausible that he could enjoy himself despite knowing that they continue to plot against him. But the claim that there is no other way, as yet unused, in which his enemies could hurt him? To believe this would require a lack of imagination—so great a lack of imagination, however, that it could have been accomplished only by imagination itself, in the form of a fiction.

Ninth Walk

As the Eighth Walk addresses prudent governance of the soul, the Ninth Walk speaks to how the prudently governed soul engages others. In its turn from the interior focus of the preceding Walk to its own exterior focus,

---

15. In paragraph 19 Rousseau notes one way in which he continues to make use of *positive* fictions, at least if he is to be believed—but it is a conscious use of fictions. I am referring to the time he spends with those whom he forthrightly identifies as "the children of my fancy whom I have created according to my heart and whose company sustains its sentiments" (VIII, 19).

the Ninth Walk parallels the Sixth. Both Walks inquire into the relation between society and philosophy. They differ, however, with respect to the perspective from which they are written. The Sixth Walk addresses the relation between society and the philosopher as seen from outside: it concerns the relation between society and the philosopher's *interests*. The Ninth Walk, by contrast, inquires into the relation between society and the philosopher considered from within: it concerns the relation between society and the philosopher's *experience*. More instructive than the Ninth Walk's parallel with the Sixth Walk, however, is its relation to the First Walk, its opposite number on the same concentric circle. Both Walks concern Rousseau's sociability in the face of extreme duress. As he had in the First Walk, here too in the Ninth he depicts himself as having been consigned to involuntary solitude. Yet whereas in the First Walk we saw him badly agitated, in the Ninth Walk he is at ease and manages to engage the world much more happily and indeed much more fruitfully. His infamous reputation still stands in the way of many ordinary social satisfactions, but he manages to navigate around the obstacles when there is a possibility to do so. He has accepted as irreversible necessity the constraints imposed on him; and having done so, he is able to summon the prudence to cloak his identity lest warmly disposed strangers discover that the seemingly good man before them is the infamous author of the *Social Contract* and *Emile*.

If Rousseau's engagement with his fellow human beings is guided by prudence, however, it is surely *motivated* by the prospect of *pleasure*. Indeed, pleasure—in particular, the pleasure of sociability for "the most sociable and the most loving of humans" (I, 1)—is the innermost theme of the Ninth Walk. This pleasure had been lost to Rousseau for some time, a casualty of his enemies' successful effort to poison his reputation. It has become available to him again in consequence of the developments recounted in the intervening Walks, culminating in the breakthroughs of the Seventh and Eighth Walks. By the end of the Eighth Walk we saw Rousseau able to secure, if not his entire life, at least his solitude against the turbulent intrusion of amour-propre. And although he wasn't always able to keep inflamed amour-propre at bay, he was able to limit the frequency, duration, and effects of the inflammation. In the Ninth Walk he goes further. He is now able, in the face of society's ongoing hostility, to recognize and enjoy such opportunities for social encounters as luck or his own contrivance can supply. That he can do so signifies that he has attained a greater degree of freedom. That he chooses to do so signifies a sounder understanding and judgment of pleasures worth pursuing. And the quality of his newfound social pleasures signifies a refinement in attention. These three attainments—freedom, judgment, and refinement—

are the respective foci of Socrates's three ostensible proofs of the superiority of the just man's or the philosopher's life to the life of the tyrant in book 9 of the *Republic*. But before turning to the particulars of these proofs and Rousseau's corresponding arguments, let us first take note of the broad relation between the *Reveries'* and the *Republic's* respective ninth divisions.

Book 9 of the *Republic* begins and ends with treatments of the complex polity of the soul. It begins with Socrates filling out his newly revised and enriched model of the soul. The tripartite soul of book 4 has become a whole effectively composed of *five* parts or forms, each of which is now conceived as a seat of desire and defined by what it desires. One part remains to be elaborated, namely, the portion of the appetitive part of the soul from which arise the antinomian desires; this is the part that rules the tyrannical man's soul. Book 9 ends with Socrates insisting on the severe limits of what can be accomplished in politics and calling for the redirection of erotic passion from the city to the soul. The city in speech that he and his interlocutors have so painstakingly constructed is to guide them in governing the polities of their own souls. In between these bookends Socrates investigates the tyrannical soul and purports to prove that the tyrannical man is miserable and that the best or most prudent man enjoys the most pleasant life. The running contrast between the worst and the best of men makes up the bulk of book 9 and crests with Socrates's three proofs.

The Ninth Walk of the *Reveries* follows the same lines. It too features an ongoing contrast between the misery of society and the pleasantness of Rousseau's own more natural sociability; and it too begins and ends by treating the possibility and limits of governing one's soul. Rousseau opens the Ninth Walk by stating that because everything exists in constant flux, happiness, understood as a permanent condition, "does not seem to be made for man here-below" (1). Notice how well this comment serves as a gloss on Socrates's tyrannical man, who wishes to impose his will on everything. Rousseau closes the Ninth Walk with a remark about hospitality whose gist is that goodness and contentment cannot be elicited by the prospect of financial gain. Indeed, the introduction of money inevitably undermines goodness and contentment (24). This point is an echo of Socrates's insistence at the end of book 9 on the impossibility of establishing anything like the city in speech he and his companions have devised. Not that the kallipolis runs on money. But Rousseau's point goes beyond money in any case. What both he and Socrates disavow is the possibility of inculcating virtue or happiness by means of external or institutional mechanisms: only education and upbringing can do the job. In between these opening and closing sections Rousseau, like Socrates, compares the pleasures of a healthy and moderate person to the purported pleasures of those tyrannized by amour-propre. He examines the good or natural person's freedom, judgment, and purity of pleasure and contrasts these with the corrupt or vain person's lack thereof. He does not purport to offer proofs, as Socrates had. But he points to and perhaps demonstrates what Socrates had purported to prove. For that matter, Socrates's proofs are dubious—*as proofs*. He too, in truth, only points and perhaps demonstrates.

Socrates's first proof (578d–580c) concerns the tyrant's lack of freedom: the supposed master is more enslaved than anyone else. For all his ostensible power, he is kept from doing even ordinary things. Most especially he is kept from *seeing* things:

> Isn't the tyrant bound in . . . a prison, he who has a nature such as we described, full of many fears and loves of all kinds? And he, whose soul is so gourmand, alone of the men in the city can't go anywhere abroad or see all the things the other free men desire to see; but, stuck in his house for the most part, he lives like a woman, envying any of the other citizens who travel abroad and see anything good. (579b–c)

Free men, by contrast, *can* see; and the freest man, the philosopher, sees furthest and most clearly. This is Socrates's teaching. It is also Rousseau's in the first third of the Ninth Walk, which corresponds to Socrates's first proof.

Rousseau's freedom is natural freedom, which was the subject of the Sixth Walk. The Ninth Walk, however, adds two important elements to that earlier treatment. First, it shows that the life of natural freedom partakes of and can be vastly enriched by sociability—this notwithstanding Rousseau's depiction of the primal savage as asocial or calling himself a solitary walker. In fact Rousseau does have kith and kin. But neither he nor his hypothetical predecessor in the state of nature is *constituted* by social relations. Indeed, none of us is so constituted in our innermost core. What distinguishes Rousseau and his savage forebear from the rest of us is that this core has not been compromised: amour-propre has not overturned the reign of amour de soi. The second element added by the Ninth Walk to the articulation of natural freedom is something that particularly resonates with Socrates's first proof. The most affecting of Rousseau's anecdotes and reflections in the Ninth Walk center on the pleasure he takes in *seeing* the happiness of others, especially children. This seeing is more than a pleasure, though. It also contributes to understanding: "If I have made any progress in understanding the human heart, it is the pleasure I have taken in seeing and observing children which has earned me this understanding" (5). Seeing is good both intrinsically and instrumentally—just as Glaucon had said in *Republic* 2, where he listed it centrally among examples of things that are good both in themselves and for the sake of other goods.

The *Republic*'s second proof (580d–583a) is an appeal to experience—not one's own experience, but that of the philosopher. Only the philosopher, according to Socrates, has experienced all classes of pleasure and thus can compare them to one another. His choice of the philosophic life is therefore an informed choice, the *only* fully informed choice. Rousseau makes no such claim—certainly not explicitly. Then again, neither do the philosophers of whom Socrates speaks. Like those philosophers, though—and like Socrates himself—Rousseau too seems to have access to the pleasures of the various ways of life. Thus he effectively claims that he too has made an informed choice and that his choice too has the authority of firsthand knowledge. Rousseau, of course, doesn't call his life or his pleasure *philosophic*. But he does better than that. He shows us his practiced ability to compare and judge among competing pleasures, including the pleasures of the philosophic life. Consider the following passage, in which he recounts two successive scenes of amusement, both from a long-ago country fair. In the first scene, a group of wellborn partygoers threw pieces of gingerbread into a crowd of peasants in order to amuse themselves at the sight of the ensuing crush and chaos. Rousseau was a member of this party and even participated in the action, though only for fear of mortification and with little enjoyment. Soon sick of the spectacle, he "left the well-bred group and went off to walk alone through the fair," where he was "entertained by a variety of objects." He relates one of these scenes in considerable detail:

> I noticed five or six Savoyard boys around a little girl who still had a dozen sorry-looking apples on her tray of which she would very much have liked to rid herself. For their part, the Savoyards would very much have liked to rid her of them; but they had only two or three pennies between them, and that was not enough to make a great dent in the apples. This tray was the garden of the Hesperides for them, and the little girl was the dragon guarding it. This comedy entertained me for a long time; I finally resolved it by paying the little girl for the apples and having her distribute them to the little boys. I then experienced one of the sweetest sights which can gratify a man's heart, that of watching joy united with the innocence of age spread all about me. For even those who were looking on shared it as they watched it; and I who shared this joy so cheaply had, in addition, that of sensing that it was my handiwork.

In comparing this entertainment with the ones I had just left, I felt with satisfaction the difference that separates healthy tastes and natural pleasures from those which opulence engenders and which are hardly anything but pleasures of mockery and exclusive tastes engendered by scorn. (15–16)

Like the philosophers in Socrates's proof, Rousseau has recognized and chosen the healthier and indeed the truer pleasure.

This episode also provides insight into the character of the natural. Of particular significance is that Rousseau's healthy and natural pleasure included the gratification of amour-propre. He makes special note of the pleasure of knowing that the charming scene was his own handiwork. That even the philosopher or natural man gratifies his amour-propre is reassuring, since amour-propre is bound to be present in almost everything we do, certainly in social life. But it is also daunting, in that the good governance of amour-propre, by which I mean keeping it moderate in magnitude and direction and most of all in influence, is a rare and difficult attainment. Good governance of amour-propre requires that amour-propre be subordinated to something else. The *citizen's* amour-propre must be subordinated to society; it must be collectivized—this is what we call virtue. In the case of the natural *man*, whether the attenuated version represented by Emile or the philosopher Rousseau, amour-propre must be subordinated to amour de soi. But to be subordinated does not mean to be subsumed. Amour-propre is still to be gratified *as* amour-propre. Amour-propre is surely a major impetus, perhaps even the mainspring, of Rousseau's political or legislative efforts. Indeed, the Ninth Walk offers us further insight into the whole business of philosopher as Legislator. Small scale and stakes notwithstanding, when Rousseau arranges things so that all members of a group of children are made happy—and he recounts more than one such episode (IX, 11–13, 15)—he bears a most definite similarity to the Legislator. He too operates behind the scenes and requires no recognition from the beneficiaries of his "rule."[16]

The difficulty of governing amour-propre seems to have intensified in the modern world as the few possible modes of good governance have become even more remote. In the wake of a universalist religion and, more recently, a secular universalism, true citizens, according to Rousseau, are

16. Another indication that Rousseau means to speak to his work as Legislator here in the Ninth Walk is his inclusion of several references to the *Letter to d'Alembert*, which was the first writing he addressed to the public at large. See Meier, *On the Happiness*, 167.

no longer to be found or even hoped for (*Emile*, 250; 165). And naturalness in the register of an Emile must contend with endless stimulants to vanity and desire. Even the life of philosophy may have become more difficult in a world that seeks not to keep it at bay but to subsume it. Nevertheless the remoteness of these pure types does not mean that one can't make considerable progress in moderating one's amour-propre. Rousseau's pure types can serve as useful orienting points and sources of self-understanding. In several important respects—including the choices of where to live, what activities to pursue, and what society to keep—they can even serve as models, as Rousseau surely meant for them to. This is especially the case concerning the philosophic life, where the articulation of the pure type is hidden within a depiction of a less remote natural life, a life that is both idle and lively, both simple and thoughtful, and appreciative to the point of piety.

Rousseau's story about the Savoyard boys and the little girl selling apples vindicates amour-propre by acknowledging its place in this most innocent of engagements. It also seems to diminish amour-propre by putting amour de soi ahead of it, not only with respect to governance but also with respect to pleasure. Rousseau's primary emphasis is on the sweetness of disinterestedly "watching joy united with the innocence of age spread all about me." The gratification of amour-propre is literally an add-on: "and I who shared this joy so cheaply had, *in addition*, that of sensing that it was my handiwork."

Yet what appears as a diminishment—what was meant to appear as a diminishment—may be no such thing when examined more closely. And a closer examination is exactly what Rousseau provides in the very next paragraph, number 17, where he seeks to explicate what distinguishes his own "healthy tastes and natural pleasures" (16) from the unhealthy tastes and unnatural pleasures of the well-bred partygoers. The first lines of the paragraph maintain the apparent diminishment of amour-propre as a source of real pleasure:

> For my part, when I have carefully thought about the kind of sensual pleasure I savored on these occasions, I have found that it consisted less in a feeling of beneficence than in the pleasure of seeing contented faces. This sight has a charm for me which, even though it penetrates all the way to my heart, seems to be solely one of sensation. If I do not see the satisfaction I cause, even though I am sure of it, I only half enjoy it. It is even a disinterested pleasure for me which does not depend on the part I might have in it. (17)

Gratifying amour-propre (through beneficence) was part of Rousseau's pleasure, but the lesser part. The greater part consisted in seeing contented faces, a pleasure in which—as it does not turn on one's own role in bringing about the contentment—amour-propre had no part. But this diminishment of amour-propre's role in natural pleasure is less decisive than it sounds, for it is derived from a comparison that is not as comprehensive as *it* sounds. Rousseau does not compare the pleasure of the "feeling of beneficence" to the pleasure of seeing contented faces *as such*, or *altogether*; he compares them only insofar as they are *sensual pleasures*. The restrictive terms of the comparison are set in place in the paragraph's opening words ("For my part, when I have carefully thought about the kind of *sensual* pleasure I savored on these occasions . . ."). The comparison leaves out, it is silent about, nonsensual pleasure. Was there no nonsensual element to Rousseau's pleasure on this occasion? We can hardly assume that there wasn't. And so we are left to wonder why he has chosen to make his comparison on these terms—and to do so slyly, that is, without explicitly acknowledging what he was doing. Why *not* make the broader comparison? One can't help suspecting that we have met here another case of Rousseau's Socratic circumspection. It would be entirely within character for Rousseau to have deliberately understated amour-propre's part in this and other pleasures, lest the quiet appeal of innocent pleasures become quieter still. (Not that readers would necessarily be wrong to pursue the gratification of amour-propre. Even if we accept that the philosophic life has been proved happiest, that doesn't prove that the life centered on more ordinary natural pleasures, the life overtly advertised in the *Reveries*, would prove happier in all cases than a life driven by the demands of amour-propre. Like Socrates in *Republic* 9, Rousseau doesn't debunk the life of the tyrant quite as effectively as one might have thought.)[17]

Rousseau does go on to acknowledge, implicitly in paragraph 17 and explicitly in paragraph 18, that "what is only a pleasure of sensation . . . certainly has a *moral* cause" (18; emphasis added). And in paragraphs 19 and 20 he elaborates on moral causality by way of examples. Yet this does nothing to expand the terms of his comparison. Indeed, it only ratifies them: to acknowledge that sensual pleasure has a moral cause while still

17. Socrates purports to demonstrate that the happiness enjoyed by different kinds of men—the kingly man or philosopher, the timocratic man, the oligarchic man, the democratic man, and the tyrannical man—corresponds to their degree of virtue, and Glaucon pronounces himself persuaded of all this (*Republic*, 580b). But his proofs speak only to the comparison between the philosopher and the tyrant. They say nothing one way or the other about the other kinds of men.

neglecting to acknowledge nonsensual or moral pleasure only serves to further obscure that neglect.[18]

Republic 9's third proof (583b–587b) concerns the subjective quality of different pleasures. Socrates develops a system of hedonistic classification that accords the highest status to *pure* pleasures, or pleasures that needn't have been preceded by pain in the way that the pleasures of eating, drinking, and sex are always preceded by hunger, thirst, and the pangs of desire (585b–e). Rousseau doesn't offer a comparable formal distinction. But his account of his own pleasures echoes Socrates's view: "If my pleasures are few and brief, I surely savor them more deeply when they come than if they were more familiar. I ruminate upon them, so to speak, by frequently remembering them; and, however few they might be, if they were *pure and without mixture*, I would perhaps be happier than I was in my prosperity" (10; emphasis added). This passage is strangely conditional ("*if* they were pure and without mixture, I *would perhaps be* happier than I was in my prosperity"). But Rousseau goes on to describe pleasures that do indeed seem "pure and without mixture." The purpose of the conditional phrasing may be to call attention to the vulnerability that remains even in one who has become a more perfect philosopher. Rousseau's new attentiveness and freedom of mind do not shield him from external sources of distress. One wonders whether his heightened attentiveness might render him *more* sensitive to certain kinds of pain even as, and for the same reasons that, it has opened him to more and deeper pleasure. Signs of pain or distress in another person cause *him* pain and distress, since his imagination causes him to identify with the suffering being: "A sign, a gesture, a glance from a stranger, suffices to disturb my pleasures or to calm my troubles. I am my own only when I am alone. Apart from that I am the plaything of all those around me" (19). A life without pain and suffering is not available to human beings, and Rousseau gives no assurance that a net surplus of pleasure

18. Rousseau's answer to Socrates's second proof allows us to appreciate all the better his estimation of the philosophic life's standing vis-à-vis other lives. No life can include all human goods, and to show this is one of Rousseau's great if sad contributions. But the philosophic life alone allows for experience and knowledge of the goods that it excludes. The proof? Rousseau the philosopher, whose life excluded, for example, the moral beauty of Emile's life, was the one who revealed that beauty to us. The philosophic life is not perfect. Neither, however, is it partial in the way that all other lives are. (For a contrary view, see Storey, "Rousseau and the Problem of Self-Knowledge." Storey shows very nicely the incompleteness or imperfection of any single life in Rousseau's view, but he seems to forget that the hero of the *Reveries*, though a seemingly solitary walker, was also a political philosopher.)

over pain might be possible. The sober note struck in the opening lines of the Ninth Walk continues to resonate: "Happiness is a permanent condition which does not seem to be made for man here-below. Everything on earth is in constant flux, which permits nothing to take on a constant form. Everything around us changes. We ourselves change, and no one can be assured he will like tomorrow what he likes today" (1).

But is this sober note perhaps too sober? Prior to the Ninth Walk Rousseau had spoken of happiness as something less remote—as a stable condition and perhaps therefore a rare one, but not a permanent and therefore impossible one. It has been only a short while since he claimed to have attained it himself, and not only once: "I again found serenity, tranquility, peace, even happiness, since each day of my life reminds me with pleasure of the previous day and since I desire no other for the morrow" (VIII, 19). Why adopt the superstrict view of happiness as a permanent condition here in the Ninth Walk? Perhaps it merely reflects the greater stringency in thought befitting a more perfect philosopher. Or perhaps it reflects the adoption of a more precise phenomenological lens: happiness as a permanent condition, he says, "does not *seem* to be made for man here-below." There may be something to these explanations, but I would like to suggest another possibility. Although Rousseau uses "happiness" (*le bonheur*) to refer to different conditions at different places in the *Reveries*, he *defines* the word only once, at the start of the Ninth Walk. Could this single definition somehow apply in all cases? Could happiness be both a permanent condition beyond human reach and a condition that Rousseau *has* reached? Obviously it could not, at least if we take the terms "permanent" and "man here-below" in their ordinary senses. But what if we take these terms in another sense, a sense we saw Rousseau employ earlier in the *Reveries*? What if we interpret "permanent" as a stand-in for *eternal*? And what if Rousseau would have us understand him as something other than a "man here-below"? If we permit ourselves this reading, the contradiction disappears: happiness becomes a possibility for Rousseau, and not only for Rousseau. But *should we* permit ourselves this reading? Would it be reasonable to do so?

It would. Everything on earth is indeed in constant flux. Yet even amid this flux—even as we ourselves are in flux—we have access to eternity, as Rousseau illustrated in the Fifth Walk. This in no way undermines the narrative arc of the *Reveries*. To the contrary, Rousseau's teaching about eternity's centrality to philosophy helps explain what drives, vindicates, and makes possible his trajectory. In seeking and ultimately attaining considerable "serenity, tranquility, even happiness," he seeks and ultimately attains a deeper and more sustained encounter with the eternal. The latter (encounter with eternity) is the stuff of the former (serenity, tranquility, happiness). Happiness is the enjoyment of our being, and enjoying our being requires that we overcome, if not the awareness of time, then the anxiety and regret that so often accompany it. (The *purest* happiness perhaps does require overcoming awareness of time. Whether the purest is necessarily the greatest is another question, both for Rousseau and for Socrates.) I take Rousseau to be indicating as much in the final paragraph of the Eighth Walk: "Whatever [men] may do, this is my *most constant* condition and the one through which, in spite of my fate, I savor a happiness for which I feel myself constituted. I have described this condition in one of my reveries. It suits me so well that I desire nothing other than its duration and fear only to see it troubled" (VIII, 23; emphasis added). The reference to one of his reveries, combined with his expressed desire for nothing other than the duration of this "most constant condition," point us to the Fifth Walk and its revelation of eternity's place in the philosophic life. If this reading is correct—if the invocation of "permanence" and "constancy" is a subtle evocation of eternity—then the one who attains this condition might indeed be regarded, in the way and for the reasons that we have already discussed, as something other than a "man here-below."

The foregoing qualification—*in the way and for the reasons that we have already discussed*—is no small thing. As he frequently reminds us, Rousseau is very much a man here-below. He knows that his days are few. He acknowledges many human, all too human weaknesses. And perhaps most tellingly of all, he still suffers the slings and arrows of fortune. But the outrage, finally, is gone, at least when he is away from company. True, he is his own only when he is alone (19); but he *is* his own then, which is something most people can't claim and something that Rousseau himself couldn't claim nearly so credibly prior to the breakthrough unfolded in the Seventh and Eighth Walks. Theoretical wisdom (insight into the soul) has yielded practical wisdom (insight into his own soul) and therewith greater calm, greater freedom, greater happiness, greater access to the eternal.

Neither eternity nor love is mentioned in the Ninth Walk—by name. Yet both are crucial to the Ninth Walk. They are also crucial to each other. To love is to wish for and to anticipate and thus in a sense to experience eternity. To experience eternity in a world in which everything is in flux is to experience the beauty and lovability of the world. In prior Walks Rousseau had highlighted the beauty and lovability of the natural order. In the Ninth Walk he highlights the beauty and lovability of human beings. Love is what moves him to sociability and what he takes *from* sociability. Rousseau the philosopher—lover of the truth, lover of learning, lover of knowledge, and therewith lover of nature and life—shares this love with his readers and in turn experiences loving communion with them, even if they are unknown to him or yet to be born. If this is so, then the solitary walker isn't entirely alone, and his solitude isn't loneliness. Not that it ever was: Rousseau announced at the outset that writing the *Reveries* "will, so to speak, double [his] existence": "In spite of mankind, I will still be able to enjoy the charm of society; and decrepit, I will live with myself in another age as if I were living with a younger friend" (I, 14). And he has only recently spoken of spending time with "the children of [his] fancy" (VIII, 19). To these companions can be added ourselves, his readers—unless we don't need to be added because we ourselves *are* his younger self or the children of his fancy. For the readers to whom Rousseau speaks are present to him as he writes, just as he is present to them—to us—as we read.

Love is thematic in the Tenth Walk too, where it *is* mentioned and indeed brought front and center. The *Reveries* concludes, whether by design (as I judge) or by chance (as most others suppose), with a brief meditation on love—not on love as such or love of a certain kind but a particular love, Rousseau's love for one woman and her love for him, a love that would call forth other loves, including the love of wisdom.

The Love of Wisdom and the Wisdom of Love

Tenth Walk

The Tenth Walk is a grateful meditation on the happy and formative years Rousseau spent at Les Charmettes when he was a young man—and on Madame de Warens, the belle esprit who opened her home and her heart to him. It was there that the two loves that would put him on the path to the philosophic life took root in his heart: love for a woman (who also loved him), and love of learning. Thus the Tenth Walk is a loving and grateful meditation on love and gratitude.

His time at Les Charmettes, Rousseau tells us, "determined [his] whole life." Thus it did not belong to that life. Neither did it belong to the life that preceded it. Rather, like his exile on St. Peter's Island, it was—and *is*—an island in time to which he can return in memory.

The Tenth Walk is unique in a number of ways. It is far briefer than the other Walks, consisting of only a single paragraph. It is dated: the Walk in which Rousseau visits an island in time is itself pinned to a precise time. It looks backward, in memory; but backward with a view to what would follow. It makes no mention of enemies, whether real or imagined. And although, like the other Walks, it has notable affinities to the corresponding book of the *Republic*, it also nods appreciatively to the Bible, classical political philosophy's most powerful historical challenger and alternative. These features set the Tenth Walk as a whole apart from the preceding nine Walks, making it a kind of coda. By concluding in this way, that is, with a coda rather than a recapitulation or general statement, *The Reveries of the Solitary Walker* mirrors its subject. Rousseau's book about the philosophic life ends as the philosophic life itself ends—with acceptance and gratitude but with no script or summation. (Only for Socrates, it seems, did the philosophic life admit of the latter.) In this one respect I will take the *Reveries* as my own model: as the *Reveries* mirrors its subject, so the present study will mirror *its*. To do otherwise would be to presume to provide what Rousseau saw no need to provide.

By stepping outside of the philosophic life and addressing itself to the source of that life, the Tenth Walk responds directly—and affirmatively—to book 10 of the *Republic*. *Republic* 10 begins with Socrates reopening the question of poetry. But instead of examining poetry from the standpoint of civic virtue, as he did in books 2 and 3, this time he examines it with respect to wisdom, that is, as philosophy's rival (607b). At first book 10's critique of poetry is bound to seem willfully obtuse and overly severe. In the end, though, the poets are invited to make an apology and petition for reentry into the kallipolis. Indeed, Socrates would like the petition to succeed, so appreciative is he of all that he has learned from poets—from Homer, in particular (607c–e). A successful petition would require that the poets recognize that poetry is and ought to be ministerial to philosophy. Ministerial in two ways: First, the poets are uniquely well positioned to develop and to communicate to the public a compelling popular teaching that is consistent with the philosophers' political wisdom. Second, the poets can bring to the philosophers a variety of insights and observations about human beings that might otherwise elude them. (One wonders whether the poets' ability to perform these roles might not bespeak a capacity, at least among the greatest poets, to become philosophers themselves—a capacity to move not *from* poetry to philosophy but *with* poetry to philosophy, as perhaps Plato did.) It would be a bit much to expect Rousseau to respond in his very brief Tenth Walk to Plato's complex reconsideration of poetry. Yet Plato's complexity on this matter is also convolution: the pith of his teaching might have been stated much more succinctly than it is. So perhaps Plato's return to poetry doesn't require such an extensive reply after all. Or perhaps Rousseau has replied with the whole of the *Reveries*. However that may be, the Tenth Walk enacts the very apologia that Socrates hoped to solicit, in two ways.

First, the Tenth Walk makes clear that a kind of poeticism if not poetry proper was necessary to Rousseau's eventual embrace of the philosophic life. It was the idyllic character of life at Les Charmettes that gave rise "in [his] heart" to a taste and a disposition that would be necessary for this embrace: namely, the "fondness for solitude and contemplation . . . along with the expansive and tender feelings made to be its nutriment." To be sure, Madame de Warens was a real woman, not the invention of a poet. And yet perhaps in a certain way she was the invention of a poet after all, for a love such as Rousseau's for her is born of the idealization of the beloved, and idealization of this sort is invention if not delusion (*Emile*, 656; 499). Second, the Tenth Walk is itself a highly poetic writing—moving, wistful, evocative—whose poeticism serves the life of philosophy by soliciting and nurturing *in the reader* the very tastes and dispositions that led Rousseau to philosophy.

Following his surprising return to the topic of poetry, Socrates just as surprisingly takes up what he calls "the greatest rewards and prizes for virtue" (608c), which, he says, are conferred only in the afterlife. This claim requires him to speak of the soul's immortality, for which he gives a remarkably offhand proof followed by the long and memorable myth of Er with which the *Republic* concludes. (By addressing the wages of justice and injustice after death Socrates goes beyond what he had been asked to do, making the bulk of *Republic* 10, like Rousseau's Tenth Walk, a coda to the main body of the work. Indeed, the *whole* of book 10 is a coda: none of it, including the return to poetry, speaks to the meaning or the intrinsic goodness of justice.) The myth of Er explains what determines both the character of one's life and the fate of one's soul after death. Similarly, the Tenth Walk gives us Rousseau's explanation of what "*determined my whole life*" (emphasis added) and describes the "period of four or five years" spent in the country with Madame de Warens in terms reminiscent of the heaven described by Er. Perhaps in keeping with its modesty vis-à-vis the *Republic*, whereas Plato's souls spend a thousand years in heaven or hell, the *Reveries* has Rousseau enjoying in these four or five years only "a *century* of life and a pure and full happiness" (emphasis added). Or maybe this isn't modesty: Rousseau's century of happiness was no myth.

Where the *theme* of the myth of Er is concerned, the parallel is just about perfect. In Plato's moral-cosmological myth, souls of the departed spend a thousand years in either of two realms after their lives on earth have ended. Those who have lived decently on earth are rewarded with a thousand years in heaven. Those who have lived badly are punished with a thousand years in a hellish underworld. Following that millennium all souls are called on to choose their next earthly lives in a lottery. Those who have been chastened by hell choose decent lives. Those who have just emerged from heaven typically do not: to them it seems that the best of lives is the life of a tyrant. Consider the implication: Those who have chosen to live decent lives have done so only for fear of punishment, only for the sake of extrinsic consequences. The just are more cautious and have been better habituated than the unjust, but like the unjust they too regard the tyrant's life as the most intrinsically satisfying life. Why *does* injustice have such appeal? Why does the life of the tyrant seem the best life? Surely the core of the answer—for both Plato and Rousseau—is the tyrant's apparent power to indulge all appetites, especially the lawless ones. And surely the appeal of lawless appetites lies less in particular objects than in the lawlessness itself, in the wholesale repudiation of constraint and the elevation of the self to godlike status.

For both Plato and Rousseau there is a way out of thralldom to the appeal of injustice. Both thinkers show us the possibility of seeing the intrinsic goodness of justice in the soul. And both thinkers identify the philosopher as the one who has achieved this insight. Plato's exemplar is Socrates; Rousseau's is himself. Not everyone will find Socrates admirable, let alone worth emulating, and fewer still will feel this way about Rousseau. But careful reading of Plato's dialogues reveals behind Socrates's professed ignorance and vexing disputatiousness a believable human wisdom. And careful reading of the *Reveries* reveals behind Rousseau's touchiness and self-pity a similarly believable wisdom. As with Socrates, so with Rousseau, one who looks intently may see, behind a dubious exterior, "divine, golden" "images within" (*Symposium*, 216e–217a). Seeing the goodness of justice requires seeing through delusions. For Plato that means seeing through tyrannical eros. For Rousseau it means seeing through amour-propre. This is what Rousseau has learned how to do over the course of the *Reveries*. Seeing through the delusions of amour-propre has allowed him finally to resign himself to the world's injustice and thereby attain and sustain a more truly philosophic way of being. He has achieved what may be the better part of human wisdom. And he has gained steadier footing from which to glimpse an even higher wisdom.

But is Rousseau's wisdom the same as Socrates's? Here we must take note of another distinctive feature of the Tenth Walk, a major and startling feature that is introduced by a seemingly small one.

The Tenth Walk is the only Walk dated by Rousseau. *Any* dating would be interesting for highlighting that, however much philosophy may center on the eternal, the philosophic life takes place in time. Dating only the Tenth Walk is more interesting yet, for it suggests that Rousseau the narrator and Rousseau the author have become one and the same person. But of course it isn't just any date that Rousseau records. The Tenth Walk begins: "Today, Palm Sunday, it is precisely fifty years since I first met Madame de Warens." Or more literally—and evocatively—it is precisely fifty years since his "first *knowledge* of" or even "first knowing *with*" (*ma première connaissance avec*) Madame de Warens. A good part of my purpose in this study has been to uncover Rousseau as a latter-day Socratic. But by dating the final Walk Palm Sunday, Rousseau recalls not Athens but Jerusalem, not Socrates but Jesus: both his triumphal entry into Jerusalem and his impending crucifixion. Does Rousseau mean to suggest that he has achieved a triumph of his own that should be understood in relation to Jesus? If so, what would that relation be?

It seems to me that Rousseau does mean to suggest a comparison, indeed two comparisons: one between himself and Jesus, the other between his thought and the religion that grew up in Jesus's name. In neither case can the result of the comparison be called pious. But only slightly less striking than the results of the comparisons are their terms. Classical political philosophy is nowhere to be seen. All we have are Rousseau and Jesus, Rousseau and Christianity.

With the mention of Palm Sunday Rousseau invites us to consider him in relation to Jesus. But by what standard, and toward what end? A plausible answer is suggested by the character of the *Reveries*. Like the *Confessions*, even if differently, the *Reveries* presents Rousseau as a model for emulation. Not a model with respect to this or that quality or in this or that situation, but a model of a way of being: a model of naturalness and goodness. What is this if not to suggest *imitatio Rousseau* in lieu of *imitatio Christi*? As we can discern from other writings, Rousseau does not regard Jesus as the best model for emulation, particularly in the modern age. Jesus, in Rousseau's view, for all the sublimity of his life, or death, is too remote from ordinary human beings to serve as the most apt model for emulation. This remoteness, moreover, isn't just a matter of being too perfect but also a matter of being too remote from *nature*. Naturalness means living in this world, not another. And it means living within oneself, not seeking one's treasure beyond oneself, which is what Rousseau takes Jesus to be advising.[1] Thus Rousseau, the man of nature, offers *himself* as a model. Not that he too isn't at a far remove from most people, but he *is* so, as we discussed in part 1, by virtue of having preserved and cultivated the same nature that lies within us all.

To present oneself as a model for emulation doesn't require that one regard oneself as the best human being in every or even in any respect. No reader will need to be reminded that Rousseau does not always shine in the *Reveries* or the *Confessions*. And yet I don't wish to diminish the merits of Rousseau's life as he sees it. He purports to have grasped the principle of natural goodness as no one else has. And by thinking through this principle and its implications he has discovered a unique way of life and a unique way of experiencing life, a uniquely *natural* and *good* way of life and experience of life. A visitor to Rousseau's tomb in the in the Panthéon

---

1. Regarding Rousseau's estimation of Jesus as a model for emulation, see Christopher Kelly's careful treatment of the matter in *Rousseau's Exemplary Life*, 54–75.

in Paris might be disappointed to find it a bit scuffed and chipped and outshone by a statue of Voltaire that stands too close for comfort. But the visitor can at least accept that the words inscribed on the tomb represent Rousseau as he represented himself: *Ici repose l'homme de la nature et de la vérité.*

The contrast Rousseau draws between his thought and Christianity is more severe than the contrast between himself and Jesus. Rousseau offers a *theoretical* critique of Christianity that, though mostly implicit, goes to fundamentals, and a *practical* critique that is equally fundamental but more overt and extensive. The theoretical critique is implicit in the principle of natural goodness, which he identifies as the basis of his entire system of thought and which he purports to have proven (*Dialogues*, 934; 211–13; *SD*, 202; 74). What he doesn't say out loud, though of course he doesn't have to, is that to prove the natural goodness of man is to disprove original sin and all that flows from it. The practical critique has two major thrusts. Rousseau faults Christianity's universalism and otherworldliness for undermining civic virtue and citizenship, and he faults Christianity's focus on doctrinal purity for fostering intolerance, fanaticism, and cruelty. For these reasons Christianity as a political force must be overcome. By what, or in favor of what? Little guidance can be expected from classical antiquity. Although classical political philosophy offers much insight into human nature, neither it nor classical political practice has much to say about the making of a good regime in a world in which both the polis and pagan religion have long been untenable. Here too, then, as he does concerning the question of the most apt model for emulation by individuals, Rousseau responds by striking out in a new direction. And here too one could argue that the new direction is consistent with classical political philosophy's practical teaching.[2] But here he departs even from his previous departure, that is, from his treatment of the question of the most apt exemplar for individuals. His response to that question centered on something of his own making, namely himself, or at least himself as portrayed in his writing. In response to the question facing peoples, by contrast, that is, the question of the most apt kind of religion, he hearkens back to something that long predates him. For although he has sketched

2. Given its democratic character, Rousseau's political teaching is bound to strike most readers as inconsistent with classical philosophy. But the principles of political right as discerned by Rousseau are not *simply* democratic. They are the principles of a democratic or universal aristocracy. Insofar as a universal aristocracy is lacking, it falls to a different aristocracy, a natural aristocracy of wisdom, to propose and persuade the populace to accept such laws as would best preserve society.

the principles of political right in the *Social Contract,* no society could be constructed or could understand itself according to these principles alone. Societies rest on beliefs and opinions that have no basis in the principles of political right or even in reason. And so much the more does the *founding* of a people require recourse to measures that lie beyond the principles of political right and reason. The Legislator must credibly invoke the divine; and the people he forms must understand itself as distinct from other peoples, in considerable part because of what it believes about its relation to the divine. In his chapter on Legislators in the *Social Contract* Rousseau pays special tribute to only two foundings. In neither case is the Legislator named, but neither one needs to be named. The laws they commended to their peoples have not ceased to command reverence and obedience even after many centuries. The staying power of these foundings testifies to the greatness of their Legislators: "The Jewish law which still endures, that of Ishmael's child which has ruled half the world for ten centuries, still proclaim today the great men who dictated them" (*SC,* 384; 157).[3] But what most signifies the wisdom of a founding and its worthiness of emulation, more than temporal duration or geographic extent, is its *character,* that is, the character of the laws and, especially, the character that these laws have impressed on the people. Rousseau looks to only one founding for this purpose: that of *Moses.*

Moses, on Rousseau's understanding, took in hand a "servile troop"[4] and made of it a people remarkable for its moral passion.[5] This passion could and frequently did run to excess, but it arose from a true love of justice and a disposition to compassion. These two fundamental moral passions, moreover, helped give rise to a national consciousness. In these ways the Mosaic law and the people it constituted stand apart from the pagan city, from Christianity, and from the main currents of modern political thought and practice. The pagan city lacked the intense passion for universal justice and (even more so) an ear for the call to compassion. Christianity, though it embraces both justice and compassion, does so from an otherworldly perspective and thus does not summon forth the moral and political vigor required by a healthy society; and as we've

---

3. Rousseau also makes specific mention of a third legislator in the chapter, namely, Lycurgus. Though he elsewhere expresses great admiration for Spartan law, however, the reference to Lycurgus in this chapter does not speak to the content of that law. It serves only to make the relatively minor point that the Legislator must eschew or vacate command over men.

4. See *On the Government of Poland,* 956; 171–72.

5. The following summary account owes much to Jonathan Marks's illuminating study "Rousseau's Use of the Jewish Example."

already noted, Christianity's universalism inhibits the development of a national consciousness, which too is a requirement of a healthy society. (The God of Moses, by contrast, preferred that there be particular peoples under His universal sovereignty and entered into a covenant with *this* particular people that it might perform a mission that would benefit all peoples.) Modern societies, finally, especially those we call liberal, though they lay claim to the mantel of this-worldly justice and compassion, do so falsely, according to Rousseau. Their claim is a cynical facade or perhaps sometimes an uncynical facade, but a facade all the same. Their vindication of self-interest and promotion of commerce pit individuals against one another. They also dilute a people's national consciousness, thereby enfeebling it or provoking feverish reaction. The corrupting effects of self-interest were not born with modernity. But they have been engorged by modern political thought and practice, especially liberal thought and practice, which vindicate and deliberately promote the pursuit of self-interest.[6] Not that the Israelites were kept by their law or their moral passion from descending on various occasions into barbaric savagery. Indeed, their moral passion sometimes seems to have been an amplifier and even a source of barbarity. Rousseau suggests as much in *The Levite of Ephraim*, in which he retells a horrific episode from the book of Judges. Even so, what Rousseau feared most for the modern world was not the excess or wildness of moral passion but rather its flattening. The moral passions can be prudently governed by wise statesmanship—where they exist. Where they are wanting, however, no statesmanship can hope to supply the deficit.[7] As Rousseau sees it, compassion and the love of justice nurture an intensity and unity of being and therewith a strength of soul that, though potentially dangerous (as every strength is potentially dangerous), is the stuff of life and all the more so of a life worth living.

Rousseau does not relate his views of Christianity and Judaism in the *Reveries*. But by mentioning Palm Sunday and thus invoking Jesus and Jerusalem he does *point to* Christianity and Judaism and to his views thereof. And this is hardly the whole of the book's relation to the world of the Bible. Rousseau also speaks to Jerusalem in more immediate ways in the *Reveries*. He even speaks, as it were, *from* Jerusalem. In this book

6. "Let human society be as highly admired as one wants; it is nonetheless true that it necessarily brings men to hate each other in proportion to the conflict of their interests, to render each other apparent services and in fact do every imaginable harm to each other" (*SD*, 202; 74).

7. See the remarkable footnote that Rousseau appended to the end of "The Profession of Faith of the Savoyard Vicar" (*Emile*, 632–35; 479–81).

about the philosophic life and its ongoing perfection—a perfection that requires overcoming the ordinary moral consciousness in favor of the cognitivist view of morality—he nevertheless gives voice to a moral passion whose intensity and focus are more reminiscent of the Hebrew prophets than of classical philosophy. He not only denounces in prophetic strains; he especially denounces the oppression of the poor and weak by the rich and powerful. Of course his repeated complaints about the injustices inflicted on himself may not strike us as very prophetic. But he is also moved to indignation by injustice done to others. "The sight of injustice and wickedness still makes my blood boil" (VI, 16)—this is hardly the voice of self-pity. And if he expresses more outrage at his own unjust suffering than at the unjust suffering of others, well, that too expresses a moral consciousness that is more Hebraic than Socratic, particularly given that his outrage always presents itself as principled indignation. Nor does his moral passion express itself only as outrage. Recall his "ardent desire" and "constant passion" "to see every heart content"—this too from the Sixth Walk (18), which is where the philosopher's political engagements are most extensively addressed. In both of these moments Rousseau seems to be worlds away from classical political philosophy. Where he is hot with purported indignation, whether real or pretended or a mixture of both, Socrates is cool and ironic. Recall how Socrates responded to the dishonor done to Philosophy by playfully remarking that his spiritedness had been "*almost*" aroused (536c). And where Rousseau speaks about his benevolence almost erotically (the "ardent desire" and "constant passion" "to see every heart content"), the classical philosophers, though they present themselves as benevolent, reserve their eros for intellectual pursuits. Rousseau, it seems, had a foot, or maybe even his heart, in Jerusalem.

Nor does Rousseau's moral passion seem to ebb in the remaining Walks, even after he has purportedly purified himself of irascible passions. Does this mean that he has not overcome the ordinary moral consciousness after all? If by "overcome" we mean extirpate, then the answer is yes, he has not overcome the ordinary moral consciousness. But such a perfectionistic standard serves only to obscure meaningful differences. In fact Rousseau *has* overcome the ordinary moral consciousness, at least on the telling of the *Reveries*—not by extirpating moral passion, which he wouldn't want in any case, but by freeing himself from its *rule*. Moral passion no longer compromises the sovereignty of amour de soi and reason in his soul. How much force the moral passions retain under the sovereignty of amour de soi and reason is not clear. Rousseau's boiling blood is heard from even after he has attained his fullest philosophic maturity, that is, after he has registered the insights recounted in the Seventh and Eighth

Walks (VIII, 23). Whether he is indignant *in spite of* his rational judgment or with its *permission* or even its *encouragement* is not fully knowable. More than likely the answer varies across these alternatives according to the episode at hand. And whatever the precise answer, wise statesmanship of the soul ought to be possible, for it entails recognizing the irreducible forces under its writ and deploying them constructively. The same is true of political statesmanship. The good statesman of any polity must own phenomena that may or may not have arisen at his behest. He must embrace them as if they *had* arisen at his behest. A fiction, perhaps, but a necessary and constructive one.

There are two more ways in which Rousseau seems to me to depart from Athens in the direction of Jerusalem—deeper ways, or at any rate ways that speak to the philosophic life and perhaps enhance it.

The first concerns something that Rousseau may have learned from Christianity's overt and sustained *challenge* to philosophy. In the Bible (which he had studied seriously for many years; see *Confessions*, 579–80; 485) and in Christian apologists Rousseau would have confronted the case for Revelation. The challenge of Revelation demanded of philosophy a more searching examination of itself and of the soul for which it believes itself to be good. For Rousseau to be able to embrace philosophy after confronting (and while *continuing* to confront) the challenge of Revelation means that he has contributed something toward this end. The confrontation with figures like Pascal seems likely to have contributed something to Rousseau's awareness of the distorting effects of amour-propre even on true philosophy. Rousseau's own critique of philosophy, his critique of all but the greatest philosophers, has a great deal in common with Pascal's and others' critique of philosophy and philosophers as such. Rousseau's attunement to amour-propre's tendency to corrupt philosophy surely made him a more perfect philosopher than he otherwise would have been. Perhaps in this respect it made him a more perfect philosopher than his classical predecessors—more perfect because *less* perfect.

The other way in which Rousseau seems to me to depart from Athens in the direction of Jerusalem is deeper still, in that it concerns a possible motive force or need that has something to do with the turn to philosophy in the first place. Consider those of Rousseau's reveries in which he turned inward, and consider the need that they met. And prior need *is* implied. To be sure, enjoyment may occur where there has been no prior pain or privation. Consider "pure" pleasures such as that of smelling flowers. But what Rousseau attained through his inward-turning reveries was nothing so superfluous. He attained the exultant experience of *sufficiency*, and this does seem to me to presume a prior pain or privation, whether or not he had felt and recognized it as such. For the precise meaning of sufficiency is the suffusion of what one hitherto had lacked to be fully oneself, and I take Rousseau to be indicating as much. His attainment of the sense of godlike sufficiency meets a need; and what is this need if not the need to have, or at least to feel or believe that one has, a connection with the divine; a need that is perhaps more pronounced in more reflective and sensitive human beings; a need that, if it should go unmet, leaves one unredeemed or un-validated or at least feeling so. Such a need is far more pronounced in the biblical view of human nature than in that of classical philosophy, certainly more than in classical philosophy's teaching about the philosophic life. If Rousseau does regard this need as real, he is implicitly criticizing the classical tradition along similar lines as Pascal, who regarded the philosophers as blinded by pride to their dependence on God.

Of course if this need smacks of the Bible, Rousseau's solution does not. There is no fear and trembling here, and the alienation he purports to overcome is not between man and God but between man and himself—between the false, other-directed, and factious self and the natural or true self. With Rousseau, the entire spiritual universe is internalized. Although he dissents from the modern project that vindicates man as godlike in his *power*, Rousseau in a certain way extends and radicalizes the modern project by vindicating man in his *being*.[8] (So much for Rousseau's alliance with Pascal. Surely that pious one would convict Rousseau of a similar—no, a worse—pride than that of his classical predecessors for claiming an even more divine self-sufficiency.) And so if Rousseau is connected to Jerusalem, it is in a most Athenian way. A most *Socratic* way. Socrates's interlocutors in the *Republic* learn near the end of their long night's discussion that their city in speech, though it will never see the light of day, can still serve as a pattern for their souls. Rousseau, perhaps, has made Jerusalem a pattern for his soul—all Jerusalem, including the Temple, including the Holy of Holies, including the Divine Presence.

---

8. For a more extensive treatment of this point, see my "Nearer My True Self to Thee."

Acknowledgments

As befits a book about a way of life, this book had more than one moment of origin.

Over the course of years studying Rousseau I developed the growing suspicion that this brilliant thinker and almost impossible human being might also have been a little bit, or more than a little bit, *wise*, so I decided to explore his understanding of the life devoted to the pursuit of wisdom. From this came a conference paper that I thought might become an article; the year was 2014. Clifford Orwin, who commented on the paper at the panel at which I presented it, boosted my enthusiasm for this inquiry, not least with his challenges. At this same conference, Joel Schlosser kindly suggested that this inquiry of mine might make a nice small book. If the book I ended up writing isn't so small, the reason can be traced to another originary moment, this one even longer ago. During a fellowship year sponsored by the Symposium on Science, Reason, and Modern Democracy at Michigan State University in 1996–97, I audited a course on Aristotle's *Ethics* taught by Arthur Melzer, whose interpretation of Aristotle's treatment of voluntariness, responsibility, and the like one February afternoon precipitated a moment of actual dizziness. Was this my very own *periagoge*? Alas, no. Or perhaps I was turned *too much* in that moment, for I came to rest in a position not very different from the one where I had begun. Not very different, but not quite the same, either. Something had registered, and in the years to come I would periodically recur to what I had seen on that day and reflect on it. And I began to notice the same insight that I had glimpsed in Aristotle in other philosophers, including Rousseau. And so began this book.

Jonathan Marks and John Scott were all one might wish for as reviewers for the University of Chicago Press. Their excellent suggestions, which were blessedly of a piece with one another, have made this book leaner and better than it otherwise would have been. Even more blessedly, their suggested excisions left my authorial vanity unscathed.

I am grateful to all those who offered me a platform from which to present my work or who provided comments that helped advance my thinking. These include Bryan Garsten and Steven B. Smith, who invited me to present my work at the Yale Political Theory Workshop; Heinrich Meier, who generously gave of his time and hospitality on another cold February day, this one in 2018; Daniel Schillinger and Matthew Mendham, who brought eyes both sympathetic and questioning to what I had written; and the conveners of a conference held in honor of Ruth Grant, from whom I long ago learned something about negotiating between the soaring insights of great thinkers and the less than soaring but no less to be cherished gifts of ordinary life.

Further testimony to the happy blend of the transcendent and the immanent can be found in the dedication to this book.

Finally, I am grateful to Carleton College for material support, warm colleagues, and students who have been wonderful partners in inquiry; to the National Endowment for the Humanities for a generous yearlong fellowship to support this project; and to editors Charles Myers and Sara Doskow and copyeditor Kathleen Kageff for their graciousness and good counsel. Like Rousseau, I am not much of an institutionalist by nature. But, also like Rousseau, I recognize the importance of institutions—even, or especially, to solitary walkers, wayward citizens, and the like.

Bibliography

Alter, Robert. *The Hebrew Bible: A Translation with Commentary*. New York: W. W. Norton, 2018.

Aristophanes. *Clouds*. Translated by Thomas G. West and Grace Starry West. In *Four Texts on Socrates*. Ithaca, NY: Cornell University Press, 1974.

Aristotle. *Nicomachean Ethics*. Translated by Joe Sachs. Newburyport, MA: Focus, 2002.

———. *The Politics*. Translated by Carnes Lord. Chicago: University of Chicago Press, 1984.

Barney, Rachel. "Ring Composition in Plato: The Case of Republic X." In *Cambridge Critical Guide to Plato's Republic*, edited by M. McPherran, 32–51. New York: Cambridge University Press, 2010.

Benardete, Seth. *Plato's "Laws."* Chicago: University of Chicago Press, 2000.

———. *Socrates' Second Sailing: On Plato's "Republic."* Chicago: University of Chicago Press, 1992.

Bloom, Harold, ed. *Jean-Jacques Rousseau*. New York: Chelsea House, 1988.

Brann, Eva. *The Music of the Republic*. Philadelphia: Paul Dry Books, 2004.

Butterworth, Charles E. "Appendix A, Description of the Notebooks Containing *The Reveries of the Solitary Walker*." In Jean-Jacques Rousseau, *The Reveries of the Solitary Walker*, translated by Charles E. Butterworth, 241–45. Indianapolis: Hackett, 1992.

———. "Interpretive Essay." In Jean-Jacques Rousseau, *The Reveries of the Solitary Walker*, translated by Charles E. Butterworth, 145–240. Indianapolis: Hackett, 1992.

———. "Preface." In Jean-Jacques Rousseau, *The Reveries of the Solitary Walker*, translated by Charles E. Butterworth, vii–xix. Indianapolis: Hackett, 1992.

———, trans. *The Reveries of the Solitary Walker*, by Jean-Jacques Rousseau. Indianapolis: Hackett, 1992.

Coleman, Patrick. *Anger, Gratitude, and the Enlightenment Writer*. New York: Oxford University Press, 2011.

Cooper, Laurence D. *Eros in Plato, Rousseau, and Nietzsche: The Politics of Infinity*. University Park: Pennsylvania State University Press, 2008.

———. "Nearer My True Self to Thee: Rousseau's Spirituality—and Ours." *Review of Politics* 74, no. 3 (2012): 465–88.

———. *Rousseau, Nature, and the Problem of the Good Life.* University Park: Pennsylvania State University Press, 2008.

Davis, Michael. *The Autobiography of Philosophy: Rousseau's "The Reveries of the Solitary Walker."* Lanham, MD: Rowman and Littlefield, 1999.

———. *The Music of Reason: Rousseau, Nietzsche, Plato.* Philadelphia: University of Pennsylvania Press, 2020.

Dent, N. J. H. *Rousseau: An Introduction to His Psychological, Social, and Political Theory.* New York: Basil Blackwell, 1988.

Descartes, René. *Discourse on Method.* Translated by Laurence J. Lafleur. Indianapolis: Library of Liberal Arts, 1950.

Fendt, Gene. *Comic Cure for Delusional Democracy: Plato's Republic.* Lanham, MD: Lexington Books, 2014.

Friedlander, Eli. *J. J. Rousseau: An Afterlife of Words.* Cambridge, MA: Harvard University Press, 2004.

Gans, Eric. "The Victim as Subject: The Esthetico-Ethical System of Rousseau's *Rêveries.*" *Studies in Romanticism* 21, no. 1 (1982): 3–31. Reprinted in Jean-Jacques Rousseau, *Critical Assessments of Leading Political Philosophers,* volume 4, *Politics, Arts, and Autobiography,* edited by John T. Scott (New York: Routledge, 2006); and in *Jean-Jacques Rousseau,* edited by Harold Bloom (New York: Chelsea House, 1988).

Gourevitch, Victor. "A Provisional Reading of Rousseau's *Reveries of the Solitary Walker.*" *Review of Politics* 74, no. 3 (2012): 489–518.

Grace, Eve. "Justice in the Soul: The *Reveries* as Rousseau's Reply to Plato's Glaucon." In *Rousseau and the Ancients / Rousseau et les anciens,* edited by Ruth Grant and Philip Stewart. Montreal: North American Association for the Study of Jean-Jacques Rousseau, 2001.

———. "Rousseau's Socratic 'Sentimentalism.'" In *The Rousseauian Mind,* edited by Eve Grace and Christopher Kelly. New York: Routledge, 2019.

Hartle, Ann. *The Modern Self in Rousseau's Confessions: A Reply to St. Augustine.* Notre Dame, IN: University of Notre Dame Press, 1983.

Hegel, G. W. F. *The Phenomenology of Spirit.* Translated by A. V. Miller. New York: Oxford University Press, 1977.

Howland, Jacob. *Glaucon's Fate: History, Myth, and Character in Plato's "Republic."* Philadelphia: Paul Dry Books, 2018.

Kass, Leon. *The Beginning of Wisdom: Reading Genesis.* New York: Free Press, 2003.

Kaufmann, Walter. *Without Guilt or Justice: From Decidophobia to Autonomy.* New York: Peter H. Wyden, 1973.

Kelly, Christopher. *Rousseau as Author: Consecrating One's Life to the Truth.* Chicago: University of Chicago Press, 2003.

———. *Rousseau's Exemplary Life: The "Confessions" as Political Philosophy.* Ithaca, NY: Cornell University Press, 1987.

Kelly, Christopher, and Alexandra Cook. "Introduction." In *The Reveries of the Solitary Walker, Botanical Writings, and Letter to Franquières,* edited by Christopher Kelly. Vol. 12 of *The Collected Writings of Rousseau,* edited by Christopher Kelly and Roger Masters. Hanover, NH: Dartmouth College Press, 2000.

Kennington, Richard. "Descartes." In *History of Political Philosophy,* edited by Leo Strauss and Joseph Cropsey. 3rd ed. Chicago: University of Chicago Press, 1987.

———. "Essays on Descartes." In *On Modern Origins: Essays on Early Modern*

Philosophy, edited by Pamela Kraus and Frank Hunt. Lanham, MD: Lexington Books, 2004.

Lampert, Laurence. *Nietzsche and Modern Times: A Study of Bacon, Descartes, and Nietzsche*. New Haven, CT: Yale University Press, 1995.

Leibowitz, David. *The Ironic Defense of Socrates: Plato's "Apology."* New York: Cambridge University Press, 2010.

Levine, Alan. *Sensual Philosophy: Toleration, Skepticism, and Montaigne's Politics of the Self*. Lanham, MD: Lexington Books, 2001.

Machiavelli, Niccolò. *The Prince*. Translated by Harvey C. Mansfield. Chicago: University of Chicago Press, 1998.

Manent, Pierre. "To Walk, to Dream, to Philosophize." In *The Rousseauian Mind*, edited by Eve Grace and Christopher Kelly. New York: Routledge, 2019.

Marks, Jonathan. "Rousseau's Use of the Jewish Example." *Review of Politics* 72, no. 3 (2010): 463–81.

Masters, Roger D. *The Political Philosophy of Rousseau*. Princeton, NJ: Princeton University Press, 1968.

Meier, Heinrich. *On the Happiness of the Philosophic Life: Reflections on Rousseau's "Rêveries."* Translated by Robert Berman. Chicago: University of Chicago Press, 2016.

———. *Political Philosophy and the Challenge of Revealed Religion*. Chicago: University of Chicago Press, 2018.

———. "Rousseau on the Philosophical Life: *Les rêveries du promeneur solitaire.*" In *Recovering Reason: Essays in Honor of Thomas L. Pangle*, edited by Timothy Burns. Lanham, MD: Lexington Books, 2010.

Melzer, Arthur M. *The Natural Goodness of Man: On the System of Rousseau's Thought*. Chicago: University of Chicago Press, 1990.

———. "The Origin of the Counter-Enlightenment: Rousseau and the New Religion of Sincerity." *American Political Science Review* 90, no. 2 (1996): 344–60.

Mercier, Sebastien. *De J. J. Rousseau considéré comme l'un des premiers auteurs de la Révolution*. Paris: Buisson, 1791.

Miller, Fiona. "Forced into Freedom: Rousseau's Strange Self-Portrait in the *Rêveries.*" In *The Nature of Rousseau's "Rêveries": Physical, Human, Aesthetic*, edited by John C. O'Neal. Oxford, UK: Voltaire Foundation, 2008.

Montaigne, Michel de. *The Complete Essays of Montaigne*. Translated by Donald Frame. Palo Alto, CA: Stanford University Press, 1980.

Nietzsche, Friedrich. *Beyond Good and Evil: Prelude to a Philosophy of the Future*. Translated by Walter Kaufmann. New York: Vintage Books, 1967.

———. *The Gay Science*. Translated by Walter Kaufmann. New York: Vintage Books, 1974.

Orwin, Clifford. "Rousseau's Socratism." *Journal of Politics* 60, no. 1 (1998): 174–87.

Orwin, Clifford, and Nathan Tarcov, eds. *The Legacy of Rousseau*. Chicago: University of Chicago Press, 1997.

Pagani, Karen. "Living Well Is the Best Revenge: Rousseau's Reveries and the (Non)-Problem of Forgiveness." *Eighteenth-Century Studies* 47, no. 4 (2014): 407–23.

———. *Man or Citizen: Anger, Forgiveness, and Authenticity in Rousseau*. University Park: Pennsylvania State University Press, 2015.

Pangle, Lorraine. *Virtue Is Knowledge: The Moral Foundations of Socratic Political Philosophy*. Chicago: University of Chicago Press, 2014.

Plato. *The Apology of Socrates*. Translated by Thomas G. West and Grace Starry West. In *Four Texts on Socrates*. Ithaca, NY: Cornell University Press, 1974.

———. *The Laws of Plato*. Translated by Thomas L. Pangle. Chicago: University of Chicago Press, 1988.

———. *Phaedo*. Translated by Eva Brann, Peter Kalkavage, and Eric Salem. Newburyport, MA: Focus, 1998.

———. *Phaedrus*. Translated by James Nichols H. Nichols. Ithaca, NY: Cornell University Press, 1998.

———. *Plato's Symposium*. Translated by Seth Benardete. Chicago: University of Chicago Press, 2001.

———. *The Republic of Plato*. Translated by Allan Bloom. 2nd ed. New York: Basic Books, 1991.

Raymond, Marcel. Introduction to the *Reveries*. In *OC* 1, lxxxvi–lxxxviii.

Reisert, Joseph. *Jean-Jacques Rousseau: A Friend of Virtue*. Ithaca, NY: Cornell University Press, 2003.

Rousseau, Jean-Jacques. *Collected Writings of Rousseau*. Edited by Christopher Kelly and Roger Masters. 13 vols. Hanover, NH: University Press of New England, 1990–2010.

———. *Œuvres complètes*. Edited by Bernard Gagnebin and Marcel Raymond. Paris: Gallimard, Bibliothèque de la Pléiade, 1959–95.

Schaefer, David Lewis. *The Political Philosophy of Montaigne*. Ithaca, NY: Cornell University Press, 1990.

Scott, John T. "Rousseau's Quixotic Quest in the *Rêveries du promeneur solitaire*." In *The Nature of Rousseau's "Rêveries": Physical, Human, Aesthetic*, edited by John C. O'Neal, 139–52. Oxford, UK: Voltaire Foundation, 2008.

Shklar, Judith. *Men and Citizens: A Study of Rousseau's Social Theory*. Cambridge: Cambridge University Press, 1969.

Storey, Benjamin. "Rousseau and the Problem of Self-Knowledge." *Review of Politics* 71, no. 2 (2009): 251–74.

Strauss, Leo. *The City and Man*. Chicago: University of Chicago Press, 1978.

Tocqueville, Alexis de. *Democracy in America*. Translated by Harvey C. Mansfield and Delba Winthrop. Chicago: University of Chicago Press, 2000.

Xenophon. *Memorabilia*. Translated by Amy L. Bonnette. Ithaca, NY: Cornell University Press, 1994.

Index